The Ethics of Working Class Autobiography

The Ethics of Working Class Autobiography

Representation of Family by Four American Authors

ELIZABETH BIDINGER

McFarland & Company, Inc., Publishers
Jefferson, North Carolina, and London

LIBRARY OF CONGRESS CATALOGUING-IN-PUBLICATION DATA

Bidinger, Elizabeth.
  The ethics of working class autobiography : representation of family by four American authors / Elizabeth Bidinger.
    p.   cm.
  Includes bibliographical references and index.

  ISBN-13: 978-0-7864-2576-1
  softcover : 50# alkaline paper ∞

  1. Authors, American — Biography — History and criticism. 2. Baker, Russell, 1925– Growing up. 3. Wideman, John Edgar. Brothers and keepers. 4. Nesaule, Agate. Woman in amber. 5. Mason, Bobbie Ann. Clear Springs. 6. Authors, American — 20th century — Biography. 7. Working class authors — United States — Biography. 8. Autobiography — Moral and ethical aspects. I. Title.
  PS129.B53   2006
  810.9'0054 — dc22   2006014352
  [B]

British Library cataloguing data are available

©2006 Elizabeth Bidinger. All rights reserved

No part of this book may be reproduced or transmitted in any form or by any means, electronic or mechanical, including photocopying or recording, or by any information storage and retrieval system, without permission in writing from the publisher.

On the cover: blue collar worker ©2006 Veer; hammer ©2006 PhotoSpin; family icon ©2006 clipart.com

Manufactured in the United States of America

McFarland & Company, Inc., Publishers
  Box 611, Jefferson, North Carolina 28640
  www.mcfarlandpub.com

For my parents

Acknowledgments

I am deeply grateful to Lynn Z. Bloom, whose brilliance and encouragement were essential to this work. I am also indebted to Veronica Makowsky and Robert Tilton; both dramatically improved not only this project but also my understanding of American literature. I am additionally honored to acknowledge William L. Andrews, whose commentary on a draft deepened my thinking about autobiography and social class.

This book would not have been possible without my husband, my parents, my daughters, the grace of God, or B.W. and T. Bidinger, who live on in my heart.

Contents

Acknowledgments	vii
Introduction	1
1. A World Apart: Working Class Autobiographers and Their Families	31
2. Life with "A Formidable Woman": Russell Baker's Ethical Representations in *Growing Up*	74
3. Inventing the Self and the (Br)Other in John Edgar Wideman's *Brothers and Keepers*	102
4. Autobiography as Healing: Agate Nesaule's *A Woman in Amber*	127
5. "My Folks and Their Country Culture": Inventing Authenticity in Bobbie Ann Mason's *Clear Springs*	155
Conclusion	188
Works Cited	193
Index	199

Introduction

It might be said that all autobiography recounts some kind of transformation in the author. As Jean Starobinksi puts it, "one would hardly have sufficient motive to write an autobiography had not some radical change occurred in his life" (78). Each of the working-class autobiographies examined in this study narrates a particular kind of transformation: one's crossing of class, cultural, and social boundaries; one's attainment of higher education than one's parents had; one's entry into a life that includes writing and abstract, analytical thinking; and the processes of self-invention and re-invention that one has undergone throughout this movement.

This book analyzes the autobiographies of writers who spent much or all of their youth in working-class circumstances, and who moved into the upper-middle class in their adulthood. The works considered here, Russell Baker's *Growing Up* (1982), John Edgar Wideman's *Brothers and Keepers* (1984), Agate Nesaule's *A Woman in Amber* (1995), and Bobbie Ann Mason's *Clear Springs* (1999), all describe the authors' evolutions from children in socially or culturally marginal families to highly educated, intellectual professionals. Broadly speaking, the study examines how these autobiographers, in their present incarnations as upper-middle-class writers, confront their working-class pasts and the people in it. More specifically, my analysis investigates how the authors' identity construction in the texts relates to the authors' portrayals of family members and significant others. Further, the book focuses on autobiography as an ethical act, seeking to illuminate ways in which the authors appropriate, exploit, "primitivize," patronize, or in some other manner diminish the dignity of their working-class family members in their texts.

The first chapter provides a broad overview of trends in the way autobiographers represented their working-class family members in American class-advancement autobiographies in the twentieth century. It discusses four autobiographies from different periods of the century, highlighting the key aspects of each text's strategy of representing the author's working-class family; it also surveys the critical reception to the books, citing in particular the reviewers' reactions to the authors' family portraits. The chapter thus provides some historical and literary precedents for the analytical chapters that follow.

All four of the main analytical chapters of this book explore the intersections of class, race, ethnicity, or region in the texts. In the process, each chapter analyzes one text and focuses on one particular facet of social identity, its interconnectedness with social mobility, and its implications for autobiography.

Chapter 2, which posits Russell Baker's *Growing Up* as a stereotypical American class-mobility memoir, discusses how the author's gender, among other factors, influences the autobiographer's portrayal of family members. This chapter also analyzes Baker's autobiography as an example of a positive model of ethical working-class autobiography, but contends that it is Baker's closer approximation to the dominant culture that simplifies to some degree his task of delineating an identity metamorphosis.

The next three chapters identify the ethical problems in the texts by Wideman, Nesaule, and Mason and demonstrate how these problems largely arise from the authors' attempts to negotiate their class and cultural duality. Chapter 3 argues that Wideman exemplifies an autobiographer's grappling with issues of race. Chapter 4 examines Nesaule's difficulty with writing autobiography about class differences. Lastly, the analysis of Mason's memoir in Chapter 5 emphasizes the author's problematic construction of a regional identity.

The purpose of the ethical analysis of these autobiographies is not to pronounce them or their writers good or bad, nor is it to suggest that any of these books should not have been written. In fact, I have chosen these texts because I regard them as estimable autobiographical works which illuminate lives and times that may be unfamiliar to many middle-class Americans. Nevertheless, the autobiographies by Wideman, Nesaule, and Mason raise questions about the authors' portrayals of working-class or racially or culturally "different" people.

Interest in the ethical aspects of autobiography is relatively new; scholars began to give serious attention to the subject in the early 1990s and have only in the past few years begun expanding their avenues of inquiry beyond privacy concerns. Paul John Eakin, one of the first to explore the impact of autobiography on real people being represented, looked initially to privacy laws for guidance in determining what is ethical for autobiographers to do. But as Eakin explains in his most recent volume on the subject, the right to privacy "has proved to be not only legally ineffective as a bulwark against invasive life writing but also conceptually problematic," because it implies "an assumption of autonomous individualism that is inadequate to model the experience of selfhood in our intensely interpersonal lives" (*Ethics* 6). Simply put, one cannot own the facts of a life that necessarily intermingles with and overlaps the lives of others.

Now scholars are approaching the ethics of autobiography from fascinatingly diverse angles, examining the complex moral dimensions of life writing from the points of view of all concerned parties—the author's, the subject's, the reader's, and even the critic's. Eakin has come to regard ethics as "the deep subject of autobiographical discourse," and many scholars concur (*Ethics* 6). One of the most important recent works on the subject is G. Thomas Couser's book *Vulnerable Subjects*, the title of which refers to a class he defines as "persons who are liable to exposure by someone with whom they are involved in an intimate or trust-based relationship but are unable to represent themselves in writing or to offer meaningful consent to their representation by someone else" (xii). When a writer undertakes to represent an especially vulnerable subject in an autobiography, Couser asserts, the author is assuming a higher level of ethical and moral responsibility than if the subject were the writer's peer.

As stated earlier, my analyses focus on the ethical quality of the authors' representations of their family members, most of whom can be considered "vulnerable" according to Couser's criteria. For Couser, subjects are rendered vulnerable by a range of conditions, including youth and old age, physical or mental impairment, and being socially or culturally disadvantaged (xii). The family members of the autobiographers I study are, generally speaking, disadvantaged because of their socioeconomic status, but some are also racial or cultural minorities.

Like Couser's, my study focuses on "intimate" life writing in which trust and proximity play strong roles. Indeed, Couser articulates well the philosophical premise for my own study when he asserts that the "ethical stakes" and the "urgent need for ethical scrutiny" increase in proportion to both the closeness of the relationship between the writer and subject, and the vulnerability of the subject (xii). Since all self-identities are relational, constructed in relation to others, all autobiographers have a great deal at stake with their portraits of family members: their autobiographical selves are delineated in part by their re-creation of their familial relationships. However, those who have moved upward socially, and who may have experienced intensely conflicted feelings about their identities in relation to their family members, may have even more at stake psychologically in how they characterize their relatives.

Ethics and "Truth"

Couser rightly notes that autobiographical writing is "far too complex and variable" to be subjected to "abstract" and "presumably universal principles" (33). It may be useful nonetheless to survey briefly the concepts, even biases, underlying my ethical assessments.

The first is the matter of truthfulness. Purveying the truth, both factually and emotionally, has long been seen as the central guiding ethical principle of autobiography by many authors and critics. Lynn Z. Bloom speaks for many when, in "Living to Tell the Tale: The Complicated Ethics of Creative Nonfiction," she concludes that a writer of creative nonfiction is not ethically obligated to keep silent about family history or any personal event that overlaps with the lives of others. The writer, Bloom asserts, owes simply the "literal and larger Truth" to both the people she writes about and her readers (288). However, scholars of autobiography are realizing that ethical ideals such as "truthfulness" can have different meanings when applied to different life writing scenarios.

Some critics, for example, now contend that literal truth and factual accuracy are not necessarily ethically required in certain kinds of autobiographies, such as those that recount trauma or oppression. Such scholars have asked: Since all truth is subjective anyway, shouldn't stories that reveal larger social truths be excused if they at times blur the line between fact and fiction? Paul Lauritzen examines, and rejects, what he calls the "big picture" argument, which such critics use to defend certain survivor accounts that have been shown to include fabrications. This view asserts that survivors such as Rigoberta Menchu, whose book *I, Rigoberta Menchu*, contains significant embellishments, testify to larger truths and that scrutinizing the details of their stories amounts to uncharitable hairsplitting.

This debate is pertinent to an ethical analysis of working-class autobiographies because narratives about one's culturally marginal background often take the shape and tone of survivor accounts. Such autobiographies have often been reviewed with relatively little skepticism. In many cases it *is* reasonable to consider the specific rhetorical situation before censuring an autobiographer for heightening his or her narrative with fiction. Early African American autobiographers, for example, knew that divulging too much information would be dangerous to other slaves, fugitives, and sympathetic whites. In another instance, as Chapter 1 explains, Richard Wright uses fiction in his autobiography, often at the expense of his family members, in order to create a devastating portrait of the psychological effects of racism on families and children. While Wright was criticized by his contemporaries for being untruthful, most scholars today see his method as necessary for imparting larger truths. As William L. Andrews contends, our present-day sensitivity to the "peculiar symbiosis of imperfect freedom and imperfect truth in the American autobiographical tradition makes it easier for us to regard the fictive elements of black autobiography as aspects of rhetorical and aesthetic strategy, not evidence of moral failure" ("First" 225). However, this is no longer the nineteenth century or the 1940s. When discussing contemporary autobiography it is fair to recognize the ethical claims of real-life subjects in works by any writer. Working-class family members of all racial and ethnic groups are vulnerable to being portrayed in biased, even distorted ways by writers who are, after all, writing to solidify their own, often tenuous, identities.

A formerly working-class autobiographer, while undoubtedly striving to be honest, may yet also often be interested in producing a particular kind of book, one that dramatizes a journey from a hard life to a better one, that solidifies his own myth of himself, that emphasizes the radicalness and heroic nature of his own transformation, and that appeals to the biases, tastes, and expectations of his upper-middle-class readers. In all of these an autobiographer has an investment, and all, undoubtedly, shape his or her representation of family members in his or her life story. Therefore, I approach the texts from a position of believing that it *does* matter that the autobiographers render themselves and others as truthfully as possible, in both the factual and philosophical senses. As Lauritzen writes: "If life writing is to be a useful resource for moral deliberation, then we must be extremely careful ... about distinguishing fact from fiction." To do justice to the "constructed character" of experience, "we must not collapse the distinction between what happened and what was imagined" (37).

For Wayne Booth, an ethical critic of fiction, an essential step in assessing the moral, political, and philosophical soundness of a literary work is to do one's best to make "appraisals of the truth-value" of the narratives (*Company* 12). How can a reader possibly know how truthfully an autobiographer is depicting his or her family members? If truth is always mediated by individual perception as well as cultural and social paradigms, not to mention the vagaries of memory, then how can a critic know whether a writer is being honest? Lauritzen rightly argues for "the moral necessity of the idea that there is a truth and a reality accessible to a careful investigator" (33). Yet it is impossible, and probably pointless, to try to adjudicate between opposing points of view even if one were to "investigate" one's representation of one's family members by interviewing the subjects.

My approach, therefore, is to raise questions, and to point out ways in which some of the authors' portrayals of proximate others are not only clearly self-serving but also potentially harmful, possibly damaging the reputation of individuals or reinforcing class, cultural, or racial stereotypes. I try to evaluate the quality of the writers' characterizations of proximate others, examining not only the complexity and balance of a given portrait, but also the autobiographer's attitude toward the person he or she is portraying, and I try to assess whether the writer appears to make a genuine attempt at truthfulness. This is, admittedly, an approach that relies heavily upon subjective interpretation.

At the core of my study, however, is an attempt to illuminate connections between the writers' life plots and the ethical problems in the texts. So the fundamental question I bring to each autobiography is, how does the author's creation of an identity in the narrative influence the author's portrayal of others? How does class mobility shape the way one sees oneself in relation to one's family members who have not left the working class?

It may be useful to consider some common characteristics of people who have elevated their class status that may shape their autobiographical identity and influence their truthfulness in representing others. Sociologists have found that professional people who had poor or culturally marginal origins often experience a deep sense of alienation throughout their lives, even after they have become solidly accepted members of mainstream culture and the middle class. This is frequently rooted in a person's having seen oneself, from a very young age, as being different from one's family. Being different becomes a key to one's identity, a factor that facilitates one's transcendence from the family's circumstances, since, as the sociologist Lillian Rubin writes, "a sense of marginality in the family, the child's feeling that he doesn't fit, lays the psychological groundwork that enables the growing child to see and grasp alternatives" (*Transcendent* 199). Seeing oneself as separate from the family feels not only familiar but important, essential to one's psychological survival as well as one's success in the world.

As adults, "transcendent children" — Rubin's term for adults who overcame difficult pasts and succeeded professionally — often perceive themselves as separate not only from their family but also from other groups or institutions, such as schools and places of employment, and from society in general. Those who lived on the periphery of their families of origin often feel they never fully belong anywhere, and so many experience isolation and loneliness even when they've "made it." There is a positive side to this sense of difference that helps fuel it as well. Rubin writes that this marginality is "so much a part of the definition of self that it seems like the wellspring of creativity and accomplishment. Therefore, people may nurture their outsider status—albeit unconsciously—even while wishing they could be rid of it" (*Transcendent* 59).

Most of the autobiographers I examine or cite in this book make their marginality a fundamental aspect of their autobiographical identity. This way of defining oneself has clear implications for one's portrayal of one's family members. One of the most common manifestations of this liminality is a writer's positioning himself or herself as an ethnographer whose task is to delineate the "otherness" of his or her family and community of origin for a mainstream audience. As the liaison between his or her family and the dominant culture, the autobiographer maintains an outsider status in both worlds, yet implicitly draws the authority to write from his or her inclusion in each realm. Many of the distortions I identify in the writers' representations of family members stem from the authors' efforts to impose and maintain this dynamic.

Former children of the working class often share another trait: a deep desire to repair or compensate for their family members' hardships and humiliations. In one of her well-known studies of working-class families Rubin found striking differences between social classes in terms of the adults' desire to help their parents. For example, a far greater percentage of interviewees with working-class parents express the goal of giving money to their families. As Rubin puts it, "Almost identical words issuing from so many lips ... give testimony to the precariousness with which their parents and some of their siblings still live, to the continuing fragility of life in these circumstances" (*Pain* 166). She adds, "For the rest of us, there is no need to think about such things. Their parents can not only take care of themselves but usually can — and often do— help the children as well" (167). In keeping with this characteristic, formerly working-class autobiographers are often inclined to share the benefits of their literary talents with their less-advantaged relatives. This often takes the form of romanticizing their culture, their hardships, and even their weak choices and character flaws; it is one of the primary ways in which many "transcendent" autobiographers are apparently tempted to place personal agendas over truth-value in their texts.

Another of the primary sources of the ethical problems I identify in these texts is the authors' passionate determination to affirm, or even largely create, an ethnic or racial identity for themselves. Couser terms this convention of autobiography "the narrative of reracination — the rediscovery or reaffirmation of ethnic identity and the rerooting of the self in traditional culture" (*Vulnerable* 58). This approach to autobiography is popular. A casual survey of the working-class, African American, and ethnic autobiographies published in the United States in the last twenty years shows that most are centered on the theme of racial and ethnic reaffirmation. Of course, one of the most important changes in American autobiography in the last three decades has been the increased publication of life stories by people of color. But even a large percentage of books by whites have emphasized the authors' ethnic or regional heritage.

Rubin explains why white Americans are so drawn to defining themselves in this way. In a country as vast and diverse as ours, identifying oneself with an ethnic group "provides a sense of belonging to some recognizable and manageable collectivity — an affiliation that has meaning because it's connected to the family where, when we were small children, we first learned about our relationship to the group" (*Fault* 179). Paradoxically, while it eases the "isolation of modern life" by making us feel we belong with a group, it also "sets us apart from others, allows us the fantasy of uniqueness — a quest given particular urgency by a psychological culture that increasingly emphasizes the development of the self and personal history" (179).

Only in recent decades, however, have these meanings of ethnicity intensified. Rubin points to both the civil rights movement and the Immigration Act of 1965, which brought an enormous wave of immigrants into the country, as key events that renewed ethnic consciousness among whites. The increased visibility of people of color, the growing solidarity and vocalness of minority groups, and the decreased political power of whites all contributed to the trend of whites becoming more focused on their ethnic and racial identification. Rubin observes that at high school and college campuses "we see white students struggling to deal with the minority presence and to find legitimacy for the kind of public expression of their identity that, in the current climate, is readily acceptable for other racial groups but not for whites as whites" (*Fault* 194). Since white students "can't comfortably ask for recognition as whites, they embrace their ethnic past and demand public acknowledgment of their newly acquired group status" (195).

Contemporary autobiographers of any race who are seeking to delineate their own and their families' uniqueness are, therefore, understandably drawn to shaping their life stories as reracination narratives. How do the requirements of this narrative convention affect the authors' truthfulness in characterizing themselves and their family members? Without making assertions about what is true and what is distorted, we can nevertheless identify characterizations in the texts that appear to fit perhaps too neatly into the reracination narrative, and point out such problems as the portrayal of family members as cultural and/or class representatives.

Ethics of Auto/biography

Though I am primarily concerned with the nature of the authors' characterizations of family members, I also examine the ethical aspects of the autobiographers' exposure of their relatives' lives as well as their appropriation of them. Eakin notes that in recent years autobiographies have become "increasingly *biographical,* featuring those others in our lives—parents, siblings, lovers, friends, and mentors—who have shaped us decisively" (*Ethics* 9). The emphasis on a proximate other is especially common in working-class autobiographies, in which authors often use portraits of family members to dramatize parts of the authors' own divided identities.

Some significant ethical aspects of biography-centered autobiography have been largely unexplored. For example, what purchase does an autobiographer get from telling the story of a family member *as a way of telling the story of oneself?* At what point does a writer's seemingly devoted act of speaking for a loved one become, in fact, the author's appropriation of another human being? Are working-class family members more susceptible than their better-educated counterparts to being exploited or appropriated by autobiographers?

Couser uses the term auto/biography for single-author texts, "memoirs of proximate others, such as close relatives or partners," that are also "collaborative in some sense or degree." In those texts "there is more than one subject, and the process of collaboration may itself be featured in the narrative" (20). Both Mason and Wideman highlight, to different degrees, the cooperation and collaboration with the proximate other at the center of the text. Couser identifies the potential ethical pitfalls in such "collaborative autobiographies," and he notes that both the "partnership" between the writer and the subject, and the writer's portrayal of the subject, can be ethically problematic. The "justice" of the portrayal "has to do with whether the text represents its subject the way the subject would like to be represented, with the control the subject has over it, and with the degree and kind of any harm or wrong done by misrepresentation." The privacy and reputations of subjects can be harmed, as can be "their integrity as individuals" (42). In my study I scrutinize both the portrayal and the partnership at the center of these texts, and find that the "collaborative" appearance of the books may be misleading, largely because of the power disparity between the author and the subject.

In fact, one of the chief ethical problems engendered by a subject's cooperation, which can range from offering up memories to reviewing drafts, is the *appearance* that the subject is a fully empowered and fully consenting participant. When an author such as Mason includes in her memoir scenes in which she interviews her mother, Christy, the implication is that Christy has had an active and significant role in the shaping of her own characterization in the text, and that she has consented to Mason's revelations about, for example, Christy's marriage. Christy's personal life is laid bare and analyzed in the text, while Mason is virtually silent about her own marriage and, indeed, about most of her private life since her twenties. By displaying her mother's involvement with one section of the book, Mason implies that her mother has willingly given up her privacy, has consented to all of the book's revelations, and that therefore Mason has covered her bases, ethically speaking.

However, as Couser notes, the granting of consent does not "foreclose the possibility of ethical conflict." This is especially true with "more vulnerable subjects" (13). The first question the situation raises is whether a vulnerable subject has, in fact, granted what Couser terms "informed consent," a principle which, in medicine, requires that consent be "freely given by an adequately informed, competent patient" (Beauchamp and Childress, qtd in Couser, 24). Can Mason's mother—a rural, elderly woman who has not read Mason's other books and who appears to lack a full understanding of the project Mason is working on—be considered "adequately informed" about what she is getting herself into when she shares her memories for her daughter's memoir? Couser asserts that in an ethnographic type of collaboration (Mason's memoir is not a collaborative work, of course, but a relational one which draws heavily on her mother's recollections because it is centered around her life) "differences of culture may impede or prevent the obtaining of truly informed consent" (48).

Other working-class autobiographers who proclaim their mother's consent or collaboration similarly cause a reader to wonder whether the mother possessed enough sophistication about contemporary autobiography to imagine how her own story might be exploited, or at least subsumed, by the writer's own interests. Writer Mary Karr prefaces her autobiography *The Liar's Club* with an acknowledgment that suggests her mother's consent to the author's exposure of her in the book: "My mother didn't read this book until it was complete. However, for two years she freely answered questions by phone and mail, and she did research for me, even when she was ill. She has been unreserved in her encouragement of this work, though much in the story pains her" (vi). Such comments in autobiographies raise questions about the intersection of an author's professional interests and his or her relationships with parents, siblings, children, and other significant people.

Jacki Lyden begins her memoir of her mother's severe mental illness,

Daughter of the Queen of Sheba, with "A Few Words": "This book was written first and foremost for my mother and my family, without whose reminiscences I could not have created it.... My mother was unsparing in allowing me access to her records, and I have been unsparing, I suppose, not only in recreating her here, but in sharing memories with the world I know she does not always share herself" (Preface). What do Karr's and Lyden's mothers, both women with very difficult and marginal lives, gain from their willingness to offer up their humiliation and pain to their successful daughters' book projects? Most certainly, they enjoy a period of extraordinary interest and attention from their adult children while the book is being researched. However, did they cooperate with a naive assumption that their children would depict them in a flattering light, or in the belief that their input would soften their daughters' judgments or perhaps curtail shaming revelations? Wideman's text provokes similar queries about the nature of the "collaboration" between the author and his much less sophisticated brother.

Of course, one should not assume that because there is a gap between the author and subject in terms of sophistication and power, the subject has been exploited or bullied. As Couser notes, "Having power or rank over someone else is not the same as overpowering that person" (37). He adds, however, that in ethnographic autobiography subjects "may indeed be vulnerable to the writer's domination, in part because they are likely to be among 'those who do not write'" (37). While none of the working-class parents of the autobiographers studied here is illiterate, none would be considered a sophisticated reader, except Nesaule's mother, whose death preceded her daughter's book. And almost all of the family members featured in the texts are significantly less educated than the autobiographers.

While they are not, perhaps, as vulnerable in a collaboration as someone of a different culture and language might be — as, for example, Black Elk was in the making of *Black Elk Speaks* with John G. Neihardt — less-educated family members are less likely than those with advanced education to negotiate for some control over their representation in the text. Couser observes that in ethnographic kinds of collaborative or cooperative autobiography "the most obvious danger is the taking of liberties — the appropriation of a life story for purposes not shared, understood, or consented to by the subject" (48). He adds that in ethnographic autobiography, "the danger tends to be that of attributing to the subject a voice and narrative not originating with him or her, and that he or she may not have edited" (48).

An imbalance of education and power between a writer and his family may make the writer more apt to speak for his relatives — with little or no objection from them. According to sociologists Richard Sennett and Jonathan Cobb, one consequence of people living in a society that places high value on personal achievement is the "powerlessness and inadequacy" felt by working people who aren't regarded as higher achievers, and their tendency to cede de facto power and authority to professionals (227). Further, the authors note that Americans place a specific and rarefied premium on intellectual achievement, even more so than on material affluence, and they assume that people who have developed their minds are and should be in a position to judge others, especially the less educated.

The deference that working-class people are likely to show their better-educated siblings or children is crucial to the dynamic between writers and their families. Significantly, Baker, whose family is closer to the mainstream culture, takes fewer liberties in representing his family than do Wideman, Nesaule, and Mason — whose families are more socially and culturally marginal — in depicting theirs. One reason, perhaps, is that Wideman, Nesaule, and Mason implicitly know that the proximate others they depict are unlikely to view themselves as having been appropriated or exploited in the texts, much less to voice an objection.

Contemporary American autobiography is often written by people young enough to have parents who are alive, not to mention siblings who are in their prime. Such autobiographers may or may not have to contend with the reactions — or anticipated reactions — of family members to their published texts; social class status may be a factor in the extent to which family members assert their "rights" in regard to a published portrayal of themselves. Sennett and Cobb's findings suggest that working-class family members are apt to accept that a more educated family member's version of family history is authoritative, above questioning or reproof.

Autobiographers who have commented on their writing process, whether within their texts or in other venues, often relate how their families' attitudes, or expected attitudes, toward the book affect the book's content. Annie Dillard, who cleared her autobiography with every member of her upper-middle-class family, exemplifies this. In "To Fashion a Text," written while she was at work on her autobiography, Dillard remarked, "I've promised my family that each may pass on the book. I've promised to take out anything that anyone objects to — anything at all" (69–70). She added, "Everybody I'm writing about is alive and well, in full possession of his faculties, and possibly willing to sue" (69).

However lighthearted the last phrase was intended to be, Dillard was signaling that she regarded her family members as peers who possess a certain amount of power in their own right; their vigilant awareness of the autobiography-in-the-making and its implications for themselves was in itself a claim of rights: "My sisters are watching this book carefully," Dillard noted (69). Whether Dillard's method of attaining family approval made *An American Childhood* a more ethically sound book is debatable for many reasons. The editing privileges she extends to her family members may accomplish more than protecting the family secrets; it may run deeper in the text, becoming an agenda to affirm the goodness and normality of one's own household, class, and family, and thus distorting the author's vision and treatment of "others." Sidonie Smith argues, for instance, that Dillard's portrait of her childhood as "idyllic" relies, in part, on the text's marginalization and containment of people who are different, people of other races and classes "whose exclusion [from the text's implied delineation of the normative] establishes the borders of Dillard's communal identification" (*Subjectivity* 137). Thus, the content of the memoir as well as Dillard's extratextual comments suggest that her portrayal of her family members was to some degree influenced by her relatives' willingness to challenge Dillard's authorial power if need be.

In light of all these arguments that suggest the elusiveness of fairness, one might wonder whether collaborative or relational autobiographies should be written at all when there is a significant disparity in power between the author and the subject. Yet I concur with Couser's statement that it would be misguided to devise ethical standards that would in essence censor whole sub-genres of autobiographical writing (55). There are, after all, benefits as well as liabilities in cooperative or collaborative situations; and, in many cases, "the recuperative benefits of ethnography outweigh its costs" (55).

Couser describes some features that he believes characterize "the most ethically responsible life writing," and the preeminent one is "acknowledgment of the face and the autonomy of the other even, or especially, when the relationship is consensual" (22). Important ways to respect the other's autonomy include giving subjects both compensation for, and some control over, their stories. Because of its pertinence to my study, it's worth quoting at length from Couser's description of an ethical relational or collaborative autobiography relationship:

> The agreement of a subject to confide in a collaborator or a life writer, then, is not carte blanche, not a waiver or privacy rights, but rather a willing sacrifice of privacy with the goal and expectation of some compensatory benefits. Ethical partnerships, then, especially with vulnerable subjects, would involve respect for the integrity of their stories and for their rights—both authorial and economic—to their own stories. That is, like other collaborators or consensual partners, subjects should have some degree of control over the shape their stories take and, in some cases, an opportunity to

share the proceeds from the sale of their stories. Or, if they cede these rights, they should do so only with "informed consent" [22–23].

Of course, people who are poorly educated or who simply lack advanced literacy may not possess the skills or the desire to exert a meaningful degree of control over their own representation in a book. One example is Wideman's effort to elicit his brother's input on *Brothers and Keepers* in the editing stage, only to find that Robby is unable to articulate any concrete suggestions. Wideman's effort, however, is significant, and it enriches the text ethically while also deepening its portrait of Robby.

One of the dangers in collaborative or auto/biographical texts that involve vulnerable subjects, Couser observes, is the author's assumption that whatever condition renders the subject vulnerable also diminishes or prevents his or her autonomy. In some cases, he adds, such as those of cognitive impairment, the writer may assume that the subject is "invulnerable to certain kinds of harm — such as psychic pain or harm to reputation" (23). For example, a common ethical problem is a double standard of privacy like the one seen in the Mason text: authors are willing to expose intimate and often humiliating details of the lives of marginal relatives but not of their own. One wonders if Wideman, Nesaule, and Mason believe, respectively, that a prisoner, a working-class alcoholic, and an elderly rural woman have less to lose in terms of privacy and reputation than do professional writers with public personas.

Autobiographies that center on a proximate other *without* that subject's consent also raise questions about privacy infringement and the betrayal of trust, especially if the portrayal is an especially revealing or a negative one. An increasing number of scholars and writers are debating the ethics of writing about a family member or former spouse, since, as Couser argues, in such relationships the preexisting intimacy "creates special liability to exposure and harm" (28). Nancy K. Miller expresses the fundamental ethical dilemma of autobiographers, suggesting that it is fairly impossible not to harm others when you write about your own life. Since every story of oneself necessarily renders relations with others, she asks, how can an autobiographer tell one's story *"from one's own perspective"* yet "without violating the other's privacy" and without being unfair? "You — the person whose life is being written about — enter willy-nilly into the public domain. Faithfully recorded or maliciously distorted, your story circulates, utterly outside your control" ("Ethics" 153). Yet most critics, even those who are deeply aware of the power exercised by writers and the potential abuse of that power, believe that writers are, in the end, ethically justified in writing about proximate others as long as its done skillfully, conscientiously, and without malice.

One of the questions I raise in my analyses is whether it is at all possible to benefit from a family member's vulnerability in an *ethical* way. Is it wrong, period, to benefit from a relationship, whether the writer and subject are on good terms or bad? After surveying a range of philosophical viewpoints concerning the ethics of relationships, Claudia Mills concludes that deriving an external benefit from personal relationships is not wrong, "so long as that benefit is not the dominant goal" of the relationship, and so long as one continues "to value the loved one appropriately" (103–4). Mills goes on to make a sensible argument that writers are ethically entitled to any financial profit they receive for published stories about others. She cites the significant skill and effort required to create a publishable work, and the fact that writers, like any other professionals, should get paid for their labor (110).

Yet Mills acknowledges that there is no simple resolution to the essential conflict between a writer's duty to a loved one and a writer's duty to one's profession: "to be a friend is to stand to another in a relationship of trust," yet to be a writer is to be loyal to "one's story," even if that necessitates a violation of trust (105). Like others before her, Mills ultimately comes down on the side of writing, even justifying the exposure of "hurtful, harmful, dark, dangerous things" because without those elements, writers won't create interesting — or publishable — material (105). I agree with Mills that we can't, in the name of ethics, expect writers to avoid their richest sources of writing — themselves and their loved ones (105).

Mills does, however, delineate some reasonable ethical conditions that autobiographies should meet. If a writer reaps benefits from the stories of others, the writer should make him- or herself equally "vulnerable" to the sharing of his or her own stories (111). Mills also proposes that writers should refrain from telling stories of their childhoods until they have had enough time and distance to heal, acquire a seasoned perspective, and even to forgive (118). Mills appears to share my belief that the ethical quality of an autobiography depends largely on the richness of the text's characterizations of others, as well as on the writer's attitude. Ethical life writing is characterized by "sensitivity and concern both for the stories themselves and even more for the persons, for the human beings, whose stories these are" (114). Further, it is essential that portraits of others, even of "our hated ones," should be sufficiently complex, "doing full justice to their unique and distinctive and suffering and joyful personhood" (115). Nancy K. Miller echoes that conclusion somewhat, suggesting that recounting events from another person's private life is not, in itself, unethical, but that *how* it is done determines its ethics. Reflecting on her own misgivings about publishing a memoir about her former marriage, Miller finally determines that "Telling my story truthfully does not necessarily constitute a betrayal of the people who shared in it, even if in the telling I illuminate some of the darker moments from my point of view" ("Ethics" 158).

Likewise, I do not approach the texts I analyze with an *a priori* assumption that, simply because these authors have written extensively and revealingly about vulnerable proximate others, they have necessarily betrayed them. Even when autobiographers expose their vulnerable subjects more than the subjects would like, the authors are not necessarily acting unethically. We can, however, analyze the nature and extent of any harm autobiographers do cause, and weigh the benefits of the text against those human costs. Couser stresses that the point is not whether harm is caused but the degree of seriousness of any harm, and whether such harm is *"justified"* (30). Therefore, when analyzing the texts I am concerned mostly with investigating any gratuitous harm to those the authors portray.

Ethics and Moral Judgment

One last area of ethics figures prominently in my analyses: autobiographers' exercise of moral judgment. How an autobiographer interprets and judges the behavior of him- or herself and others affects the reader's ethical experience of the book perhaps more than any other single aspect. Yet for probably a number of reasons, including the traditional hesitation of literary critics to invoke moral values in textual analyses, scholars have only recently begun to theorize about what constitutes "ethically instructive" judgment, to use John D. Barbour's words, in autobiography (97). He suggests that "an ideal of good or fair judgment" is a crucial tool for discussing the ethics of autobiographies because consciously or not, it is the standard we often use to assess the work of life writers (92).

For Barbour, autobiographers have an opportunity to demonstrate for readers "a paradigm of what moral deliberation" should be in real life, by providing a concrete example of "complex and fair judgment" which is "conscientiously made" (96). To this point we can add that autobiographers who write about especially vulnerable subjects have a particularly valuable opportunity to model good judgment of people who are often judged harshly by mainstream society.

Barbour admires writers who make a strenuous effort to understand how a person's history and context influence one's actions and, potentially, mitigate one's moral responsibility. The fundamental element of good judgment in Barbour's view, it seems, is a writer's recognition that "moral agency is circumscribed," and that in any life much happens that is outside of one's control, subject to what Barbour calls "moral luck." Therefore, certain choices "may be neither simply voluntary nor involuntary," and there may be factors that "diminish a person's responsibility without entirely eliminating it" (91). Barbour argues that since it is so difficult to measure responsibility with exactness, "good judgment sometimes resembles not judging," which is to say, making assessments "with a good deal of caution, tentativeness, and acknowledgment of ambiguity" (91).

The autobiographer's ethical duty to examine the limits of moral agency in the lives of others is especially relevant to autobiographies centered on working-class subjects. Writers should ideally be scrupulous in exploring the socioeconomic and cultural factors that shape their subjects' lives. This is not because such persons should not be regarded as moral agents, but because many readers may be prejudiced against the poor and the working class, with little awareness of it.

Sociologists have repeatedly found that a great number of middle- and upper-middle-class Americans view working-class people as morally inferior. Lillian Rubin, noting that "the dictates of a culture become part of the psychology of its people," contends that Americans place more value on people who move up socially. She writes that "'climbing up'" isn't a neutral term. It means "going somewhere, getting out, moving ahead. 'Upwardly mobile,' we say — the words spoken almost reverently, an accolade, an acknowledgment of an accomplishment. It's an idea whose value is deeply embedded in the American culture, a powerful idea that has profound consequences both for those who move up and for those who do not" (*Fault* 40–41).

According to Rubin, one reason why middle-class people tend to blame poorer people for their plight is that people who are struggling sometimes *do* behave differently than do people with more comfortable lives. Life in the working class can be "difficult and problematic," and the people who live it often express a different outlook than do people of higher social status (*Pain* 133). Rubin describes the world of the working class as an environment in which a dearth of choices "is the reality of most lives — no friends or relatives around who see a future with plenty of possibilities stretching before them; no one who expects very much because experience has taught them that such expectations end painfully" (*Pain* 163). In such a climate of little hope, "the fatalism, passivity, and resignation of the working class grow." It is tempting, Rubin explains, for middle-class observers to regard these qualities as inherent character failings. This view palliates middle-class guilt "about the inequalities in American life — inequalities that are at such odds with our most cherished ideological myth of egalitarianism" (163). Rubin argues that these self-destructive attitudes are often simply "realistic responses" to the social environment in which most working-class men, women, and children "live, grow, and come to define themselves, their expectations, and their relationship to the world around them" (*Pain* 163).

The American tendency to view social class status as a reflection of moral character has such long and deep roots that it has become a largely unquestioned perception. Sennett and Cobb trace the "morality of social class" in America from its articulation in *The Autobiography of Benjamin Franklin* to its flowering in the first great industrial expansion in the decades following the Civil War (71). For Franklin, self-improvement and moral character were indistinguishable, and virtuous behavior was not practiced for its own sake but as a way to succeed. The authors explain that Franklin was practicing a secular brand of Puritanism that flourished into an enduring "peculiar morality" that justified the acquiring of surplus capital (172).

Sennett and Cobb explain that the early Protestant practice of self-abnegation was adopted by early capitalist entrepreneurs, so that "an industrious boy [like Franklin] who started with nothing" could earn respect "by denying himself present pleasures, in order someday to elevate his social standing" (172). They note that the Enlightenment ideal of equal opportunity existing for every man to transcend his social origins brought with it the belief that both success and failure had to do with a person's moral character and strength: "If all men start on some basis of equal potential ability, then the inequalities they experience in their lives are not arbitrary, they are the logical consequence of different personal drives to use those powers—in other words, social differences can now appear as questions of character, or moral resolve, will, and competence" (256). The authors also explain how this moral view of class was reflected and reinforced in nineteenth-century popular literature, including the Horatio Alger stories. Significantly, in contemporaneous European novels such as *Vanity Fair,* a fall in social standing appears "as a matter of bad luck," whereas in the United States, "a move downward more often had moral overtones" (72). Sennett and Cobb argue that these roots engendered a modern American society that regards success as "the badge of individual worth" (77–78). It is fair to say, then, that autobiographers who portray actual living working-class people and pass judgment on them, whether explicitly or implicitly, are doing so within a cultural context of deeply rooted assumptions about such people.

Nonetheless, Barbour emphasizes that good judgment does not mean excusing others from moral assessment. When autobiographers are writing about their parents or siblings, the writers often confuse a posture of forgiveness with a policy of avoiding any moral evaluation whatsoever. Barbour notes the common misconception that "forgiveness is often contrasted with judgment," as if the act of forgiving eliminates or precludes the act of judgment. But forgiveness "is not a refusal to judge"; on the contrary, to decide that something needs to be forgiven is to have made a judgment, Barbour asserts (93). Indeed, "forgiveness *depends* on accurate moral judgment" (my emphasis) (95).

Barbour wonders whether a life writer's desire to forgive a parent may distort his or her judgment, implying that such distortion may be an inevitability. My analyses suggest that ethical problems often stem from the writers' powerful, and completely understandable, need to be a good daughter or son. However, a failure to ascribe moral responsibility properly can undermine the ethical integrity of a text as much as a lack of psychological understanding does. As Barbour suggests, idealizing one's parent may compromise one's discernment and assessment as much as does an attitude of angry rejection (89). Moreover, because the writers I analyze represent members of social, racial, and cultural minority groups, and because their texts are widely circulated, well-regarded literary works, their moral interpretations of family members have ethical implications that extend beyond the limits of their own personal relationships.

In applying these criteria to a reading of four autobiographies, this book suggests that a central part of analyzing the experience of an autobiography is examining how judiciously the author wields his enormous power in representing the real people he has known intimately. For the memoir always, as Nancy K. Miller notes, "expresses a form of power over its subjects" (*Bequest* 14).

The autobiographies I analyze provide a rich opportunity to explore ethics because the upper-middle-class authors have a great advantage over their subjects, the working-class family members they feature prominently in their works. Moreover, the autobiographers' greater professional success in relation to their families is central to the self-identities the writers clarify in their texts. Indeed, all four of the authors are what might be called family redeemers, individuals whose role in their families is to attain enough professional success to vindicate the family's hardship, sacrifice, or, simply, its ordinariness. Whether explicitly or covertly, these autobiographies are very much about the power difference between the authors and the proximate others they depict. Interestingly, many of the texts' ethical problems stem from the authors' apparent ambivalence about the power disparity between themselves and their families, and from the autobiographers' attempt to compensate for what they perceive as a parent's or sibling's vulnerability.

Generally speaking, all four autobiographers analyzed adhere to a common pattern in depicting or describing the shape of their lives. Susanna Egan has identified this plot, which often takes the form of a quest or a "journey entailing separation, death or wounding, and rebirth or return," as "a common feature of the narrative imagination" and one frequently adopted by autobiographers, especially when writing about their youth (*Patterns* 107). For the writers in this study, the object of their youthful quest is, in Mason's words, "to become sophisticated" (xi); that is, to attain the higher education and upper-middle-class status that was inaccessible to their parents. For Wideman, Nesaule, and Mason their journey also entails assimilation into the dominant culture. While Wideman and Nesaule make some allusions to journeys in their texts, especially in referring to the social, cultural, and emotional "distance" they've put between themselves and their families, Mason employs the journey as the central theme that structures her narrative. Baker, who "traveled" less distance culturally in his quest than the others, only once explicitly compares his life to a journey. However, with or without the journey metaphor, all four depict their identity transformations as following the plot formula from which the journey metaphor derives.

Egan surveys the numerous sources of this narrative convention and discovers certain features of the formula to be consistent. The journey plot often contains both "a struggle in which the hero is wounded but victorious and a magic power or redemptive gift that the hero brings back from his ordeal" (107). Further, quoting Joseph Campbell, Egan notes that the "'standard path of the mythological adventure of the hero'" can be seen as a "'a magnification of the formula represented in the rites of passage: separation — initiation — return.'" Egan adds:

> When the mythological hero sets out on his adventures, he too is separated from his family and his society and must struggle with the hardships of his way. Specifically, he encounters fabulous forces, is victorious over them, and returns with the power to bestow a boon on his fellow men [107].

Furthermore, in Egan's analysis of the journey motif in autobiography, the autobiography itself often "becomes the gift described by [Vladimir] Propp, the knowledge or power ascribed by [Arnold] Toynbee and Campbell as the achievement of the journey" (111).

Baker's *Growing Up* is a typical — though extraordinarily well-written — American autobiography about class ascendancy for many reasons, including its unabashed celebration of Franklinesque virtues and its conscious efforts to demonstrate that hard work and education can lead to middle-class prosperity. It is also a normative example of how an autobiographer "returns" from his journey and bestows the gift of the autobiography on his family. For Baker, the return leg of his journey is really just a visit, figuratively speaking; his autobiography is a traditional act of affectionate, respectful reminiscing of the people in his past. Having attained prestige as an author and a *New York Times* columnist, he turns his considerable authority and skill to writing a memoir that pays tribute to the sturdy character of his family members and that acknowledges in particular his mother's significant role in his success. Writing from the perspective of middle-age and having experienced parenthood himself, Baker has, he suggests, greater awareness of the strength and grit his mother possessed during his childhood and adolescence.

Baker's appreciation for his relatives, however, is put forth in moderation. Not seeking to canonize his mother or other family members, Baker succeeds in portraying them with realism, psychological complexity, and flaws. Unlike the textualized identities of Wideman, Nesaule, and Mason, Baker's identity is not staked on his metaphorical "return" to his past. As an autobiographical narrator he does not yearn to move home, literally or figuratively, as do the other authors. In addition, as Chapter 2 argues, Baker's text demonstrates the author's relative ease with his social class liminality; he identifies with both the middle-class values of his mother and the working-class sensibilities of his paternal relatives and his wife. Not perceiving himself as alienated from his origins, he doesn't apologize for being upper-middle-class, nor does he overstate his commonality with his family members.

The other three authors make more problematic use of the return element of the journey plot. For Wideman, Nesaule, and Mason, writing an autobiography in mid-life is more than an act of revisiting the past; it is an act of re-inventing oneself as a loyal and authentic member of the racial, ethnic, or cultural community in which they were raised. More or less following the separation — initiation — return formula outlined by Egan, Wideman, Nesaule, and Mason each depict their adult lives as following a pattern of three stages: separation from their family and community of origin; a painful period of confronting, being oppressed by, and yet trying to assimilate into, the dominant culture; and finally a metaphorical return home, signified by a renewed identification with, respectively, their black, Latvian, or southern family members. Baker's move away from family didn't represent an immersion into a vastly different world, nor did it require him to suppress a large part of his identity; consequently, he isn't compelled to "return" home to recapture a lost part of himself.

Wideman posits his book as a reunion with his imprisoned brother; and he implies that, after a misguided young adulthood in which he wanted to emulate whites, this "collaboration" with Robby demonstrates his solidarity not only with Robby and other people from home but also with other black prisoners. Nesaule depicts her twenty-two-year marriage to Joe as a period in which she was pressured, by her husband and by the mainstream culture, to repress her Latvian identity and to alienate herself from her family and the Latvian community. She suggests that both her divorce from Joe and her new relationship with a man who urges her to express the "Latvian part" of herself have enabled her to return to her Latvian roots (270). And Mason portrays her literal relocation to Kentucky as stemming from her recognition that, during her years up North, where she earned a doctorate and found acclaim as an author, "my folks and their country culture were always present in the deepest part of my being" (xi).

The metaphorical return home of Wideman, Nesaule, and Mason is a sentimental construct that is doomed to be problematic because it is founded on the fallacy that one can, in his or her middle-age, reverse or ignore the transforming effects of higher education, professional status, affluence, and assimilation. In order to construct renewed identification with their roots, Wideman, Nesaule, and Mason sometimes romanticize, excuse, or patronize their original family members in their portrayals of them. The authors also exploit (and exaggerate) the cultural "otherness" of their family members for the authors' own re-invented identities. In addition, they often inadvertently reinforce stereotypes about blacks, southerners, and working-class people.

In many ways the texts by Wideman, Nesaule, and Mason strain to pay tribute to or perform some kind of service for the relatively vulnerable family members the authors left behind. In one interview Wideman claims to have written *Brothers and Keepers* to "help Robby" (Coleman 160). Similarly, Nesaule, wanting to give a voice to her fellow Latvian refugees, especially her own family, begins her book with an "Author's Note" in which she pleads "for greater understanding for all [war] victims" (viii). She adds, "I want tenderness for them long after atrocities end" (viii). In her text she shows not only sympathy to those victims but also bias against those who are not of that group, measuring morality very differently depending on whether or not one is a Latvian war refugee. For her part, Mason plainly wants to create an appreciation in middle-class urban and suburban readers for the simple agrarian lifestyle led by her parents, and to prove that her mother's life as a farm wife is, despite appearances, "*extraordinary*," as Mason declares near the end of the book (274).

Only Baker avoids engaging in what Lynn Z. Bloom calls "special pleading" ("Living" 288). Though Baker brings to light many admirable qualities of his relatives, he primarily wants to tell his own story. In contrast, the other authors write more about their family members than themselves; Wideman and Mason even purport to have written their books about Robby and about Mason's mother, respectively. The decision of these writers to base their own autobiographies on a family member reflects the high level of obligation they feel toward their families. The greater the gap between the author and his or her family in terms of quality of life, the more the memoir is devoted to chronicling the life of a family member rather than the life of the writer.

It's also interesting to note that the greater the disparity between a writer and his family, the more the writer insists on a newly recognized oneness with one or more family members. Wideman, whose life could not be more different than his brother's, discovers "a simple truth: I could never run fast enough or far enough. Robby was inside me" (4). Mason, near the end of her book, declares, "After all my comings and goings, now I see that I *am* my mother — and all of my forebears" (281). Nesaule strongly implies that she's reclaiming her "real" self by embracing the symbols of her Latvian family, such as her mother's amber, some sand from Latvia, and even her family's hatred of Joe, her former husband.

An examination of the obvious social and cultural differences between Russell Baker and the other authors can provide insight into the reasons behind the ethical problems in the works by Wideman, Nesaule, and Mason. As an autobiographer Baker has far less to contend with in delineating an identity. To begin with, he has no problematic large-group identity like the racial, ethnic, or regional identities of the other authors. He is, of course, a member of an ethnic group (WASP), but because he identifies with the "normal" majority and the dominant culture, he hasn't had, either in life or in writing his text, to overcome any real sense of being different or inferior, as have Wideman, Nesaule, and Mason.

As a white Anglo-Saxon Protestant man who was raised by a mother and other relatives who espoused, as Baker portrays them as doing, Franklinesque values such as self-improvement and industriousness, Baker moved into the middle class more smoothly than the other authors. The working-class aspects of his childhood that made him feel different were easily made invisible when he entered college and later the field of journalism since, after all, he had no dark skin, accent, or ethnic name to set him apart. Unlike Wideman, Nesaule, and Mason, as an autobiographer Baker does not face the daunting task of integrating radically different worlds of his past and present.

In contrast, the other writers face an additional burden in constructing a persona; they not only delineate a personal self but also an ethnic identity, which the psychoanalytic theorist Vamik Volkan considers analogous to a second layer of clothing:

> Think in terms of learning to wear, from childhood on, two layers of clothing. The first layer fits snugly. This is one's personal identity. The second layer, the ethnic (emotionally bonded large group) layer, is a loose covering that protects the individual in the way that a parent, close family members, or other caregiver protects one [27].

Wideman, Nesaule, and Mason all identify themselves with a racial or ethnic group (Chapter 5 argues that Mason equates her southern "country" heritage with an ethnic identity) that has been deemed inferior or backward by the dominant culture. As all three of them suggest in their memoirs, their large-group identities are associated with shame, powerlessness, and, for Wideman and Nesaule in particular, trauma. Certainly for these three authors social class, lifestyle, and ethnicity are intertwined. Consequently, Wideman, Nesaule, and Mason all experienced their move into the upper-middle-class as a threat to their racial, ethnic, or regional identity. Baker's cultural background was not at odds with the values and lifestyle of the middle class; indeed, in his mother's household, class mobility and social respectability were foundational values.

Wideman and Mason both write about their belief, held during their youth and young adulthood, that they couldn't be both middle-class, and, respectively, black or southern "country." Nesaule suggests that throughout her young adulthood she believed that being emotionally healthy and professionally successful were incompatible with being a "real" Latvian-American. All three of them also write about feeling pressured by professors and others to erase their cultural differences in order to succeed academically and socially. However, their texts also suggest that this pressure really came mostly from themselves and that they felt guilty for wanting to shed their racial or ethnic identities. Baker, in contrast, doesn't characterize his class change as a betrayal; in fact, his matriculation at a university fulfilled his mother's nearly feverish ambition for him.

After experiencing such a deeply disorienting shift in their identities, Wideman, Nesaule, and Mason write with a strong psychological imperative to re-assert their racial or ethnic selves, and even to invent a self that is perhaps more "ethnic" than the authors had been before they left home. Volkan explains that people who feel that their large-group identity is in danger of erasure will emphasize even more this aspect of their identity. Using a Finn as an example, Volkan writes that "going to the sauna ... remains a national habit for a Finn, but he is proud of being a Finn even when he is not in the sauna" (91). However, "Should Finland or his Finnishness be threatened ... he will adhere more stubbornly to his sense of ethnicity, because to give it up would feel like giving up part of his own being, part of his own identity. He will also exaggerate his tradition and perhaps go to a sauna more often to affirm his concrete link with his shared we-ness" (92). Since Baker didn't attempt to shed his cultural identity — he didn't have to — he doesn't write from a desire either to assert an ethnic self or defend his native culture.

Another major difference between Baker and the other writers is the psychological dynamic between the authors and their parents. Although his mother endured losses and hardship, Baker does not see her as a victim. Even though she was a woman living in an era of gender inequality, Baker does not portray her as powerless; for example, she managed to accomplish her goals of independently supporting her children and making her son eligible for a college scholarship. Consequently, Baker wants to pay homage to his mother's character, but he clearly doesn't feel the need to compensate for (or ignore) her limitations by romanticizing her in his text. He writes that as a child, he felt he had to make up for her thwarted dreams for her own life; he outgrew that, however, and as a middle-aged autobiographer he plainly isn't driven to explain her failures or lament her victimization. Significantly, the mother he portrays didn't see herself as a victim.

Wideman, Nesaule, and Mason, on the contrary, all regard the proximate others around which they center their texts as victims in life, and the authors explicitly connect that person's experience of trauma, shame, and powerlessness to his or her racial or ethnic group — to a status as black, "country," or Latvian "exile." A crucial aspect of these writers' relationships with their parents is the adult child's deep sense of his or her parents' powerlessness. Wideman writes about his mother's overwhelming feelings of bitterness, futility, and paranoia as a black person in a world in which whites, she believes, "have a master plan that leaves little to accident, that most of the ugliest things happening to black people are not accidental but the predictable results of the working of the plan" (72). Throughout Nesaule's memoir her parents are mistreated, controlled, and exploited, first by soldiers and later by greedy landlords and employers. Mason portrays her mother as a neglected orphan who was later dominated throughout her adulthood by her mother-in-law; Mason also characterizes her mother as having been locked into a life of child-raising and endless farm chores because of her lack of education.

This perception of powerlessness in their parents is an important key to the identities of Wideman, Nesaule, and Mason as delineated in their texts. The parent-child dynamic demonstrated in these authors' memoirs is one that Volkan explains in his discussion:

> Transgenerational transmission is when an older person unconsciously externalizes his traumatized self onto a developing child's personality. A child then becomes a reservoir for the unwanted, troublesome parts of an older generation. Because the elders have influence on a child, the child absorbs their wishes and expectations and is driven to act on them. It becomes the child's task to mourn, to reverse the humiliation and feelings of helplessness pertaining to the trauma of his forebears [43].

As stated earlier, all the authors in this book are family redeemers; however, as autobiographers Wideman, Nesaule, and Mason also assume the role of family hero or heroine by using their writing to solicit sympathy and admiration for their family members—and dislike for those whom the writers perceive as having bullied or discriminated against their families. As autobiographers they are trying to reverse the powerlessness of their family members who lack the authors' strength, intellectual gifts, literary talent, and other advantages. To do this they mount a passionate defense of their family members and their native cultures, at times placing loyalty before truth-value. Near the end of his memoir, Wideman disingenuously asserts that his imprisoned brother is a "better man" than Wideman himself (202); similarly, Mason tries to portray her ordinary mother as "amazing" (110). Nesaule doesn't romanticize her mother as much as she wields her prose to fight a fierce battle on her mother's behalf, vilifying her ex-husband Joe in large part for his lack of compassion for her mother and other Latvian war refugees.

Baker's family suffered, too, but their traumas were not connected to their identity; neither Baker's mother nor Baker himself perceived their poverty to be a result of who they were. Their struggle was largely due to the Depression—an experience shared by nearly every segment of society. As an autobiographer, Baker wants people to like his mother—who doesn't?—but he trusts his readers to like her in spite of her flaws. Wideman, Nesaule, and Mason, who have experienced prejudice against their cultural communities, don't trust their readers to like their family members without persuasion.

Sennett and Cobb cite one of the psychological and emotional complications resulting from class mobility as "status incongruity," a "tangle of feelings" amounting to more than a mere sense of being "caught between two worlds" (20). A person who has raised his class status, the authors assert, experiences "a profound dislocation" in his life, but also "a feeling of inadequate defenses in the very midst of success" (26). The move upward creates a range of conflicts involving a person's relationships with his family and community. These include a guilt similar to survivor's guilt; a feeling of having betrayed his family (183); a sense of having to choose between the rewards of achievement and the enjoyment of "fraternity" with the people with whom his "loyalties and social bonds remain" (110); and a great sense of division in himself in which his "active, performing self" is alienated from "the passive self that just wants to be, to enjoy family and friends, to love them" (194).

A sense of having betrayed one's family by surpassing them is enhanced, the autobiographies in this study suggest, when one's family members have led particularly difficult lives. The ethical problems in the texts of Wideman, Nesaule, and Mason are often engendered by the authors' focus on the obstacles faced by their family members, rather than on the achievements of the author. In trying to explain why their parents or siblings didn't raise their class status, these authors often employ distorted logic or disingenuous rhetoric, and sometimes intellectually dishonest characterizations. As autobiographers, Wideman, Nesaule, and Mason are caught in a bind created by the wide disparity between themselves and their relatives. To give a more deeply truthful account of their transformation, they would have to acknowledge not necessarily the shortcomings of their family members but the extraordinary strengths the authors themselves possess—a difficult approach to undertake when one wants to remain modest. Yet Wideman, Nesaule, and Mason all overcame tremendous odds in order to escape the worlds of their childhood. Their texts would be stronger if they had emphasized that point—that being extraordinary is what it takes to get out of, respectively, the Homewood ghetto, the impoverished Latvian-American community of Indianapolis, and the Kentucky farm.

Baker's memoir demonstrates a way out of this ethical bind with his focus on how and why he was able to move beyond his working-class origins. He does acknowledge (in one paragraph) that his sister Doris was greatly disadvantaged by the "defect" of being a girl in a time when girls were expected to become housewives, nurses, or teachers (10). But mostly he tells the story of how his mother's shrewd guidance facilitated his intellectual development and fostered his success. It is a positive approach that helps him avoid the ethical pitfalls that ensnare the other writers. Baker's depiction of his mother as the ambitious one and himself as the reluctant achiever is an ingenious device that enables him to trace his own achievements while not appearing to take himself too seriously. By drawing his mother as the driving force behind his upward rise, he can recount a Franklinesque story of hard work leading to success without boasting of his own self-discipline.

However, by documenting the life of a white male from an ordinary working-class family, Baker's story goes against the current trend in contemporary autobiography (though his book was a bestseller). In modern-day America it is more glamorous to return to one's racial, ethnic, and regional origins than to return to one's working-class roots. In fact the romanticization of one's cultural difference has itself become an American convention. According to Werner Sollors, "In contemporary usage ethnicity has largely been transformed from a heathenish liability into a sacred asset, from a trait to be overcome in a conversion and rebirth experience to a very desirable identity feature to be achieved through yet another regeneration" (33). It is, moreover, easier to re-invent oneself as "authentically" black or southern than it is to erase the class gap between oneself and one's family created by higher education and professional success.

Indeed, the autobiographies by Wideman, Nesaule, and Mason illustrate how conditionally, even strategically, class, ethnic, and regional identities can be constructed, with one or the other emphasized or suppressed according to an author's needs. For example, as part of re-identifying with her original family, Nesaule focuses on class differences between her husband and herself and her family members. In contrast, Wideman, in order to establish more commonality between himself and his brother, foregrounds his racial identity as an African American, and de-emphasizes the class difference between himself and Robby. Mason is able to depict her similarity with her rural, high-school-educated mother by constructing a southern "country" identity for herself—her version of "country" being rural and homey rather than the cowboy-culture style promoted by Nashville—and by virtually omitting details about her present life as an affluent, upper-middle-class author. Further, Mason magnifies the "country" aspect of her parents' life above the southern quality of it, thereby skirting the more negative connotations and stereotypes of southern life. Yet Baker succeeds in large part because, without the "edge" of cultural difference, he has to do the literary work of making relatively ordinary people interesting and lovable, rather than relying on—and exploiting—as do the other writers, the exotic "otherness" of family members.

As all four of the texts in this book demonstrate, an autobiographical identity is a construct that provides a shape and a meaning for the narrative, as Egan observes about an autobiography's theme (*Patterns* 21). Though fiction is an inevitable and necessary aspect of any work of artful autobiography (including Baker's, which perhaps too consistently keeps us in the world of the Franklinesque), the identities that Wideman, Nesaule, and Mason construct nonetheless engender some of the distortions, omissions, and simplifications that make their texts ethically problematic.

The ethical analysis undertaken in this study attempts to recognize that "truth," the sought-after virtue of ethical writing, is never a single person's perception but is a product of social and cultural collaboration. Yet by making "appraisals of truth-value" in these texts, this book will, it is hoped, raise awareness of ethical problems than can arise when even highly skilled and well-intentioned writers undertake to textualize complicated self-identities amidst complex circumstances. The study also seeks to enhance understanding of the ethical bind working-class autobiographers face; writing about one's class transition is as conflict-ridden as living through it, and both require courage. Even the ethical problems of these texts testify, in some ways, to the fortitude of their authors, who defend their families— albeit edited versions of them — with the same determination that brought the writers out of the working-class circumstances into which they were born.

1

A World Apart:
Working Class Autobiographers
and Their Families

When the *New York Times* writer Rick Bragg published his best-selling autobiography, *All Over but the Shoutin'* (1997), he chose as his epigraph a verse from the song "Pancho and Lefty," by T. Van Zandt. The verse describes a hard-shelled hero who lives on the road, free of emotional ties. This man was loved by his family, was even considered the special one — his mother's favorite son; but, the lyrics suggest, his life of constant motion, of perpetual pursuit of achievement, has hardened him, leaving him emotionally inaccessible and, it is implied, incapable of forming deep attachments. The verse ends with an image recalling the young man bidding farewell to his family, bound to his dreams, while his mother cries.

Van Zandt's image of the rugged hero departing to pursue his ambitions, leaving behind his weeping mother, is a Country-Westernized version of a convention in American rags-to-riches literature that dates back at least to Horatio Alger. That Bragg uses it suggests that for him, the lyrics capture the essence of his story, which chronicles his transformation from a poor southern boy to a Pulitzer Prize-winning reporter, and which is dedicated to "My momma and my brothers." It also underscores the extent to which that conventional imagery, which masculinizes the upwardly-mobile individual and feminizes (and sentimentalizes) the people back home, informed the characterizations in his book. As has been well noted by autobiography scholars, life writers often draw, either unconsciously or with intention, upon available models of identity to provide shape for their own self-portraits. Bragg's characterization of himself and his mother hew closely to those in Van Zandt's song. That Bragg's memoir was enormously popular suggests the powerful appeal of the American success story, and also, partly, of these familiar characterizations. The song's gender roles are reassuring cliches, even in our modern society, in which an ambitious male is yet a more cherished figure than a power-seeking female. Indeed, as a group, twentieth-century autobiographies by women who crossed class barriers indicate that women have experienced much greater resistance to, and familial complications because of, their professional achievements than have their male counterparts.

Van Zandt's lyrics also reinforce subtle but pervasive class characterizations in which the working classes are depicted as passive, emotional, or saintly, among other "feminine" qualities. Like many narrators of class-advancement stories, Bragg is an active, performing self who moves through time, while his mother and siblings are depicted as remaining in a world that is enclosed, seemingly unchanging, and relatively static. This dichotomizing approach to portraying the two worlds of the autobiographer's life, the working-class past and the upper-middle-class present, is typical of American autobiographies that trace the authors' departure from working-class origins.

Raymond Williams identified a similar problem in twentieth-century British fiction. After the first World War, writers who had grown up in the working class began producing novels, and they often sought to re-create the world of that community—"typically the world of childhood or of the family, while cancelling their present selves from this original situation" (271–72). Williams described these "separated novels" as depicting the working-class community as "the enclosed class as a regional zone of experience" (272). Later in the century, narratives about working-class childhoods were centered on the theme of escape from this life: "They lacked any sense of the continuity of working-class life, which does not cease just because one individual moves out of it, but which also itself changes internally" (272).

The problem, Williams recognized, is not just a literary one but a human one, the challenge of characterizing a particular way of life that is different from the author's present, without portraying the people who live it as monolithic, ossified, and "other." For twentieth-century American autobiographers, this challenge was complicated by various additional influences, often, for instance, political ones. From the slave narratives on, American autobiography has been an effective tool for social change, and a great deal of the working-class autobiographies published in the last century were aimed at enlightening mainstream readers about lives on the periphery. In such books autobiographers of various races and ethnic groups often tailored their portrayals of their early lives to support their ideological purpose. Other motives also engendered certain autobiographical practices: Richard Rodriguez narrated his personal history as part of his argument against bilingual education and affirmative action, while authors such as Mary Karr and Michael Patrick MacDonald (*All Souls: A Family Story from Southie*, 1999) published gritty memoirs of their working-class families and became media celebrities.

This chapter will trace some of the more significant strategies in portraying one's working-class origins that emerged over the last century in American life narratives, as represented in four texts. These strategies frequently reflect the authors' times, including the prevailing cultural attitudes towards the poor; literary vogues; and, especially, social and political pressure on marginal writers to portray "others" in certain ways for the largely-white middle-class readership to whom publishers catered for much of the century. The autobiography by Dreiser represents the start of at least two major developments in American autobiography that may have peaked in the 1990s: the unabashed showcasing of the family's dirty linen; and, the exploiting of one's poor origins to enhance one's literary identity. Richard Wright exemplifies an autobiographer's privileging of an ideological agenda over complex and nuanced characterizations of his family members; but *Black Boy* also represents a rhetorical situation in which such distortions may be ethically justified. Yezierska's text illustrates the stereotypical identity crisis of immigrants, the Old World/New World conflict, but with a postmodern twist: the author's guilt about "betraying" her family by leaving their culture has been replaced, in her later years, by remorse for having exploited and misrepresented them in her fiction. For her part, Angelou inaugurated a significant trend in the genre by launching a literary career with her autobiography, but she also provides a rare example of working-class memoir that resists the typical tendency to emphasize the "otherness" of one's socially marginal relatives. My discussions center on the critical reception of these books, so that the chapter will also trace the development of critics' views on autobiographers' portrayals of their working-class families over the century, and in particular critics' implied ethical judgments.

Theodore Dreiser's *Dawn* (1931) is the first autobiography by a major American writer in which the author not only explicitly depicts the poverty of his childhood but also clearly seeks to exploit that background to solidify his identity as a writer of fiction. In fact, Dreiser's career represented several social and literary breakthroughs. Biographer F. O. Matthiessen noted that Dreiser was "the first American writer whose family name was not English or Scotch Irish" (Matthiessen 10). Ellen Moers adds that he was "the first to be brought up Catholic; the first to hear a foreign language spoken at home; the first whose people were not only very poor, but unrespectable" (xiv). From his adolescence into his adulthood, Dreiser felt very deeply the "snobbery" of middle-class people who considered him inferior because of his impoverished upbringing. During his single, improbable year as a scholarship student at Indiana University, Dreiser was "palpably conscious" of being considered "undesirable" for "lack of a little money, savoir faire, social experience, and the like" (*Dawn* 390). But more painful to him than being excluded socially was his deep sense that a professional life was out of his reach, in spite of his intellectual drive and abilities. He recalls admiring a particular professor and envying him "The delight of living in such a refined and nobly intellectual world! Ah, why was I born to be a dub?" (413).

Of course he did become a writer, but that sense of being judged as vulgar and inferior stayed with him. Moreover, the success Dreiser eventually achieved was in large part the result of his ability to transform his deprived childhood, and the insights he drew from it, into his chief asset. When he was twenty-eight, Dreiser's literary career was launched amidst a controversy that sealed his image as a chronicler and champion of the poor — but also as an underdog defending the worthiness of his material against the genteel, elitist literary establishment. *Sister Carrie* was published in 1900, but only after its publisher, the Doubleday, Page Company, had attempted to break its contract and not publish it; legally bound, the publisher begrudgingly issued the book and, Dreiser claimed, failed to promote it. As Marsha S. Moyer explains, Frank Norris, who was a reader at Doubleday, invented a story that the publisher's wife, Mrs. Doubleday, was scandalized by the novel and insisted that it be suppressed. For Dreiser, who eagerly spread the tale, the story undoubtedly soothed the humiliation caused by the novel's meager sales, but it also provided him with an identity as an important cultural figure. As Moyer notes, instead of feeling like a failed novelist, he could see himself as the victim of Mrs. Doubleday, a "cultural symbol" who represented "the confining genteel code held in place by the sanctity of home and virtuous womanhood, a code which shaped the cultural discourse that influenced the negative reception to his first book" (41).

It is true that the reviews of *Sister Carrie* were centered on class and the questionable desirability of working-class characters as literary subjects. A word that frequently appears in the reviews is "reeks," as in the *Louisville Times* reviewer's description of Dreiser's realism: "It is sometimes morbid and sometimes forbidding. At its best it is grim and shadowy. It reeks of life's sordid endeavor; of the lowly home and the hopelessly restricted existence" (Salzman 1). The novel follows an unsophisticated young woman's journey from a small town into the theater world of Chicago, where she quickly engages in an illicit liaison with one man, then leaves him to become the mistress of an embezzler. Denounced by many critics as immoral and evil, the book was ignored by influential critics such as William Dean Howells and Hamlin Garland. Dreiser's biographer Swanberg explains that Carrie "was an affront to current mores at a time" (87). Certainly, Carrie's illicit sex and her ambiguous position at the end — she wasn't sufficiently punished for her sins, some critics suggested — explain some of the negative reaction to the novel. But as Swanberg notes, critics were repelled by the notion of working-class characters as a subject for a novel: "It dealt with uneducated people who spoke colloquially," and thus "it was vulgar" (88). Further, "Dreiser obviously *liked* these characters, compounding his crime by showing great sympathy for these vulgarians in their sordid tribulations" (88). With the exception of a rather small group of intellectuals, readers were threatened by Dreiser's humanizing, rather than sentimentalizing or demonizing, of uneducated people outside the realm of respectability, and by his suggestion that their moral agency is diminished by the harshness of their circumstances.

The cool reception to *Sister Carrie* first sent Dreiser into a depression, then caused him to burn with a sense that he was "fighting a struggle not only against provincial moral standards, but aesthetic values, sociopolitical issues, and economic injustices" (Moyer 45). Over the next fifteen years, having published five more books, Dreiser was gradually becoming a central figure in critical debates. By the late teens, when he began writing *Dawn*, he was entering into a period of "renewed [critical] effort to establish Dreiser as a serious writer in America" (Moyer 49). During this "glory" period he was "hailed as 'the culmination of an American progressive tradition with eighteenth-century roots.'" He was seen as a "folk-hero who wrote in plain language" for the broader public (Moyer 49). Though published in 1931, *Dawn* was written some twelve or so years earlier, when Dreiser was gaining strength in his literary reputation, but was not yet as solidly established as he would be after the publication of *An American Tragedy* in 1925. Thus, it is fair to read the autobiography as Dreiser's attempt to solidify his image as an authentic and authoritative voice of working-class America.

Though *Dawn* is hardly read anymore, it was recognized by Dreiser's critics as an important development in American autobiography, primarily because of the author's unsparing depiction of his family and their struggles, which no other major writer had done. Along with the majority of reviewers, Henry Hazlitt in the *Nation* praised the book for its "unparalleled candor" (Salzman 605), and William Soskin, of the *New York Evening Post*, called *Dawn* "the most ferociously frank and sensitively candid biographies I have ever read," adding that "Dreiser's candor is brutal and deep" (Salzman 590). One reviewer called it "the most talked of book in America today" (Salzman 610).

Clearly, it was not simply the author's willingness to reveal all that stirred up so much excitement but the sensational nature of the revelations. From his father's pathetic failure to provide for his family, to his mother's visions and superstitions, to the drunkenness and illicit sexual relationships of some siblings, Dreiser details not only his impoverished childhood but also his family members' lack of respectability in their adult lives. Harry Hansen in the *New York Evening World Telegram* declared, "There never was an autobiography like this.... Dreiser tells everything. He makes no attempt to romanticize the unattractive household in which he grew up.... His brother's difficulties, his sisters' amorous adventures—these are laid frankly before the reader" (Salzman 592). *Dawn* is, Hansen added, "An honest record, uncolored and unashamed" (Salzman 593).

Dreiser's chief autobiographical strategy, as he suggests on his first page, is to proclaim himself free of shame about his past and his family, and then to prove his claim by baring all. The "average" person, he writes, "has frequently the greatest hesitation in revealing the net of flesh and emotion and human relationship into which he was born and which conditioned his early efforts at living and too often his subsequent place in life and society. I am free to say here and now that I am in no way troubled by any such thoughts or feelings" (3). He goes on to express pity for anyone who "is so fearful of life and so poorly grounded in an understanding of things that he is terrorized lest someone discover that his uncle was a horse thief or his sister a prostitute or his father a bank-wrecker" (3). Dreiser doesn't share that terror because "What has that to do with me, an individual has a right to ask himself?" Shame is unnecessary, not because social status shouldn't be cause for shame, but because "One does not make one's relatives or oneself or the world." The most "interesting" thing one can do is to "observe or rearrange or explain" (3).

Significantly, then, Dreiser suggests that by being analytical about his past and his family, he can avoid the feelings of shame that might plague the "average earthling" in his circumstance. Further, because of his ability and his intention to "observe" and "explain," he needn't be morally reluctant to unveil the family secrets; it will be obvious, he remarks, that he is "moved only by motives of analysis which are as honest and sympathetic as I hope to make them revealing" (3).

Indeed, Dreiser's primary strategy in portraying his family, with the exception of his mother, is one of fairly detached observation, as if they were sociological specimens. In one passage he summarizes the fates of some of his siblings in a tone that approaches indifference: "Rome drank himself into failure if not death. The girls, all of them, married, but by what devious routes! One, at thirty-seven, was killed by a train; another at forty, died of cancer. And so it has gone" (11). Dreiser self-consciously holds up his family as examples of lives lived on a particular social rung in the Midwest, and he knowingly depicts this life, to use his word, as a "spectacle," which, as he describes his early childhood home in Terre Haute, "must have offered as interesting an example of mental nebulosity and lack of social placement and skill as one would care to find" (21).

Critics were enthusiastic about *Dawn*'s "genuine value as sociology," as the *New Republic* put it, because of Dreiser's thorough portrait of bleakness (Salzman 615). Harry Emerson Wildes in the *Philadelphia Public Ledger* ranked *Dawn* among "the classic autobiographies" because of its vivid depiction of a life of "*pathos*": "Its slabs of raw red meat, its reek of slum-like atmosphere attest to its starkly realistic atmosphere." Only Dreiser's "skill in understanding" saves his book "from filth and horror" (Salzman 587). Readers, Wildes advised, will "unquestionably wince at Dreiser's method, you'll shudder at his candor" and find the book's honesty "repellent"; but this immersion into sordidness, Wildes noted, is worthwhile because Dreiser's "data are indispensable to those who earnestly desire to know the real life of submerged classes" (Salzman 587). In *Dawn*, then, reviewers saw a successful piece of literary realism which fulfilled the purpose of all works of realism, to document and represent the underclasses.

Realism as an artistic mode is, in itself, rife with ethical contradictions, and when an autobiographer applies that method to portraying his own family it is even more ethically problematic. E. L. Doctorow defines the aesthetic principle of realism as one "which proposes that the business of fiction is not to draw an idealized picture of human beings for the instruction or sentimental satisfaction of readers, but rather to portray life as it is really lived under specific circumstances of time and place" (viii). Amy Kaplan has observed that realism, while having sprung from progressive motives, was not, as it was typically manifested during the early decades of the last century, as deeply radical as its proponents liked to think: realism "strives to pave a common ground for diverse social classes by extending literary representation to 'the other half' while reassuring middle-class readers that social difference can be effaced in the mirror of the commonplace" (46). Moreover, realism often reinforced the "otherness" of the poor.

Realism blossomed around the beginning of the twentieth century, amidst a relatively new, intense awareness of class division in the country. A number of social changes in the 1890's, such as a great wave of immigration and the organization of workers, left middle-class Americans feeling threatened by the lower classes. Violent outbreaks like the 1890 Haymarket Riot of Chicago sparked fears of class warfare, as Kaplan notes; popular writers of the time, such as Josiah Strong, characterized the working classes as a "rumbling" mob and likened them to "'cannibals of some far off coast'" (Kaplan 45). Artists, intellectuals, and social activists, on the other hand, had spent that decade discovering the urban poor as an "important" and exotic subject of art as well as a social-reform project. Jacob Riis's best-selling book, *How the Other Half Lives* (1890), a photographic and journalistic study of a New York tenement, exemplifies the way middle-class culture tended to approach the spectacle of urban poverty during this period, in that it is a well-intentioned project that nonetheless primitivizes its subjects. As Kaplan observes, although Riis's book "aims to improve the living conditions of the poor, it appeals more immediately to the hearts and minds of his readers — the other 'other half.' Playing on fears of urban violence, Riis highlights the alien features of the immigrants to fix the foreign-born as 'other' in the eyes of his readers" (46).

Dreiser's literary identity was founded on his realism and his expertise in crafting working-class characters, and it is understandable that he would apply the method that worked so well in his fiction to the writing of his own life. But *Dawn* demonstrates the inherent problems, both literary and ethical, in treating one's family members somewhat as sociological case-studies. The book suggests that, in order to render his relatives' lives so thoroughly, and thus to strip them so entirely of their privacy, Dreiser has to refrain from seeing them as actual people, and from emotionally engaging with them as family members. For example, when he relates the story of his sister Amy's out-of-wedlock pregnancy, he uses a tone of condescension that he rarely, if ever, uses toward his fictional characters. He writes that, to Don Ashley, the young man who had seduced Amy, "Amy was really little more than a street girl ... a mere temporary diversion. (I cannot say that I can quarrel with his lack of interest; outside of this one bent, Amy, as I see it now, could scarcely, at that time at least, have inspired any man to real love)" (260). At one point he envisions Amy during this crisis as being "soaked, no doubt, in the best type of melodramatic misery. If she had only gained a clearer working conception of the realities, it would have been worth the cost. As it was, merely endless tangled steps, ending in confusion" (261).

Elsewhere Dreiser details another sister's scheming to obtain a married man, as well as several occasions during his youth when his sisters were sexually exploited by local boys. He also offers up scenes in which his troubled brother Rome steals, vandalizes, and debases himself in various ways while inebriated. Reviewers registered some shock at Dreiser's revelations, but virtually all of them applauded him because, they reasoned, his family's humiliations were all part of the complete and truthful picture. Albert Mordell in the *Philadelphia Record* noted that Dreiser was surprisingly "hindered by no filial ties"; consequently, "I can think of no work that gives a better picture of the troubles of a poor American family, with their poverty, conflicts, quarrels. There is no hypocrisy, no evading of facts or conclusions" (Salzman 595). For their part, the reviewers rehashed for readers the juiciest nuggets of Dreiser's family's hardships. Thus, Dreiser and his critics colluded in relieving the author's relatives of their dignity and humanity, all of them implying that the reputations and other personal rights of these "unrespectable" people mattered less than the cause of Literature. One wonders if the attitudes of the author and the critics would have been different if Dreiser's subjects were prominent citizens, but certainly, as several critics of the day noted, American autobiographers to that point had almost always been more reticent about their families, and dutiful about keeping their secrets.

One might also wonder if critics of Dreiser's day gave much consideration to the ethical aspects of an autobiographer's representation of family members; on the whole, the evidence suggests that they did not, but at least one reviewer of *Dawn* could not help but respond to the book from an ethical point of view. Henry Hazlitt, in the *Nation*, observed that "Few autobiographers, surely, have treated their immediate family as he has," adding that "only [Dreiser's] mother comes out ... well by the ordinary moral standards." Hazlitt did not explore the philosophical implications of Dreiser's treatment of his family members, but he did express concern about Dreiser's penchant for kissing-and-telling: "When he mentions his own sexual adventures or those of others, he almost invariably mentions the real name ... of the girl involved, together with her town, her neighborhood, or the business firm for which she worked" (Salzman 605).

Unlike virtually any other reviewer of *Dawn*, Hazlitt approached an ethical analysis of this autobiography when he suggested the possibility that Dreiser's book could have very real and potentially destructive effects on the women he boasts of seducing: "Many of these women are now presumably the mothers of grown families: let us sincerely hope that none of their husbands, children, friends, or enemies chance to read this book" (Salzman 606). But just when Hazlitt seemed ready to assert that Dreiser's subjects may have certain ethical claims, he cited the inverted moral logic that, he believed, producers of literature had to follow: "but we must remember that in autobiography ... the vices of the man are the virtues of the writer" (606). Such "unparalleled candor," Hazlitt concluded, is "surely the greatest single merit that any autobiographer can have" (605).

While no critic, then, ultimately condemned Dreiser for exposing his family members (and others) so egregiously, some reviewers found his characterizations to be shallow and undeveloped. They suggested that, in contrast to the way he humanized his fictional characters, brilliantly bestowing them with dimension and complexity, in his autobiography Dreiser analyzed people instead of bringing them to life. Robert Herrick, in the *Saturday Review of Literature*, observed that "in spite of his proclaimed freedom in dealing with intimate facts, Mr. Dreiser has succeeded in hacking out but one distinct character from the family ... his mother." Herrick pointed out that "never once ... is [Dreiser's mother] allowed to speak for herself in convincing accents. Nor any of the brothers and sisters: they are presented through the novel's woolly analyses" (Salzman 608). Consequently, Herrick found Dreiser's siblings "hard to distinguish" from one another and "impossible to remember," and, thus, "their frailties of conduct as well as their virtues are insignificant" (608).

In spite of its problems, *Dawn* was an important literary and cultural breakthrough, the first time a white American writer dared to write so revealingly a personal story of growing up poor. Moreover, Dreiser was not just exposing his family, he was also exposing himself, and some of the reception to *Dawn* was as mean-spirited as some of the reaction to *Sister Carrie* had been. The review of *Dawn* in the *New Republic*, for example, manifested the biting class-snobbery that often lurked in the literary culture of the time. Newton Arvin declared "social envy and social ambitiousness" to be Dreiser's main theme and central character trait (Salzman 615). He asserted that Dreiser's "interest in people has never been simple and studious," that his novels were no more than "the expression of a will to power, a passion for worldly success" (615–16). Arvin found it only natural, he implied, that such an amoral person as Dreiser came from the lower classes: Dreiser "has been a richly characteristic product of a depersonalized and predatory society" (617). Arvin's attitude underscores the courage that Dreiser displayed in writing and publishing *Dawn*.

More than seventy-five years after its publication, Dreiser's autobiography illustrates some of the basic dilemmas faced by twentieth-century autobiographers who crossed class barriers. As a writer, his first-hand knowledge of the poor was one of his greatest commodities, and he may have felt that revealing his past so fully would prove himself an authentic voice of the working-class. Despite his glaring ethical violations, the book as a whole suggests that, rather than seeking to hurt his family or even to diminish their humanity, Dreiser was, in his mind, simply choosing to fulfill his duty as a writer. As Chekhov was reported to have said, to do one's job as a writer, one has to turn one's heart to ice, and many autobiographers of both Dreiser's time and ours have assumed that attitude.

In the *New Yorker*, Dorothy Parker snidely suggested that Dreiser was mining his past for its "literary good fortune": "for when, in print, was the shanty not more glamorous than the salon?" (Salzman 601). However, to read *Dawn* only as a cynical, opportunistic sell-out of his family for his own image, is unfair to both the man and the book. It is more likely that, while Dreiser undoubtedly felt that his financial security and his literary reputation hinged on his continuing to act as the "bell-wether of realism," as one critic called him, he also believed that an unsparing portrait of real people struggling in poverty would both deepen the middle classes' understanding of the poor and advance the national literature.

Richard Wright's autobiography, *Black Boy* (1945), also tells the story of the author's childhood in a poor family and of his growing determination to pull himself into a better life — a resolve that stemmed from some innate differences in him and from his exposure to literature and writing. However, the similarities between the men's lives and their life narratives largely end there. While Dreiser's book was well-received by his contemporaries, his critics' predictions that *Dawn* would become a classic American autobiography on par with those of Franklin and Adams have proven off the mark. *Black Boy*, published fourteen years after *Dawn*, was a bestseller that sealed Wright's stature as an important writer, yet the initial critical response was far more controversial than the reaction to *Dawn*, and even vituperative in some cases. But the work has become the classic that *Dawn* did not. Its emotional power and literary artistry make *Dawn* pale in comparison; but to be fair to Dreiser, the two men wrote their autobiographies with two radically different purposes and while operating under very different definitions of "autobiography" as a genre. Dreiser treated the form strictly as non-fiction, a record of his early life as seen and analyzed by his mature self. He wrote *Dawn*, in part, for business reasons, because his publisher, Horace Liveright, suggested an autobiography as part of their multi-book contract.

In contrast, Wright produced *Black Boy* from a passionate sense of heeding a call to speak "the truth" on behalf of African Americans. In 1943 Wright gave a talk about growing up in Mississippi and Memphis at Tennessee's Fisk University, and the response from his audience made him believe that blacks urgently needed for someone of his stature (he had, three years earlier, published his novel *Native Son* to wide acclaim) to write about the reality of life for blacks in the South. According to Wright's biographer, Michael Fabre, "both white and black" intellectuals who heard

Wright's speech were struck by his bold revelations, and saw him as, in the words of one black educator, "the first man to tell the truth in this town!" (249). Wright began working on *Black Boy* immediately.

While *Black Boy* sprang from the writer's strong sense of ideological purpose, Wright's text makes it clear that the author was not simply writing a sociological tract, not merely setting out to deliver a message. In *Black Boy,* he created a work of literature plainly meant to be read aesthetically as well as historically, a book that, as Albert Stone notes, not only depicts a time and place but also traces the development of Wright as an artist and genius. Wright, then, approached life writing with multilayered intentions, creating an "autobiography" that is both an historical record of his own life and a novelistic representation of black life in the South.

The differences between *Dawn* and *Black Boy* in terms of their authors' portrayal of their family members reflect the vast disparity in the autobiographers' intentions. While Dreiser did want to shed light on a particular social milieu, the tone of his narrative does not suggest an indictment of society, nor does the author implicitly seek social change; his portraits of his relatives are not suffused with the anger that characterize Wright's family depictions. Moreover, according to Dreiser's biographers, *Dawn* appears to be mostly faithful to the major facts of the author's family, with the exception of some name and birth-order changes that Dreiser acknowledges making in order to protect his relatives' privacy. On his first page he rather solemnly declares his intention to testify truthfully, and even invokes the language of legal oath-taking: "I will not say that this is a true record.... It is — as they say in law — *to the best of my knowledge and belief.* I may add, though, that these very sincere impressions and transcriptions are as nearly accurate as memory can guarantee" (3–4).

In contrast, Wright's strategy is to record history and, simultaneously, to manipulate it — and his characterizations of his relatives — to convey the disastrous human consequences of a racist society. While on one hand he largely depicts real scenes from his own childhood, he also clearly employs fiction as well as what Stone calls "startling emphases and omissions" in his representations of his family members in order to make his ideological message more effective (*Autobiographical* 123). Stone observes that Wright, "in dramatizing one future writer's encounter with naked oppression, ... warps social reality in order ... to stress his solitary and imaginative beginnings." Stone regards this strategy as unavoidable: "In the process he necessarily misrepresents the diversity and warmth of the actual folk culture historically available to himself and to other Mississippi children as emotional supports — including particularly the extended family, church, farm, and street-corner communities" (123).

What Wright emphasizes about the people who raised him, his parents, his maternal grandparents, and some aunts and uncles, are their harsh and irrational punishments of him, their lack of kindness and nurturing, their seeming indifference to his suffering, and their inability to understand or sympathize with his motives. Wright virtually omits evidence of deep love or generosity coming from any relative, and his family members are fairly devoid of joy and humor. His mother shows some caring in a few instances, but Wright's portrait of her is overwhelmingly centered on her anger and her helplessness.

Wright plainly wanted to portray himself, and, by extrapolation, the other "black boys" who are implicitly included in his title, as a victim of his intimate environment, which he in turn shows to be a product of the wider, white-controlled racist South. The main characteristics of his experience within his family are hunger, both physical and emotional; frustration at being radically misunderstood; and anger at his cruel treatment by the adults who are supposed to love and protect him.

Black Boy was universally praised as a "forceful indictment of race prejudice," as the *Omaha World-Herald* called it, echoing the words of most critics in noting that it was "one of the most powerful appeals for understanding ever penned in America" (Reilly 118). But many reviewers, including influential African Americans such as W. E. B. Du Bois, were troubled by Wright's portrayal of his family. Most reviewers who felt this way saw Wright's depiction of his family as part of a broader problem of the author's negative representation of the black community. Such critics were indignant at Wright's generalizations about blacks based on his observations about his family; they cited, for example, the passage in which Wright ponders "the strange absence of real kindness in Negroes, how unstable was our tenderness, how lacking in genuine passion we were" (45). Many labeled Wright a racist. Beatrice M. Murphy wrote in *Pulse* that Wright had used his pen "as a sword to stab his own race in the back" (Reilly 160). Ben Burns in the *Chicago Defender* called Wright "a self-centered, anti-social rebel" who "is without feeling of solidarity with the Negro people"; "he has seen fit to picture Negroes generally as sombre, barren, listless, bitter, helpless" (Reilly 128). Du Bois, writing in the *New York Herald Tribune Weekly Book Review*, noted that in *Black Boy* "The Negroes whom he paints have almost no redeeming qualities. Some work hard, some are sly, many are resentful; but there is none who is ambitious, successful or really intelligent" (Reilly 133).

The primary concern of these reviewers, of course, was that Wright, by depicting an entire cast of African American relatives as having few admirable traits, was disparaging all blacks. However, there was some reaction that focused specifically on Wright's ethics in his treatment of his family as individuals. While those critics naturally didn't use the critical language or theoretical concepts that ethics scholars use today, they implicitly questioned the ethics of an autobiographical approach in which the author deliberately distorts his representation of real people in order to further his own agenda. They questioned his conscientiousness in his representation of these people. Many were disturbed, for example, by what they saw as Wright's lack of deep affection for his mother. The appalled *Pulse* reviewer described the protagonist of *Black Boy* as "a child who displays throughout the book no moving sympathy or affection for his crippled, broken mother who carried the family burden alone" (Reilly 160). The critic for *Book List* observed that Wright's "recollections of intimate family life show no warmth of affection, or understanding" (Reilly 171).

Du Bois offered some of the most passionate and insightful criticism of Wright's portrayal of his family members. Du Bois was troubled by the lack of nuance in Wright's characterizations ("The family which he paints is a distressing aggregation"), but he, too, was struck by the autobiographer's apparent lack of sympathy for his mother. Significantly, Du Bois believed that Wright's failure to express "love or affection" toward his mother undermines the credibility of Wright's portrait of her (Reilly 132). As Du Bois saw it, the author's detached attitude toward his mother and other family members, his tendency to intellectualize their suffering rather than to feel it, kept Wright from portraying them convincingly. Du Bois remarked, "He wonders why this poor woman, deserted by her husband, toiling and baffled, broken by paralysis and disappointed, should suffer as she does. But his wonder is intellectual inability to explain the suffering. It doesn't seem for a moment to be personal sorrow at this poor, bowed figure of pain and ignorance" (132). Du Bois also saw Wright as primitivizing his father, who is "painted as gross and bestial, with little of human sensibility." In these and other representations of relatives, Du Bois viewed Wright's lack of "sympathy" as a failure of "the artist in Richard Wright" (Reilly 133). Du Bois concluded that Wright was not being truthful in his depictions of his family members: "The reader must regard [*Black Boy*] as creative writing rather than simply a record of life."

Yet Du Bois admitted to being "baffled" by the book, because "Nothing that Richard Wright says is in itself unbelievable or impossible; it is the total picture that is not convincing" (133). Du Bois's review suggests that the critic was unsettled by Wright's failure (as Du Bois read it) to balance his unsparing portraits of his family with an explicit and compassionate exploration of the factors that shaped them and drove their behavior. Du Bois's comments implicitly raised the question of whether an autobiographer has an ethical obligation to embed moral judgment of family members within a context of human understanding. Indeed, his review demonstrated a sensitivity to ethical issues in autobiographical writing that was far ahead of his time. Du Bois's emphasis on Wright's mother's absolute defenselessness, and his concern about the author's father being drawn as animalistic, reflected an awareness of the ways in which powerful autobiographers can potentially if unintentionally victimize vulnerable family members in their representation of them.

Other critics, however, believed that Wright blatantly drew connections between his family members' actions and their own victimization by white racism. Echoing other reviewers, Robert Malloy in the *New York Sun* read in Wright's depiction of them that Wright's relatives' harsh treatment of him was a reflection of their own "twisted lives and difficulties" (Reilly 127). R.L. Duffus in the *New York Times Book Review* understood that Wright's "family troubles and dissensions were intensified by the fact of race and racial discrimination" (Reilly 134). A careful reading of some of the scenes in which Wright's family members mistreat him does make it clear that Wright was intentionally tracing their actions to their own fears and to their desire to prepare Richard for life as a black male in the South.

One such passage is when Richard presses his mother to explain the apparent whiteness of his grandmother, who married a black man and is, therefore, considered "colored":

> "Did Granny become colored when she married Grandpa?"
> "Will you stop asking silly questions!"
> "But did she?"
> "Granny didn't become colored," my mother said angrily. "She was born the color she is now." Again I was being shut out of the secret, the thing, the reality I felt somewhere beneath all the words and silences [56].

Richard persists in trying to understand, and finally asks his mother, "Why don't you want to talk to me?" At this, "She slapped me and I cried" (56). The author goes on to relate that his mother did, later, "grudgingly" explain that his grandmother was of Scots-Irish lineage into which "Negro blood had somewhere and somehow been infused." Significantly, Wright describes his mother as having stripped herself of emotion when she delivers this information: "her emotions were not involved at all" (56). As the conversation continues, the boy becomes angry because "I knew that there was something my mother was holding back. She was not concealing facts, but feelings, attitudes, convictions which she did not want me to know; and she became angry when I prodded her" (58). Wright's mother's anger at her son, her attempt to slap him into silence, and then her masking of her feelings in order to keep from him the truth he's desperately seeking, are, in this passage, obviously rooted in her own double-bind as the mother of a black child. She is, in this scene, delivering the news to him that "They'll call you a colored man when you grow up," and trying to teach him in coded ways the implications of that status and the best way to survive psychologically: to resist insight and repress emotion (57).

Wright ingeniously follows this passage with a scene in which Richard experiences his first bee sting. In the previous passage, upon hearing that he was "colored," Richard had decided that "It was fine. I did not know enough to be afraid or to anticipate in a concrete manner.... If anybody tried to kill me, then I would kill them first" (58). Now, having arrived at his aunt Maggie's house in the country, Richard is pleased to see that he is able to kill bees with his hand. His mother warns him that he would "eventually be stung." But he "felt confident of outwitting any bee." When, having at last been stung by an "enormous" bee, he runs home screaming, only to have his mother comment "dryly": "Good enough for you" (58). In trying to save her son's life lest he become too confident around whites, his mother has unwittingly become an instrument of racism in her desire to instill fear and passivity in her son.

Even among those critics who believed that Wright showed understanding in his portrayal of his family members, some saw another problem in Wright's depiction of himself as completely self-made. They found it hard to believe that none of the qualities that enabled Wright to escape the South and become a writer were present in any adult around him. Augusta J. Strong in the *Congress View* praised the book but criticized Wright for so plainly "regard[ing] himself as an exception among his own people" (Reilly 164). F.K. Richter in the *Negro Story* declared it "disturbing" that Wright gives the impression that "Richard always succeeded by his own efforts. He himself overcame all obstacles ... it was he who dragged himself out of that mess." Richter was certain that "friendly light and warmth and fertile earth" must have been present in Wright's life for the seed of his genius to grow, and that Wright simply "omit[ted] these facts" and thus wrote "fiction" more than autobiography (Reilly 171). Even Lillian Smith, a southern writer known for her realistic portrayals of racism in the South, wrote in *PM* that she found Wright's omission of goodness in his family members to be unconvincing: "What early experiences of warmth and tenderness ... did he have that convinced him of his own dignity, that tied him to reality and kept him from totally rejecting the good with the bad? We should know. Yet his book does not tell us" (Reilly 136).

Wright defines himself in opposition to his family; his pole consists of curiosity, intelligence, ambition, sensitivity, and awareness, and theirs is defined by the lack of these qualities. Wright may have been sincerely trying to relate what his experience of his family life was actually like; certainly there was a huge gap between himself and his family, since they were relatively unschooled and he was a literary genius in the making. But his critics were posing a fair question in wondering whether his sharp dichotomizing between himself and his family members may have been an exaggeration. The temptation of working-class autobiographers to emphasize the differences between themselves and their family members is one of the central ethical issues addressed in the study at hand, and Wright and his critics were early examples of both this ethical problem and the nascent critical awareness of it.

Notwithstanding the concern over Wright's "slandering" of his own people, as one reviewer termed it, many critics regarded Wright's refusal to romanticize either his family or his racial community as one mark of the autobiography's greatness. James Ivy, an African American reviewer for the *Crisis,* saw Wright as telling "unpalatable truths about himself, his family, his race, and the white South"; Wright "does not play up nor glorify Negro virtues, and he is thoroughly unabashed in recounting our vices and shortcomings. Or specifically, the integrity and the failings of those he knew" (Reilly 159). Duffus in the *New York Times Book Review* appreciated that "Mr. Wright does not idealize either his relatives or his race.... They were what they were" (Reilly 134). The *Washington Star* critic asserted that Wright "present[s] Negro society objectively" (Reilly 138). However, some of the voices who approved of Wright's "honesty" exuded racist undertones. The unnamed reviewer for *Time* offered this back-handed compliment: "More honest than most Communists, he has never tried to sweeten up his down-trodden Negroes." That critic had no difficulty accepting that Wright, as an intelligent and thoughtful black person, was a rare exception indeed; s/he called *Black Boy* "the story of a man set apart from his own race by sensitivity and intellect" (Reilly 138).

Wright's book illustrates the challenge that many working-class autobiographers face in trying to portray one's own experience of being different from one's family members while at the same time managing to endow the people back home with roundedness and complexity. *Black Boy,* in the end, is *Wright's* own story, and he was, like authors of slave narratives to which he has been compared, focused on delineating the conditions of his early life that made escape the only bearable option.

One passage that has often been criticized for its depiction of Wright's father as a stereotypical sharecropper is, in fact, a brilliant evocation of Wright's own predicament as a grown son whose life so starkly and painfully contrasts with that of his father's. He recalls visiting his father at a Mississippi plantation, seeing him for the first time since the father deserted the family twenty-five years earlier. Wright does describe his father's appearance in stereotypical terms: he was "standing alone upon the red clay ... clad in ragged overalls, holding a muddy hoe in his gnarled, veined hands"; the father who once had a "fearsome aspect" is now "smiling toothlessly, his hair whitened, his body bent, his eyes glazed with dim recollection" (42). As this passage develops, however, this portrait of his father takes on several meanings. Seeing his father as a stunted human being whose "soul was imprisoned by the slow flow of the seasons, by wind and rain and sun," and sensing "how chained were his actions and emotions to the direct, animalistic impulses of his withering body," Wright is "overwhelmed" by the disparity between himself and his father (42). He is overcome with sadness at the realization that he and his father "were forever strangers, speaking a different language, living on vastly distant planes of reality." One of the most painful ironies of Wright's success, this passage suggests, is that his own father will never be able to appreciate the degree of Wright's transformation or the enormity of his achievement: "I was overwhelmed to realize that he could never understand me or the scalding experiences that had swept me beyond his life and into an area of living that he could never know" (42).

Wright's mind is "aching" as he takes in the pathos and limitations of his father's life, and then the son has an insight that enables him to see his father as more than his cliched appearance. Wright sees that his father's life has been shaped by "the white landowners above him" who have not given him "a chance to learn the meaning of loyalty, of sentiment, of tradition," or of joy. More important, though, is Wright's recognition that his father was not originally so different from himself, but had once been a young man who had wanted more for his own life, "a black peasant who had gone to the city seeking life, but who had failed in the city." This insight allows Wright to forgive his father and to pity him, but it also illuminates the sad mystery of the two men's lives: that a similar quest made by them both crushed the spirit of one and caused the other one's to soar. His father's life "had been hopelessly snarled in the city ... the same city which had lifted me in its burning arms and borne me toward alien and undreamed-of shores of knowing" (43). In this and other passages in *Black Boy*, Wright articulates perhaps more eloquently and insightfully than any American autobiographer before him the enduring emotional costs of traveling such a distance from one's origins.

Like Wright, Anzia Yezierska escaped the poverty and oppression into which she was born by writing about it successfully. Around the turn of the last century, Yezierska (who was probably born around 1885) emigrated with her family from a *shtetl* in Russian Poland and settled in Manhattan's

Lower East Side, in a ghetto densely populated by other Orthodox Jews. Her father was a Torah scholar who, in keeping with the religious tradition from the Old World, studied at home while his wife and children worked in sweatshops to support the household. Working days, Yezierska went to school at night and eventually earned a degree from Columbia Teachers College in 1904. She began publishing stories about immigrants struggling to survive and adjust to their new country. An agent collected them and sold the volume, *Hungry Hearts*, to a movie studio in 1920, thereby launching Yezierska's career in a dramatic way.

Yezierska's most autobiographical novel, *Bread Givers* (1925), was a bestseller that secured her place in the American literary canon, and it resembles the autobiographies of Dreiser and Wright in its chronicling of a gifted young person born into poverty and cultural marginality who enters the middle class through education. Like many immigrant autobiographies and novels of the early decades of the twentieth century, *Bread Givers* is what Werner Sollors identifies as a consent-descent drama. This construct delineates "a conflict between contractual and hereditary, self-made and ancestral, definitions of American identity" (151). *Bread Givers* is a classic example of this construct, as its subtitle illustrates: "A struggle between a father of the Old World and a daughter of the New."

As Sollors notes, in consent-descent symbolism "ethnicity may function as a construct evocative of blood, nature, and descent, whereas national identity may be relegated to the order of law, conduct, and consent" (151). Yezierska's novel presents the world of the heroine's family as being in polar opposition to the wider world of America. The heroine's father and other family members embody the past, tradition, religious restrictions, poverty, and other values associated with their ethnic identity, while assimilation represents the future, education, autonomy, affluence, and, most important, a sense of control over one's life. Like the other consent-descent narratives that were popular in the period, Yezierska's novel resonated with the thousands of ambitious immigrants and children of immigrants who worried that assimilation and success in the New World constituted a betrayal of both their parents and their own "true" selves.

As she had done with her collection *Hungry Hearts*, Yezierska led her critics and interviewers to believe that *Bread Givers* was more autobiographical than it in fact was. This melodramatic story of a poor young woman who chose "freedom" over "oppression," and was harshly rejected by her family because of it, made for a compelling, heroic identity for Yezierska. As the author recalled decades later in her autobiography, her publishers shamelessly exploited this "Cinderella rise from rags to riches" image to sell her books (122), contriving, in one instance, to hold a literary dinner in her honor at the Waldorf Astoria and publicizing the fact that she had once applied to work there as a chambermaid (124). In reality, however, people are too complex, their motives and behavior too contradictory and layered to conform to the rigid construct of *Bread Givers*, and the author's profession that the characters in that novel were portraits of her actual family amounted to a self-serving misrepresentation of them. As her autobiography, *Red Ribbon on a White Horse* (1950), demonstrates, Yezierska spent the rest of her life privately regretting this fictionalizing of her family, yet stubbornly maintaining her stereotypical versions of them in interviews and her published works.

In contrast to Dreiser and Wright, Yezierska did not write her autobiography as a young woman in the prime of her career but when she was nearly seventy; it was the last of her seven books to be published, after an eighteen-year period in which she was unable to write. Though Orville Prescott in the *New York Times* called it "inadequate" as a literary performance, he also rightly described it as a "revealing and touching human document" (21). From the perspective of the early twenty-first century it is especially unique as a portrait of class mobility and its potentially crippling aftermath. It is undoubtedly the first American autobiography to show the psychological consequences of commodifying one's family's poverty and pain in one's writing, and being financially rewarded for doing so.

In a radical departure from the autobiographies of Dreiser and Wright, instead of recounting the author's childhood and tracing her climb out of the ghetto, *Red Ribbon on a White Horse* (1950) begins when Yezierska is about thirty-five and her first book is being sold to Hollywood. The autobiography then chronicles the author's slow descent from fame, productivity, and wealth, to obscurity, writer's block, and poverty revisited. Thus, while the typical arc in most class-ascension autobiographies traces the author's rise to success, Yezierska's narrative goes against that norm by following an inverted arc. While her fiction related the story of her escape from poverty, her autobiography explicitly examines the fallout from her success. On its deeper levels, the memoir reveals the complex reasons for Yezierska's descent beyond the explanation she provides, her fear of losing her soul with wealth. As a book that relies on metaphorical rather than literal expressions of truth, *Red Ribbon* in coded ways shows how mining her family for fiction, and especially portraying them as "other," created enduring and insurmountable guilt in her.

In an afterword to *Red Ribbon*, Yezierska's daughter, Louise Levitas Henriksen, advises the reader that much of the book is not literally true:

"it contains as much fiction as fact" (222). Moreover, Henriksen writes, "Less than anyone I can think of could [Yezierska] be trusted to tell the unadorned truth" (221). Indeed, the first scene in the memoir is so heavy-handed in its symbolism that it is almost certainly apocryphal, but it reveals much about the author's view of her career and her treatment of her family. The scene begins with Yezierska still living in a tenement (though in real life she had, at this point, been away from Hester Street for two decades), too poor to satisfy her hunger, when she receives a telegram from her agent. The note announces that Yezierska is now rich: Hollywood wants to make a movie out of *Hungry Hearts*, and to market it as the true story of Yezierska's life.

In order to accept the deal, the author has to pawn something to get the carfare to her agent's office. She chooses her late mother's shawl. It is not only one of a kind and representative of the Old Country — she writes that it had been unique in their village in Poland — it also embodies the author's life with her family. Yezierska describes it as a vessel containing memories of her childhood, an object that "redeemed the squalor" of and provided texture and beauty to her impoverished present (26). With this vignette, she implies that selling her book to the movies was her only alternative to starvation. This was not true, since by this time she had a university education and had taught school (facts she often denied, according to Henriksen) (Afterword 222). Yet, while she tries in this way to justify her choice, she also, in this scene, conveys the human cost of "selling" her family to Hollywood, by using the shawl as a metaphor of her family memories. For, to achieve the fame and fortune that Hollywood promised, she had first to transform the shawl/her memories into something common and marketable, then sell it/them cheaply. Yezierska describes later returning to the shop to retrieve the shawl, only to learn it had been sold and was lost forever. This episode is emblematic of Yezierska's autobiographical self. Full of regret for having sold her memories while she was a young adult, she also defends her actions by reminding the reader (and herself) of the alternative, as she perceived it: starvation — emotional and intellectual, if not physical. Her childhood, and her observations of her family members and others in her community, were all she had to sell, she suggests.

Yet, as this initial scene demonstrates, her perennial sense of guilt is a prominent theme in the book. In one of many passages in which she imaginatively confronts her late father, she confesses to betraying him in her pursuit of success, a confession that is repeated throughout the text. Her father, she realized, would never be accepted by the "new world" because of his divine calling, and she, his daughter, had "abandoned him for the things of this world, had joined the world against him" (32). While she openly admits feeling like a traitor for rebelling against her father's wishes, for acquiring wealth when it violated the family's religious and cultural mores, and for defying Jewish Orthodoxy's rules for women, on a figurative level the author reveals another, deeper source of guilt: her deliberate misrepresentation of her family, in her writing and in interviews, in order to enhance her own public identity.

Beneath its surface the pawnshop scene is about the author wanting to sell her past as a unique thing of beauty, into which "people's lives are woven," and naively believing that it will be appreciated for its richness, yet having finally to sell it cheaply as "an old rag" (27). The negotiation with the pawnbroker dramatizes the process by which an item of personal value becomes reduced to its utilitarian value, its street price. Yezierska assures Zaretsky that "this shawl is rarer than diamonds—an antique from Poland"; it is "pure wool ... hand-woven, hand-dyed." To Zaretsky, who, with his "dirty, bony fingers" and a body "crooked from squeezing pennies out of despairing people," personifies greed, the shawl is a "moth-eaten rag full of holes." He adds that "for what is past, nobody pays. Now it's junk—falling apart" (27). The transaction is a synecdoche of her literary career as she portrays it in *Red Ribbon*: a stripping away of her family's human complexity and distinctiveness in order to market them.

Later in the memoir, in a scene that echoes this meaning of the pawnshop episode, the author learns that a writer who is known for "burlesquing Jews" in *The Saturday Evening Post* is going to be working on the movie script of her loosely-autobiographical *Hungry Hearts* (81). Montague Glass, who "turned out caricatures of Jews like sausage meat," will provide "laughs and a happy ending," as well as "advertising" to enhance profits. Yezierska replies that her book is "my life!" and that she won't let the studio "murder it with slapstick!" (82). At the end of the scene the author suggests that, as she had done by pawning her mother's shawl, by writing about her past for money she has allowed her past to be cheapened and falsified. She discovered, she writes, that "this was the price of my sudden riches!" For forging a check, she notes, you went to prison, but for "forging the truth, you sat with the famous of the hour" (82).

Interestingly, Yezierska shows herself in that scene being reminded that she had willingly given over control of "her story" when she signed a contract. In other passages that cover her stay in Hollywood she likewise depicts herself as on the one hand being misrepresented by the movie studio's publicists, and on the other hand, participating in the fabrications, though her own cooperation is suggested rather than acknowledged. As she portrays it, she was plagued by disillusionment and identity confusion from her first day in California. Her text indicates that much of her angst came from what she saw as the phoniness of the Hollywood-ized image created for her, such as the movie studio's promotion of her as the "Sweatshop Cinderella." She recalls that she "couldn't recognize myself" in either the picture of her above those captions, or in the newspapers' "stories of my 'success'" (40).

She does not identify which aspects of this public identity were wrong, but she repeatedly suggests that her words and actions were always being twisted and that consequently, she and her life were being continuously misconstrued. When the studio publicist announces a newspaper's intention to print her "life story," Yezierska demurs because, she claims, all of her previously printed interviews were "distortions" (80). Later she describes herself as having been misread and misquoted throughout her entire tenure with Goldwyn; she complains that she was in "a glass house with crooked mirrors" in which her words and actions were continuously twisted and exploited to further the sale of the book and the movie (81).

Yet, significantly, when given the opportunity to provide information directly to the press, to offer them a truer version of herself, she is evasive and even deceptive, lying, for example, about her age. When the publicist asks her for "'the facts'" she resists: "'Facts?' I drew away" (80). What Yezierska hints at but does not openly acknowledge is the active role she took in creating the "Hollywood myths" that grew up around her, as Henriksen puts it (Kessler-Harris ix). According to Alice Kessler-Harris, who extensively interviewed Yezierska's family members, "at different times, in interviews as well as for the documentary record, [Yezierska] made up everything, from her date of birth to her family relationships, her work experience, and her education" (x).

The most insidious way in which Yezierska misled the public about herself and her family was her encouragement of readers and critics to read her fiction as autobiography. *Red Ribbon* shows the author frequently implying to others that the characters in *Hungry Hearts* and *Bread Givers* are real people, including her family members and neighbors. In one passage she recalls visiting her father soon after *Bread Givers* was published. Throughout her account of their conversation, and her own state of mind during that time, Yezierska suggests that the novel's heroine was/is interchangeable with herself. She felt, she writes, that the novel had explained her choices to her family, that she had "justified" herself in the book for remaining single and childless (216). She goes on to relate her father's reaction to the publication. He remarks that he heard that she wrote a book about him; he then asks her how she could write about someone she doesn't know (216). Instead of asserting that the book is not about him, that it is a work of fiction, she simply replies, "'I know you.'"

In the scenes that depict her collaborating with the *Hungry Hearts* screenwriter, Yezierska offers up detailed memories of her family life that get directly put into the script. Indeed, one of the most symbolic aspects of *Red Ribbon* is the fact that virtually all of the very few childhood memories that the author relates to the reader are told within the context of the script-writing process. Once told, those memories get immediately "built up" by the screenwriter (48). This oddity suggests the deep extent to which for Yezierska, her life and her fiction became irretrievably merged. It also indicates how she lost her past by altering it in order to sell it.

The betrayal of her family to which Yezierska repeatedly but vaguely alludes in her autobiography, then, is *her* distortion of their lives in her books. The differences between her family members and the characters "based on" them are, of course, designed to make the heroine/Yezierska appear more heroic, exceptional, and sympathetic to the reader. According to Henriksen, in interviews and her writing, Yezierska often revised the lives of her family members to make them conform to the sharp dichotomy between patriarchal tradition and personal fulfillment that was at the center of all of her fiction, and that provided the basis for her own identity as well. Yezierska "sharpened the drama of real events by eliminating muddy contradictions" (qtd in Kessler-Harris, x). In *Bread Givers*, the author "had chosen not to include characters who represented any of the six brothers who had formed her own family. And she altered the lives of her sisters—who had not been forced into marriages, and whose lives were for the most part happy—in order to enhance the significance of her own rebellion" (Kessler-Harris x-xi).

In *Red Ribbon* Yezierska perpetuates these stereotypical and misleading portrayals of her family members. She summarizes her characterizations of her fictional heroine's sisters in *Bread Givers*, but describes them as if they were her *own* sisters: in *Bread Givers*, she writes, "I described how my sisters, who had married according to my father's will, spent themselves childbearing in poverty" (216). In her autobiography her father is rendered as a type, an unconvincingly one-dimensional personification of religious blindness and patriarchal tyranny. In the exchange about *Bread Givers* he rails, "'You're not human!"; he rants about her "evil worship of Mammon" and accuses her of having a "barren heart" (217). Again, as Kessler-Harris notes, Henriksen insists that these characterizations of Yezierska's sisters and father were exaggerated, if not fabricated: "Her sisters were not the unhappy creatures of their father's will; they led fulfilled and satisfying lives. Their father was less tyrannical than traditional" (x).

Perhaps because, with the exception of her father, Yezierska virtually ignores her original family members in her autobiography, critics mostly did, too. Many reviewers clearly assumed that her personal history had been written in her novels. One reviewer, however, was critical of the fact that these people were absent from her autobiography, attributing their omission to the author's being "much too self-absorbed to give more than perfunctory attention to externals" (Langbaum 105). One could get that impression: the author never mentions having brothers; alludes to her sisters only as a group, in the single sentence quoted above; mentions her mother just twice, briefly; never refers to any family member by name; and, except for the one scene with her father mentioned above, is silent about any relationships she had with family members since leaving home as a teenager.

Yezierska's near-elision of her family from her life narrative signifies more than her undeniable solipsism. The text suggests that, even though Yezierska maintained relationships with her family—according to her daughter—she was unable to include them in a non-fiction account of her life because she did not want to contradict her fictional characterizations of them. For example, her assertions over the years that her sisters had been enslaved and impoverished by forced marriages would be undermined by any reference to them as individuals moving forward through time, acting and choosing and experiencing joy in their lives. By having relegated her original family to a fictional world in which they represented extremes, including the unchanging past, Yezierska cannot afford to include them in the present or grant them the human dimensions that would undoubtedly introduce "muddy contradictions" into her neatly-ordered scheme.

Yezierska not only had to keep her relatives out of her self-portrait, she also apparently felt the need to amputate parts of herself that didn't conform to her role in the Old World-New World drama. In several places in *Red Ribbon* she cites her father's criticism of her for being unmarried and "barren." Near the end of the book she strongly implies that she never married or had children, writing, "I too had children. My children were the people I wrote about." She asserts that she gave her literary characters, her "children, born of loneliness," as much of her life as her sisters gave of theirs to their flesh-and-blood children (216). The fictional identity of herself as a heroine who rebels against patriarchal and religious oppression and becomes a "pure" artist can only be maintained if she omits her two marriages and her very-real daughter from her narrative. It is also likely that she didn't want to have to explain the fact that, according to Kessler-Harris, Yezierska gave up her daughter when she was just four, sending her across the country to be raised by her father and paternal grandmother. As sympathetic as one may be toward Yezierska because of the social/cultural predicament in which she was born, and the painful division of self that led her to misrepresent the lives of her family members throughout her lifetime, her erasure of her daughter from her "autobiography" strikes one as unforgivable. But because none apparently knew about Louise's existence, the critics of *Red Ribbon* made no mention of this startlingly unethical aspect of the book.

Though she does not grant complexity to her family members in her portrayal of them, Yezierska conveys the complicated facets of her own identity with a degree of honesty and self-awareness that Dreiser and Wright do not. Yezierska was perhaps the first to identify a paradox that often characterizes the lives of formerly-marginal writers, a problem also lamented by John Edgar Wideman in *Brothers and Keepers* thirty-four years later: that the capacity for self-invention that enables them to succeed also, ironically, enables them to create false selves so successfully that they are unable to be completely "real" with anyone. Both authors suggest that the habit of masking their racial/ethnic/class identities in mainstream society bought them acceptance by middle-class whites, yet eroded their capacity for authentic interaction with others. In *Red Ribbon* Yezierska often chastises herself for being "a fool and a faker" (70), while Wideman admits that during college, "I had no feelings apart from the series of roles and masquerades I found myself playing," and that even now "I can blend with my surroundings, become invisible" (32, 34).

Yezierska and Wideman both create more complex autobiographical personas than do most other writers in this study, and it is not coincidental that both write extensively about their lives as successful, assimilated adults. This sets them apart not only from Dreiser and Wright, but also from the majority of American autobiographers who have crossed significant class and cultural barriers, since conventionally such life narratives end with the narrator leaving home and beginning life in a new social/cultural realm; the ramifications of that transition, therefore, are often left mostly unexplored. Yezierska's venture into this territory, however, while courageous and original, engenders both aesthetic and ethical problems in her text. Yezierska is one of the early examples of autobiographers who compromise their texts by contriving a false return home at the end. She does this by claiming, near the book's end, to realize at last the truth of her father's oft-repeated dictum, that poverty "becomes a Jew like a red ribbon on a white horse" (217).

While throughout *Red Ribbon* she recalls experiencing her sudden wealth as a betrayal of her family and especially of her father's values, she also vehemently justifies her choices. But in the brief final chapter she portrays herself as having an epiphany that her "will to lift [her] head up out of the squalor and anonymity of the poor" had come from "poverty of the spirit," and that her loss of success in American terms is actually her attainment, at last, of true success (218). In these pages she describes herself riding on a train, symbolically returning to the East Side of New York, and being struck with a new understanding of her life. She saw that "Hollywood was not my success," nor was her present "poverty and anonymity, failure" (219). This recognition caused "a warm wave of happiness" to well up in her: "Why had I no premonition in the wandering years when I was hungering and thirsting for recognition, that this quiet joy, this sanctuary, was waiting for me after I had sunk back to anonymity?" She realized, she writes, that her striving to succeed as an author was a straining for the acceptance of "important" people — a goal that was meaningless, since "the glimpses of truth I reached for everywhere, was in myself" (220). As mentioned in the Introduction, this circular journey pattern is a typical construct in working-class autobiographies, especially those appearing in the last two decades. One of the main differences between Yezierska's execution of this strategy and, say, Bobbie Ann Mason's, is the former's comparative lack of sophistication and subtlety.

In a brief review in which s/he describes *Red Ribbon* as "unevenly written," the critic for the *New Yorker* remarked that Yezierska's "conclusion—that poverty is the condition most becoming to her spiritually— doesn't carry the conviction she intended" (122). And it doesn't. One of the great strengths of her oeuvre, including this work, is its refusal to romanticize poverty. In a scene in *Red Ribbon,* when a wealthy author disingenuously murmurs, "I wish I could live in a little hall room with a trunk under my bed," Yezierska's tart reply is that if the author really had to live in a hall room with a trunk under her bed, she "wouldn't find it so romantic" (138).

In another passage the author expresses her deep ambivalence toward the poor people of her childhood neighborhood, a "strange" mixture of "love and hate" to which Wideman also confesses in *Brothers and Keepers* (*Red Ribbon* 94). The episode, (which, like many others in the book, was completely fabricated by Yezierska, according to her daughter), depicts the author being deeply moved by a letter from an elderly Polish immigrant, a Torah scholar like her father, who, having read about Yezierska's success, begs her for money to return to Poland to die. She returns to Hester Street to seek him out, and on first arriving she is "consumed with homesickness and longing for my own kind": "In every bearded old Jew ... I saw my father — ghosts of the people I had abandoned to 'make of myself a person in the world'" (94). However, after spending a few minutes with the man's widow, a "toothless," "bony" woman who exuded an "aura of dirt and poverty," the narrator is "terrified by the hungry way she grabbed at me, sickened by the smells and the dirt" (95, 97). The author's compassion is overwhelmed by "disgust — revulsion." With characteristic insight into the "crushing" effects of poverty, the author ends the scene by articulating the psychological dilemma of the formerly-poor. Once one knew what poor people suffered "it kept gnawing at you. You'd been there yourself." Yet, the urge to help the poor is tempered by the threat they represent: becoming involved brings the fear that one "might be dragged back into the abyss" (97).

Though Yezierska's last-minute embrace of poverty in the text rings false, it is convincing testimony of her desire to re-identify with her ethnic roots. It also reveals how powerfully for Yezierska her ethnicity is enmeshed with class status. On her train journey home, she "recalls" her father telling her that because she has money she is "no longer a Jew." Her wealth, he stated, made her a traitor, "an enemy of your own people" (217). This view of poverty as an intrinsic part of an "authentic" ethnic or racial essence is at the heart of the identity confusion that Wideman, Nesaule, Mason, as well as many other working-class autobiographers, grapple with in their narratives. Yet unlike those writers, who romanticize their poor relatives without actually reverting to that status themselves, Yezierska idealizes poverty only after she has herself become poor and obscure again; her posture, then, is in part an attempt to ennoble her own failure. Also unlike those writers, Yezierska does not glamorize her family in her text; even at the end, when she suddenly re-interprets her father's narrow-mindedness as "the purity of a child," and his harshness as "the zeal of a man in love with God," she nevertheless continues to portray him as mean (217).

Whether she is accusing him of being a tyrant — an "ancient patriarch condemning unrighteousness" — or attributing to him a preternatural "radiance that the evils of the world could not mar," the problem, ultimately, is the shallow, stereotypical portrait of him (216–17). Yezierska's thinly-drawn conversion to her father's beliefs is a strategy to avoid genuine examination of her father's character and the nuances of their relationship. As ethnography theorists have shown, using a stereotypical image to idealize the poor or the indigenous is no better than using one to demonize them; the problem is the image itself. Yezierska's one-dimensional depiction of her father is but a more extreme case of the difficulty many working-class autobiographers have with portraying family members as distinctive individuals rather than as representatives of a class and/or racial or ethnic group.

In this regard, Maya Angelou's *I Know Why the Caged Bird Sings* (1970) represents a special achievement because of the author's unique ability to individualize her family members. It also represents a major turning point in working-class American autobiography because, as James Olney notes, it was the first autobiography by a black woman to be treated as serious literature, with a body of criticism growing up around it within the first few years of its publication. The critical devotion to Angelou's book was also unusual at that time for an autobiography that was the author's *first* book (Olney 15). As Olney observes, this unprecedented attention to such a seemingly-marginal text was not to be "attributed solely to the undoubted quality of Maya Angelou's book" but also to the "critical/cultural times"; the scholarly community was ready, apparently, to grant "something like full literary enfranchisement" to "black writers, women writers, and autobiography itself" (15–16).

Angelou's autobiography is not typically read as a narrative of upward mobility. Stephen Butterfield, whose *Black Autobiography in America* (1974) was among the earliest works to include *Caged Bird* in the canon, chose it in part because, like the other texts he selected, he felt it was *not* a "middle-class success stor[y]" (6). Likewise, the *New York Times* reviewer, Christopher Lehmann-Haupt, stressed the fact that, as he saw it, *I Know Why the Caged Bird Sings* does not narrate the story of the author's professional rise: "For though Miss Angelou has made it as a dancer, an actress, and a writer, her autobiography is not concerned with career, or even with making it in public terms." He defined *Caged Bird* as the opposite of a book about "making it" because "instead" it traces the narrator's growth to an "interior identity" (45). To illustrate his point, Lehmann-Haupt contrasted Angelou's book with another autobiography he was reviewing, *Sugar Ray,* a book about the black boxer Sugar Ray Robinson, ghost-written by sportswriter Dave Anderson. Headlined "Masculine and Feminine," Lehmann-Haupt's review suggested that these autobiographies typified the difference between life narratives by men and women because of their divergent emphases on public and private identities.

Though Angelou's autobiography employs a different structure than that of the typical success story, it *is*, in fact, about the narrator's intellectual and artistic growth, as well as the formation of her identity as an ambitious black woman who desires and attains a degree of recognition and power in the public realm. She records such public achievements as graduating in a "top place" from the eighth grade, being a star student whose "academic work was among the best of the year," and becoming, at sixteen, the first black conductor on the San Francisco trolley system (172, 269). It is not coincidental, however, that Angelou's life narrative presents an alternative shape to a story about "making it," a shape that reflects her perspective as a woman and as an African American.

Sidonie Smith explains that often underlying the structural pattern in the stereotypical American autobiography that traces the author's journey to success "is the myth of the Horatio Alger hero": "From a lowly beginning on the fringes of society, the hard-working and virtuous individual rises slowly yet steadily to success and social prominence: self-realization is fulfilled by social arrival" (*Where* 30). For the black American, though, "this pattern becomes especially expressive and often painfully ironic since he begins on the furthest fringe of the social scale (the fluidity of his movement is problematic) and the odds against him are greater (his unlimited possibilities are in fact narrowly limited)" (30). Moreover, as Angelou discovered as a girl, Horatio Alger's heroes "were always boys" (Angelou 75). Thus, in *Caged Bird* Angelou tells the story of a *girl's* journey to success, and more precisely, a black girl's. Just as Frederick Douglass in his *Narrative* does not describe his flight from slavery but instead traces the intellectual and psychological transformation that made his escape not only possible but necessary, Angelou focuses on the development of an "interior identity" that precipitated her eventual public success.

She also provides a positive model of ethical representations of working-class family members in autobiography, and this can be attributed in part to the structure of her text, which differs in meaningful ways from the texts previously discussed. One difference is that, unlike those of Dreiser, Wright, and Yezierska, Angelou's autobiography does not portray her entrance into adulthood as an escape from an "other" world of her family and childhood. For example, she does not end her book by describing one of the professional achievements that brought her prominence as an actress and television writer. In a more typical class-mobility book such an ending signals the narrator's definitive break with his or her family's working-class world, as does, for instance, Wright's trip north. Instead, as will be explained, Angelou ends with a story that suggests the birth of her adult self, and her entrance into an adulthood that is separate but parallel with that of her mother's. Moreover, ending her book with what middle-class white readers might consider the *opposite* of success—her having a baby at sixteen—is an intentional inversion of the Alger-myth structure, part of a pattern in the book of reversals and inversions of white society's myths about social class.

One aspect of her text that makes it an exemplar of ethics is her complex portrayal of her family members and of southern blacks in general. In fact, the initial critical response to Angelou's text, which was fairly unanimous in its praise, focused on the richness of the author's characterizations of her family members. Lehmann-Haupt described the author's paternal grandmother, "Momma," as "only one of several remarkably well-drawn characters in Miss Angelou's story." He noted that Angelou portrayed her as a woman of many facets, as being a "stern ... disciplinarian" who nevertheless "laid down a firm foundation of love" (45).

Critics appreciated that Angelou did not represent African Americans only in terms of their victimization by whites, which, we recall, was a chief complaint against *Black Boy*. While Angelou unsparingly limned the indignities and injustices that her family members and other blacks in Stamps, Arkansas, endured because of their skin color, reviewers suggested, she also painted these people as possessing a wide range of qualities, including many positive attributes that directly nurtured her own intellect and character. The *Newsweek* reviewer wrote that the autobiography "quietly and gracefully portrays and pays tribute to the courage, dignity and endurance of the small, rural Southern black community in which she spent most of her early years in the 1930s" (79).

In fact, in sharp contrast to Dreiser, Wright, and Yezierska, Angelou implies that her creativity, ambition, and insight were engendered as much by her family, the black community of Stamps, black culture, and religion, as by her own innate qualities and efforts. As *Newsweek* remarked, "Miss Angelou describes an underlying warmth, generosity and humanity in the community" (80). Richard Wright's critics, we remember, were dismayed that Wright represented himself as absolutely self-made, omitting any positive aspects of either his family or the black community that contributed to his success. Some of Dreiser's reviewers lodged similar criticism against *Dawn*. Unlike those writers, however, Angelou does not suggest that her intellectual and artistic gifts, as well as her middle-class status as an adult, make her completely alien from her family members.

While Dreiser's family members are childish, "ignorant," and irresponsible in his depiction, Angelou's grandmothers and her mother are capable and independent in hers. She writes, for example, that her mother, Vivian, was "a firm believer in self-sufficiency" who saw herself as "the original 'do-it-yourself girl'" and as a woman with "gumption" (264). Wright's relatives are powerless, and resistant to the self-knowledge that Richard craves, whereas Angelou's uncle Willie, brother Bailey, and her mother impart valuable insights to *her*. And in contrast to Yezierska's portrait of her family as joyless, passive people who resist progress, Angelou paints her grandmother and her mother as urging her to succeed in the world: Vivian preaches that life will reward Maya in proportion to her efforts, and she advises her to "Put your whole heart in everything you do" (269).

Indeed, Angelou's ethical representations are related to her underlying argument about southern white society's social class system, in which blacks could enact the Franklinesque virtues of self-improvement but still find it impossible to enter the middle class. She presents Momma, Bailey, and her mother as embodying many of the values that, according to the American Dream myth, lead to prosperity and social respectability. Unlike the conventional Horatio Alger-like autobiographer, Angelou does not stress how far she had to go from her origins, culturally and socially, in order to "make it," but instead emphasizes how her family members as well as other individuals in Stamps had raised her with the middle-class values of hard work, cleanliness, studiousness, charity, respect for others, and so on.

It is significant that Angelou presents the home she shared with Momma, Uncle Willie, and Bailey for most of her first thirteen years as the environment in which her identity as an intellectual first took root. She recalls that when she and Bailey were five and six, they used to "rattle off the times tables with the speed I was later to see Chinese children in San Francisco employ on their abacuses" because their uncle Willie drilled them every day (10). When Maya was eight and she and her brother moved to St. Louis to live with their mother for a year, the children discovered "how shockingly backward" the city students were; she and Bailey performed math at an advanced level because of their work in Momma's store, and they read well because "in Stamps there wasn't anything else to do" (63). They were even moved up a grade because teachers thought Maya and Bailey would make their classmates "feel inferior" (63).

As many scholars have noted, one dilemma that twentieth-century black autobiographers faced when writing success stories was how to relate the importance of their educational experiences without appearing to endorse the white school system that excluded and/or discriminated against them. James Baldwin echoed many black writers when he asserted in his essay "Dark Days" (1980) that "the educational system of this country is, in short, designed to destroy the black child" (88). In the 1960s and '70s, in particular, many black activists and literary scholars suggested that black autobiographers who did not vehemently assert this view were politically unaware. Stephen Butterfield was among the critics who contributed to this bind by condemning black autobiographers who wrote about finding professional success by way of white-dominated avenues. As William L. Andrews observes, like many critical works in that period, Butterfield's 1974 book "argues that black autobiographers who did not take a stand against the American Dream usually were co-opted by it" ("African American" 200).

Angelou negotiates her own solution to this problem: she traces her intellectual growth and credits its nurturing to the black community. As she presents it, in addition to the knowledge she mastered because of Momma, Uncle Willie, and the black school in Stamps, her introduction to literature came by way of a local black woman, Mrs. Bertha Flowers, who, the author writes, "threw me my first life line" (92). Mrs. Flowers, "the aristocrat of Black Stamps," read Dickens aloud to Maya, who recalls the experience as hearing "poetry" for the first time in her life (93, 100). She loaned Maya books, encouraged her to memorize poems, and, while serving her tea, gave her "lessons in living," which amounted to a primer in upper-middle-class attitudes.

It is important to note that Angelou does not depict either her grandmother in Stamps or her mother as intellectuals, or as highly educated people, which they were not. Nor does she romanticize them, or, for that matter, rural southern blacks as a group. As a girl, she saw her grandmother as a person of "power and strength," but also as a sometimes-harsh woman who was reluctant to show tenderness or affection (46), and whose world-view was circumscribed by "work, duty, religion and 'her place'" (57). When Maya asked Momma if she loved her she "brushed me off" and replied that "God is love" (57).

Yet Angelou's portrayal of Stamps offers a pointed rebuttal to the stereotype of a rural black community. It is not only a place in which a black woman runs a prosperous business, it is where the author "met and fell in love with William Shakespeare" (13). Further, Angelou's emphasis on the middle-class aspects of her life with Momma went against the social/cultural trend of the 1960s and '70s in which the image of the poor black was romanticized and, as Shelby Steele notes, "imbued with strong moral authority" (100). Steele writes in his 1990 essay "On Being Black and Middle Class" that during the civil rights movement, "victimization more than any other variable ... identified and unified" African Americans, and that consequently, "the purest black was the poor black": "It was images of him that clustered around the positive pole of the race polarity; all other blacks were, in effect, required to identify with him in order to confirm their own blackness" (101). As a graduate student in 1969, Steele recalls feeling pressured by the prevailing cultural attitudes of the period to "repress" his "class background" because he had been raised in a family with "solid middle-class values" such as "hard work, family life, property ownership, and education" (98).

However, while Angelou portrays her grandmother and other blacks in Stamps as valuing learning and hard work, she repeatedly makes the point that, during the period of her childhood in the 1930s and '40s, African Americans could never really move up socially, no matter how much knowledge or property they acquired, or how "aristocratic" were their manners. For, however "refined" she acted and educated she was, Mrs. Flowers would never be considered by "whitefolks" to be their equal (95). Indeed, Angelou writes that her admiration of her mentor would have been "shattered" had she ever met with Mrs. Flowers in the presence of "powhitefolks," who thought of their "whiteness as an evenizer" and who would've undoubtedly treated the cultivated woman with disrespect (95).

The author demonstrates this phenomenon of accomplished, relatively successful blacks being treated as inferior by poor, uncultivated whites in a metaphorical scene that contrasts Momma, a proprietor, property owner, and pillar of the black community, with the "powhitetrash" girls who taunt her in front of her store (30). The episode, which Angelou recalls as "the most painful and confusing experience" she'd ever had with her grandmother, climaxes when one of the girls, having run out of ways to mock the older woman, finally does a hand stand, presenting her drawerless bottom as the ultimate insult (31). Angelou crafts the scene as one in which Momma, by standing still and singing hymns, quietly triumphs over the girls, who are oblivious to their moral defeat. After the girls' departure, Maya, who had watched everything from inside the house, was left "crying in rage," but Momma "was a brown moon that shone on me. She was beautiful" and even "happy" (33). In spite of Momma's triumph of dignity, Maya absorbed the painful truth that had been enacted: the irrelevance of a black person's accomplishments and character in the eyes of white society, who would never see him or her as anything but inferior.

The irony of the dignified, propertied grandmother being disrespected by dirty, "greasy" young women too poor for underwear and too ignorant to bathe, is captured in the image of the upside-down girl, a perfect metaphor for the inverted logic of white society's system of social class. For, as Maya saw, "My grandmother had more money than all the powhitetrash" (50). Angelou makes it clear that it was not just poor whites that used their race to trump the more-prosperous Momma. For example, the white dentist whose business would have gone under but for the money Momma had loaned him refused to treat Maya's toothache, remarking that his "policy is I'd rather stick my hand in a dog's mouth than in a nigger's" (189).

The autobiographer's most direct indictment of both white social hierarchy and the American Dream myth is the passage about her eighth-grade graduation ceremony. She leads up to the event by detailing not only her own academic accomplishments but those of other black children such as the class valedictorian, Henry Reed, who memorized a speech from *Hamlet* for the occasion. As the author narrates it, Maya's and Henry's view of themselves as intellectuals-in-the-making is shattered by the white superintendent's speech to the audience. The speaker describes the recent improvements in the white school: microscopes, a new art teacher, and chemistry equipment; and he then promises that the Lafayette County Training School for black children would, for its part, have non-academic additions, such as a paved playing field and new equipment for home economics and the workshop (181).

For Maya the message is painfully transparent: "The meticulous maps, drawn in three colors of ink, learning and spelling decasyllabic words, memorizing the whole of *The Rape of Lucrece* — it was for nothing" (180). Entering the professional class, she sees, is an American Dream for whites, not blacks: "We were maids and farmers, handymen and washerwomen, and anything higher that we aspired to was farcical and presumptuous" (181).

Moments such as this, when the narrator as a girl is struck by the disparity between her own aspirations and society's expectations of her, are emblematic of Angelou's complicated class identity. Her awareness of the fact that her intellectual gifts, and those of many other blacks, would likely remain invisible to whites, forms a central aspect of her autobiographical self. It is not surprising, therefore, that Angelou would eschew the conventional patterns of American success stories and choose not to close her autobiography with an event signifying either a momentous departure from the working class or a dramatic arrival in a higher social realm. Indeed, the brief, final three chapters of her book reflect the strategy she uses throughout the text in portraying herself in relation to her family, which accounts for her ethical characterizations: she resists defining her successful self against the poorer and less sophisticated people who surrounded her in her home and community. She also refuses to define poor blacks in opposition to middle-class whites, whether by casting the former as essentially purer, nobler, or as essentially "other" in any way.

Chapter 34 narrates the process by which Maya, at fifteen, conceived of the idea to become a conductor on the San Francisco streetcars, confronted the racist policy that sought to thwart her ambition, won the job, and was at last "swinging on the back of the rackety trolley, smiling sweetly and persuading my charges to 'step forward in the car, please'" (269–70). The episode, as she relates it, is a synecdoche of the book's broader but understated plot, the development of her achieving self and of her determination to attain the fluidity of movement across class barriers that whites have. After being informed that "they don't accept colored people on the streetcars," Maya undergoes a condensed version of the transformation that began with her recognition, at her eighth-grade graduation, that "It was awful to be Negro and have no control over my life" (265, 180). She recalls, "From disappointment, I gradually ascended the emotional ladder to haughty indignation, and finally to that state of stubbornness where the mind is locked like the jaws of an enraged bulldog" (265). She *would* get a job on the streetcars.

As does a moving train, which has often been used as a metaphor for social mobility (James Baldwin, for example, titled his collected essays *The Price of the Ticket*), the streetcar in Angelou's text enables movement across geographical districts that represent racial, cultural, and economic subdivisions in society. Her job provides Maya with freedom from the fixed racial/class identity she had known. On the streetcars "I shimmied up and scooted down" the hills of San Francisco. "I lost some of my need for the Black ghetto's shielding-sponge quality, as I clanged and cleared my way down Market Street, with its honky-tonk homes for homeless sailors ... and along closed undwelled-in-looking dwellings of the Sunset District" (270). On a metaphorical level, the narrator has not so much left her class/cultural origins as she has acquired the psychological freedom to imagine different identity choices for herself.

Significantly, Angelou portrays her mother, Vivian, as being an essential source of support for that liberation. Vivian regarded Maya's weeks-long pursuit of the position as a job in itself, and "every morning she made breakfast, gave me carfare and lunch money, as if I were going to work" (268). As the author describes it, this period marked her entrance into adulthood, a transition in which she and her mother gained more respect for each other, taking their "first steps on the long path toward mutual adult admiration" (268).

The last chapter of the book relates Maya's pregnancy at sixteen, the mysterious fact that her mother doesn't notice it until Maya is nearly due, and the first weeks of her life with a baby. The way this story is told suggests deeper levels of meaning: it symbolizes the autobiographer's birthing of a new, autonomous self. It is meaningful that the author frames the sexual encounter that engendered the pregnancy as the result of Maya's determination to discover who she is: "A boyfriend would clarify my position to the world and, even more importantly, to myself" (280). The process of inventing one's self is necessarily a solitary one. Consequently, she endures the pregnancy crisis alone, and during it transforms her self-image from that of a victim to that of a responsible agent: "For eons, it seemed, I had accepted my plight as the hapless, put-upon victim of fate and the Furies, but this time I had to face the fact that I had brought my new catastrophe upon myself" (284). Importantly, during this period "school recovered its lost magic" and for "the first time since Stamps" she again sees herself as an intellectual for whom learning is "exciting" (286).

One thing she loves most about her baby is that he is "beautiful and mine," and that, for the most part, she created this life herself: "No one had bought him for me. No one had helped me endure the sickly gray months. I had had help in the child's conception, but no one could deny that I had had an immaculate pregnancy" (288). Metaphorically, the being to which she has given birth is the thinking, ambitious self that had been nearly destroyed by racism, but which now has a fragile new life. Maya is terrified by her infant's vulnerability: "I was sure to roll over and crush out his life or break those fragile bones" (288). The autobiographer recalls that her "fears were so powerful," but that the absence of sadness in her mother's voice "helped me to break the bonds of terror" (289). Meaningfully, the narrator's fear of failure, and of disappointing her mother, is overcome because of her mother's support. Vivian urges her to enjoy her baby, assuring her daughter that since Maya is "for the right thing," she will do the right thing, and succeed (289).

It is not an accident that Angelou portrays Maya as developing a troubling new dimension of herself during her pregnancy/metamorphosis: duplicity. Before this crisis, she had held to "a code which never varied. I didn't lie" (285). Now, however, in hiding her pregnancy from her mother, Maya learns that she is not, after all, "beyond deceit." In fact, all of her energy was devoted to "pretending to be that guileless schoolgirl" who was worried about nothing more than her school exams (285). If we see the baby growing in her as a metaphor for the creative, achieving self that is Angelou as an adult, it is significant that the author underscores the subversive aspect of the development of this self, and the need to hide it from her mother and the outside world for as long as possible. Maya's cultivation of an intellectual, artistic self who is determined to succeed in mainstream society is a subversion of both the "rules" of white society and the expectations of her relatives. The secrecy surrounding it is reminiscent of Frederick Douglass learning to read covertly; of Richard Wright borrowing library books with a forged card, and hiding his books as well as his literary aspirations from his family members; and even of Angelou herself as a girl concealing from Momma her love for Shakespeare because he "was white" (14). Wideman also writes about hiding his ambitious self from his black friends and family members, and suppressing his "blackness" around whites. With her metaphorical story about a "secret" pregnancy, Angelou conveys the same point: that duplicity as well as duality are unavoidable components of the self-identity of a successful black person in America.

In an essay titled "The First Century of Afro-American Autobiography: Theory and Explication" (1984), William L. Andrews observes that "What could not be reported explicitly in Afro-American experience had to be explored through metaphor" (229). Angelou's dramatization of her burgeoning adult self through metaphor enables her to assert the *difference* between herself and her mother without flaunting the obvious gap in terms of intellectual and artistic abilities. The adolescent Maya is, of course, a future renowned writer, and the mature Angelou wants to delineate her own uniqueness (as do all autobiographers), but also to acknowledge, in a coded way, the feelings of being "treacherous" that accompanied her journey to success (287).

In the last two decades of the twentieth century, many autobiographers with working-class origins felt compelled, as did Yezierska, Wideman, Nesaule, and Mason, to declare the hereditary side of their identity, and thus to construct a class/race/culture myth. A distinguished exception worth noting in this chapter is *Hunger of Memory* (1982) by Richard Rodriguez, which embeds the story of the author's social rise within an extended meditation on the privileges his education has accorded him. Critics recognized it as a powerful book, not only because of Rodriguez's extraordinary insight into language and other aspects of acculturation, but also because of the autobiographer's honesty about the ways in which assimilation and education have necessarily distanced him from his immigrant Mexican parents. Among the many admiring reviews that *Hunger* received, Le Anne Schreiber in the *New York Times* wrote that "It would be hard to find a more honest and intelligent account of how education can alter a life" (C15), and in the *Times Book Review* Paul Zweig praised Rodriguez's "exquisite clarity" and "attention to nuance that, one senses, is not only esthetic but moral" (BR1).

Rodriguez indeed went against the current of the ethnic revival movement of the 1970s by celebrating, as G. Thomas Couser has noted, "his accession to a public identity by means of his monolingual education" (*Altered* 214). On the second page of his memoir, Rodriguez provocatively announces his intention to disappoint "those in White America who would anoint me to play out for them some drama of ancestral reconciliation." He suggests that because of his "indelible" skin color some whites might "suppose that I am unchanged by social mobility, that I can claim unbroken ties with my past" (5). He later observes that the middle class "is tempted by the pastoral impulse to deny its difference from the lower class—even to attempt cheap imitations of lower-class life." He vows to resist this "decadent solution" (6). Rodriguez adds that such "romantic solutions" (5) are "dangerous, because in trying to imitate the lower class, the middle class blurs the distinction so crucial to social reform. One can no longer easily say what exactly distinguishes the alien poor" (6).

Perhaps inevitably, Rodriguez's book was controversial, and with the acclaim came passionate criticism from reviewers and others who felt that Rodriguez, by not regretting his "Americanization," was betraying his parents and his Mexican heritage. In a *Times Book Review* essay, for example, Earl Shorris labeled *Hunger of Memory* "the work of a person who intends to obliterate the influence of his parents by denying the validity of their culture"; the author "seems, in his opposition to affirmative action and bilingual education, not only to address his work to the *gringos* but to aim to please their most ethnocentric numbers" (BR1). In the years since its publication, some scholars have argued that Rodriguez's text suggests more ambivalence about his assimilation than the author claims to feel. Couser, for instance, contends that *Hunger* "sometimes induces invalid conclusions from his experience. In particular, his views on bilingualism do not cohere or convince. His narrative is certainly better at describing the pain that attended his progressive alienation from the intimacy of his Hispanic family than it is at arguing the necessity and desirability of that process" (*Altered* 215).

It is also true that Rodriguez may overstate the alienating effects of his education, attributing the emotional distance between himself and his parents entirely to his long schooling ("I think," he writes his mother in a letter, "that education has divided the family") when there are also other likely contributing factors, such as his sexual orientation (189). In subsequent books Rodriguez has written openly about being gay, but in *Hunger of Memory* he does not mention it and so does not explore its effect on his relationship with his deeply religious, Catholic parents. Nevertheless, among the late-century's working-class autobiographies, Rodriguez's text is a rare and invaluable challenge to the sentimentalizing and essentializing of ethnicity that would later become prevalent in the sub-genre.

I want to conclude this chapter by returning to Rick Bragg's *All Over but the Shoutin'* (1997), which is a quintessential American social mobility autobiography, and, in unfortunate ways, representative of the popular memoirs that proliferated in the 1990s. This brief discussion will highlight the aspects of his representation of his mother that make his book epitomize the working-class autobiographies of recent decades. Bragg tells of his dramatic rise from poverty to prestige, beginning with the story of how his young mother single-handedly raised him and his two brothers in the Alabama foothills, picking cotton and ironing clothes to supplement their welfare income. His mother, Margaret, is depicted as a figure of pathos: having dropped out of school, she married a violent alcoholic (Bragg's father) who beat her, routinely deserted her and the children, then finally abandoned her for good when the author was seven. Bragg, who attended a local university for a semester, worked as a sportswriter for the college paper and thus began a journalistic career that culminated in a job as a Foreign Correspondent at the *New York Times*.

The reception of this long-running bestseller was mostly enthusiastically favorable. In truth, Bragg creates an immensely likable persona. He is witty and intelligent, and, in spite of (or because of) his southern-boy swagger, conveys genuine vulnerability. He admits to not liking rich people much, especially the southern rich (268), and refers frequently to the "chip" on his shoulder that makes him hypersensitive to being treated condescendingly by Yankees or "sophisticated" people (217, 224). Acknowledging this wariness of people of privilege apparently enables Bragg to avoid, to a large extent, the simplistic, generalizing characterizations of classes and cultures that weakens texts such as Mason's *Clear Springs*. His experiences up north, for a nine-month fellowship residency at Harvard, and later, working six months in New York for the *Times*, are rendered, predictably, as fish-out-of-water episodes, but in relating them the author portrays both of these hallowed institutions as including some warm-blooded people, some of whom even managed to influence Bragg for the better. And, though he identifies himself thoroughly and in every way as a southerner, he does not, as Bobbie Ann Mason does, attempt to sell the South as a pastoral idyll, or its inhabitants as pure and authentic products of the land. Unlike Mason's, Bragg's South is an evolving, heterogeneous, and fluid culture, populated not only by country folks but also by educated professionals (a few, anyway).

The structure of *All Over but the Shoutin,'* however, is the familiar, mythic one in which the author returns home from his conquests to bestow a boon on his family. One of the gifts Bragg gives his mother is the Pulitzer Prize he won for reporting in 1996; at the ceremony he receives it and immediately hands it to Margaret. In the chapter titled "Validation," the autobiographer describes the prize as the thing that will compensate for her "sacrifice" (296). The other gift is a new brick home, paid for with money he saved over twenty years for that purpose. Throughout the text, Bragg refers to the home he intends to buy for his mother one day as an outstanding "debt," and he explains that he cannot build his own personal life — commit to a wife, have children — until he has paid this debt to his mother (272). Bragg's bestowal of both the symbol of his career pinnacle, and his life savings, on his mother, reflects the profound level at which he feels driven to repair the losses and reverse the helplessness of his mother's life. Yet, while Bragg describes his own young adulthood as being directed at helping his mother, he simultaneously reveals his inability to help himself.

As Bragg describes it, his "debt" to his mother prevents his development of a whole self: until he fixes her, he cannot become fully himself. The truth of this is borne out when, as he narrates his career ascension, he traces a parallel rise: the growing tally of failed romantic relationships in his wake. Bragg's text suggests that the author's extraordinary focus on helping his mother is a strategy for avoiding the risks of building a personal life, and a home, of his own. It is also an attempt to heal himself, yet without engaging in the extensive self-searching that deep emotional healing requires. In his autobiography, his portrayal of his mother as a saintly and passive person in need of his rescuing is a substitution as well, a casting of her as a representation of his own painful past, in which his own helplessness as a child, exemplified by his inability to protect his mother from his father's beatings, was unbearable. Consequently, Bragg's narration of his acts of devotion to his mother ironically enacts and reinforces her helplessness; rather than empowering her in his text, he unwittingly appropriates her.

The use of his mother as a stand-in for the weak and wounded side of himself is ethically problematic for many reasons, and chief among them is his portrayal of her as being only and perennially a victim. Repeatedly through the memoir she is described in terms of her deprivations, her ever-present "sadnesses," her passivity, and her inability to stand up for herself (290). Throughout the book, when Bragg mentions his mother, he frequently refers to the "sacrifice" she made for her children when they were young (114): her "forget[ting] to eat" so they could have enough, her wearing shoes with holes (277), her taking on "backbreaking stoop labor," and so on (74). Yet, while Bragg vehemently attests to her strength of character, he never really allows the reader to glimpse it in action, much less to hear it issuing from her own lips. For, despite the fact that a photo of Bragg's mother is the centerpiece of the book's jacket cover, Margaret does not speak very much in the book, nor does Bragg dramatize much of his own interaction with her. Though he professes her to be the emotional center of his life, she is not depicted as a vital presence in his adult life, and she is not a vivid character in his book. As the author portrays her, she is a symbol of the unchanging past; he writes about her near the end of the book, "Nothing seemed to change, on her side, except the calender" (290). Of course, real people *do* change with time, even if they do not grow or progress in their lives. They also have other dimensions to their personalities, including moments of selfishness, anger, and other expressions of self-interest. Yet, with a few, barely noticeable exceptions, Bragg does not include these aspects in his portrait of Margaret, just as he does not provide opportunities for her to display any expertise in something, any real intelligence or humor, or any adult understanding or guidance.

The chapter in which Bragg reaches the peak of his career, winning the Pulitzer, is also the culmination of Bragg's depiction of his mother as childlike and dependent. Flying with his mother to New York for the award ceremony, Bragg explains the airplane for her as one does for a child, answering such questions as, "How did the man flying the plane know where to go? How did he keep from getting lost above the clouds?" (301). Later, while walking around Manhattan and "seeing her experience those big city things," Bragg worries about losing her, and tries to hold her hand, even though she is only sixty years old and in good health (303).

If Bragg had balanced such scenes in which his mother is like a wide-eyed child, intimidated by a new and different world, with dramatizations (rather than descriptions) of her speaking and performing as a competent adult, then the infantilization of her in this section of the book might be less troubling. As it is, however, he depicts her only as a defenseless and naive woman, and this, of course, serves to make his redemption of her, with his professional success and money, appear all the more valiant. His Pulitzer, he writes, would bring his mother the "attention, respect," that had always eluded her (296). It was "validation of my mother's sacrifice. It was payment — not in full, but a payment nonetheless — for her sweat, and her blood" (296). Bragg's book suggests that the only way he can make peace with his superiority to his mother and brothers in terms of intellectual cultivation and professional accomplishment is to frame his success as a gift to them. Though his desire to help his mother is undoubtedly sincere, and his pain for her suffering profound, in his text Bragg constructs a heroic identity for himself at her expense, rather than allowing her autonomy to be expressed. Consequently, Bragg does not succeed at making the reader feel as deeply for his mother as he clearly has sought to do.

Rather, Bragg is most moving when he shares his own experiences of being made to feel like "poor white trash," and when he applies his hard-won insight into being an outsider to his analyses of others (297). Such a moment is when Bragg writes that a part of him "understood" Susan Smith, the young, working-class mother from South Carolina who drowned her two boys. Reporting on the story, Bragg learned that Smith had believed that, with her children gone, the town "Catch" — a wealthy man who had trifled with her — would marry her. Horrified by her actions, Bragg can nonetheless identify with Smith's "desire to be something else" (287), and he expresses pity for the false hope Smith had of being accepted by a spoiled young man: "Someone should have told her how hard it is to fight your way from one side of the tracks to the other. Someone should have told her that just because they invite you to a dark room, that doesn't mean they'll take you to the dance" (283).

Bragg also appears to understand Smith's anger at being rejected. In relating his own tales of being discriminated against because he was poor, he, too, is angry, at people who underestimated and insulted him and his family. This righteous anger, stemming from a clear-eyed perception of injustice, lends some integrity to Bragg's self-portrait. It is also central to his identity as a writer. He recalls that, early in his career, he decided that stories of "struggle by people at risk, people in trouble ... made all other stories seem trivial.... I wanted to write them, only them" (139). Many of the news stories he reproduces in his autobiography are those in which his reporting benefitted his victimized subjects, such as the article that cleared the name of a boy living in the projects who had been falsely accused of molestation.

Lending a voice to those on the margin is, of course, a noble motive that has inspired many of our finest writers. However, when such writers become autobiographers, and their family members are their disadvantaged subjects, the authors can unwittingly silence their subjects by imposing a voice *onto* them. Revealingly, the most memorable words spoken by Margaret Bragg are uttered during the single instance in the text when she reacts angrily to her son. Near the end of the book, when Bragg asks her whether he had given her a new house that she really hadn't wanted, his mother replies, "I wish everybody would quit telling me how I feel.... They don't know nothin'" (315). Sometimes, the power to rescue someone can be confused with the right to speak for them. Like many other working-class autobiographers of the last two decades, Bragg's extraordinary social rise has redefined his mother's life; in writing about their shared past, the author's internal conflicts affect her as well.

2

Life with "A Formidable Woman": Russell Baker's Ethical Representations in *Growing Up*

Russell Baker's *Growing Up* is a traditional autobiography of a young man's rise into the upper-middle class of America. A widow's son growing up during the Great Depression, the narrator of Baker's memoir succeeds because of his hard work, his studiousness, and his mother's instilling in him the belief that "The Lord helps those who help themselves" (10). Though Baker's postmodern, self-deprecating persona couldn't be more different from Benjamin Franklin's self-celebrating one in his *Autobiography*, Baker's memoir affirms Franklin's middle-class value-system — as purveyed by Baker's mother — as the formula for success.

Like Franklin, Baker presents his class mobility as unmitigated good fortune, with no discernible downside. Unlike the other autobiographers discussed in this study, Baker didn't experience the loss of part of his cultural or social identity by moving into the middle-class. This apparent lack of ambivalence about his class transition, as well as the fact that he was raised with middle-class values — which made his class transition relatively smooth — explain in part how Baker is able to write about his working-class family members with exceptional diplomacy and realism.

As this chapter argues, Baker's memoir is a positive model of ethical representations of working-class family members in autobiography. He portrays less-educated, less-sophisticated people as highly individual, psychologically complex human beings who are as variously flawed, dignified, interesting, bland, courageous, shallow, inspiring, and so on as middle-class people are. The author pointedly resists sentimentalizing or romanticizing his parents or their working-class families, and he manages to reveal the admirable character of some of these relatives without insisting on their being pure, extraordinary, or some other variation of the noble primitive. Indeed, Baker's balanced, heterogeneous characterizations are consistent with the humane view that high moral character, likableness, and an engaging personality can be attributes of people from all social classes and with various levels of education or intelligence.

This chapter will identify some of Baker's ethical representations. It will also demonstrate that Baker's advantage as a white male raised with Franklinesque values, in addition to a particular family background that enables him to identify with both working- and middle-class sensibilities, create an autobiographical perspective with a minimal amount of conflicted emotions about class mobility and an unusual level of generosity and human understanding. Such a perspective, this chapter argues, facilitates ethical characterizations in autobiography.

Baker wrote *Growing Up* because his elderly mother's onset of "hopeless" senility and impending death made him "wish I had not thrown off my own past so carelessly. We all come from the past and children ought to know what it was that went into their making" (8). Writing a memoir in the wake of losing one's second parent, Nancy K. Miller asserts, often entails reconstructing family stories in such a way that helps the autobiographer comes to terms with the author's own self-identity, as well as with his or her parents: "A parent's history is a life narrative against which the memorialist ceaselessly shapes and reshapes the past and tries to live in the present" (*Bequest* 5). Purportedly for the benefit of his own children, Baker begins his autobiography by delving into his parents' family histories; he recounts his parents as young people meeting and marrying, and evokes the people and customs of the tiny mountain hamlet of Morrisonville, Virginia, in which Baker spent his first five years. With only sketchy memories of his own and few living relatives who remember that period, Baker's narrative of life in the Blue Ridge mountains a half century earlier is clearly a construct in which he imposes shape and meaning onto people and events. Baker's recreation of "what it was that went into [his] making" is a way, of course, of constructing a self.

Through the story of his parents' marriage, Baker reveals the formation of his own identity as one who embraces such middle-class values as education and self-improvement, and yet who also has a heart for rural, undereducated people like his paternal relatives. It is a story about Baker being born in the middle of his parents' class and culture clash, with Baker cast as the bridge between two disparate worlds. The author characterizes his mother, Lucy, as a woman whose family had grand middle-class aspirations but little means, providing Lucy with ambition and a respect for education but with only a year of college. As Baker portrays her, Lucy holds tenaciously to a sense of herself as having come from better people than her husband Benny, Baker's father. The author writes that his mother had come from "the genteel old Tidewater culture, where her family had been 'quality folk' for 250 years" (20).

After her father's death her search for work as a schoolteacher took her into "primitive backwaters where mountain children came barefoot to school and dropped out after fourth grade to take dollar-a-week work in the fields" (20). Baker depicts Benny as the rough-hewn local boy with whom Lucy fell in love. Baker pictures him as having "workman's hands" that were "rough, callused, competent" and a "graceless mountaineer style"; to Lucy, Baker imagines, Benny was "obviously no gentleman" (22). They nevertheless married when Lucy became pregnant, and their marriage lasted six years, until Benny, a diabetic, died at thirty-three.

The key aspect of his own identity that Baker delineates in his narrative of his parents' marriage is his sense of himself as "happily occup[ying] both worlds," as he describes his early boyhood (32). The two worlds he shuttled between were the households of his country paternal grandmother, Ida Rebecca, and his mother, in houses situated across the road from each other. As a narrator he continues to mediate between them. While he's sympathetic to both sides, he counters his mother's advantage — her greater sophistication and education — with a generous, though not patronizing, view of Ida Rebecca. He notes that Lucy likely would have exuded superiority around the Bakers. He writes that his young mother was "always education-proud" and imagines that around her mother-in-law she "wouldn't have hesitated to talk too much and show off her learning," and that she would likely have "mentioned how backward the children around Morrisonville seemed, compared to the youngsters where she came from" (29).

To further balance the scale, Baker portrays Ida Rebecca as a source of love and earthy pleasures, and relegates his mother to the role of purveying sensibleness and discipline. His grandmother plies the young Russell with "forbidden treats" like jelly bread and his mother objects (33); Ida Rebecca captivates him with her sightings of ghosts, which his mother derides as "ignorant superstition" (56). By dividing the worlds of his father's family and his mother into camps of pleasure versus edification, Baker is coming to the defense of his paternal relatives, who throughout Baker's life with Lucy were implicitly if not explicitly dismissed by his mother as poor and ignorant, and therefore as slovenly and as lacking the "gumption" to make something of themselves.

Baker tells the story of the earliest Christmas he can remember, in which his father's relatives purchased a toy steam shovel for him. The author now sees the gift as an indication of his father's and his father's relatives' expectations for his own future:

> To my grandmother and father and uncles it must have seemed like an educational toy. Metalworkers, stonemasons, carpenters, people with a tradition of craftsmanship and building, they naturally assumed that giving me a toy steam shovel was giving me something more lasting than a toy. They were also giving me a way to start thinking about my life [35].

Baker suggests that his parents would have had very different notions of what an "educational toy" might be: "Left to her own devices, my mother, I suspect, would not have thought of such a beautiful, ingenious machine but would have given me a book" (35).

Barrett J. Mandel argues that conscious memories, or what he calls "pictures of the past," are not really the source of "true" autobiography: "Autobiographies, like all works of art, emanate ultimately from the deeper reality of being" (50). Mandel goes on to insist that a writer must transcend a picture of the past "so that a true experience of being can fuel the writing" (51):

> Everyone has pictures about his or her life; some people abandon them sufficiently so that they can write middling autobiographies; others—far fewer—trust themselves to let the truth of their experience illuminate the deeper relevance of these pictures in the context of their total existence. It is the *context* disclosed through writing that is autobiography [52].

The story of the Bakers' Christmas gift has significance not because it happened but because of the meaning Baker reads into it. Baker's interpretation of the steam shovel as an educational toy reflects his years of conditioning by Lucy to see his father's family primarily in terms of their working-class life and perspective. He takes their side, however, suggesting that these less sophisticated people nonetheless had a greater sensitivity than his mother to the desires of a boy and a greater willingness to indulge them.

Baker's defense of his father's family stems from a foundational aspect of his identity development: what he terms the "battle" he and his mother fought "almost as long as [he] could remember":

> It probably started even before memory began, when I was a country child in northern Virginia and my mother, dissatisfied with my father's plain workman's life, determined that I would not grow up like him and his people, with calluses on their hands, overalls on their backs, and fourth-grade educations in their heads [14].

Though Lucy succeeded in directing Baker toward a "better life" of "desks and white collars, well-pressed suits, evenings of reading and lively talk," Baker's text suggests that an essential part of his personality was shaped by his resistance to Lucy's snobbish denigration of his father, and by extension, others whom Russell perceived as lower-class outsiders (14).

However, Baker defends his father's relatives not by sentimentalizing their rural culture or their poverty but by fleshing them out as complex human beings. He is clear-eyed about the Blue Ridge culture's crippling skepticism of any intellectual pursuit, wryly noting Ida Rebecca's disdain for "book learning," and her belief that "Man was born to work, not to sit around with his nose in a book" (29). As Baker acknowledges, as charming as country life was when he was a boy, it would have proved severely limiting to grow into adulthood there: "Morrisonville was a poor place to prepare for a struggle with the twentieth century, but a delightful place to spend a childhood" (42).

The author's characterizations provide a striking contrast to Mason's depiction of the rural South. In *Clear Springs* Mason creates a pastoralized and often primitivist portrait of rural Kentucky in large part by using her mother, a passive farmer's wife who "always knows where the moon is, and when to plant seed potatoes, and what potion to paint on a sick child's chest" and "how to read the sky," as the central figure to represent the working-class South (282). Throughout *Clear Springs* Christy Mason, whom Marianna Torgovnick's primitivist terms aptly describe ("gentle, in tune with nature, paradisal, ideal"), is either adored or exploited by northerners for her rural "authenticity" and naturalness (Torgovnick 3). The passive, somewhat tragic quality of Mason's mother's life is used by Mason to represent what we are clearly meant to see as the passive, exploited innocence of uneducated southern country people and their dying country culture.

In contrast, the tone and essence of Baker's description of his father's family are largely determined by Baker's choice to use Ida Rebecca as the representative figure of the clan. Like Mason, he chooses a woman to be the primary face of his country relatives, but the matriarch of the Baker family could not be more different than Christy Mason in temperament and demeanor. Interestingly, Baker could have chosen to focus more on his own father in his recollections of Morrisonville, but instead casts Ida Rebecca as the central figure. Benny is drawn as a likeable, innocuous young man with a taste for whiskey and "a sense of fun" (22), and who, though once defying Ida Rebecca with his marriage to Lucy Elizabeth, is nonetheless mostly shown as docile, and as often dominated by Baker's mother: "When he came home smelling of whiskey, she abused him fiercely in cries loud enough to be heard across the road at Ida Rebecca's. He never shouted back, nor argued, nor attempted to defend himself, but always sat motionless as her anger poured down on his bowed head — sick, contrite, and beaten" (38).

The choice to emphasize Ida Rebecca puts a face of strength, capableness, and humanity on the Bakers. Ida Rebecca's strength, though, is not of the saintly kind: we're told she is a "fierce" and "domineering woman, who had trained her sons to march to her command" (24). Baker repeatedly stresses her forceful personality and sternness; he imagines how his grandmother must have appeared to his mother at their first meeting: "The long jaw under her bonnet was combatively prominent. Her hair was a glistening silver white. Peering through steel-rimmed spectacles were chilly gray eyes that found little to be amused by. What my mother saw was an overpowering figure accustomed to command" (28–29).

The reader does not see her as a brute, as we're meant to regard the working-class Joe, for example, in Nesaule's text. This is in part because she is a woman, but it is also because of the ways Baker humanizes Ida Rebecca, deepening her character with other, softer dimensions. She is shown to have a loving, intimate relationship with her grandson: "Walking through Morrisonville to survey her kingdom, my grandmother took my hand and led me beside her. In her vegetable garden she taught me how to pick potato bugs. In her dark cellar kitchen she showed me how to lay the kindling and pour kerosene to fire her wood-burning stove," and so on (32). As a young boy Baker is assured of his grandmother's deep affection for him: "I loved my grandmother dearly and knew she loved me just as much" (32). Yet by emphasizing her strength and assertiveness, Baker conveys the hard realities and limitations of her life — and by extension, the lives of his other Morrisonville relatives — without painting her, or them, as pitiable.

For instance, he juxtaposes the fact of her "small book learning" with a description of her "highly developed sensitivity, particularly when it came to outsiders," in a brief passage that endows her with strong opinions and keen perception: "In Morrisonville outsiders were under suspicion until they proved they could fit comfortably into Morrisonville society. Ida Rebecca must have sensed immediately what her eleventh son failed to: that this book-proud schoolteacher who gave herself airs about her fancy family would never accommodate to Morrisonville" (30).

Baker's ethical depictions of the Baker clan are facilitated by the author's distance from their world. He left their sphere and all of its disadvantages at the age of five, when his mother moved him and his sister Doris to New Jersey. By not growing up in close proximity with these poor, country relatives, the author was spared the experience of seeing through adult eyes their vulnerability and hardships. The texts of Wideman,

Nesaule, and Mason suggest that this kind of experience is not only deeply painful but also guilt-inducing when one has escaped the same fate. Because he doesn't closely identify with the Bakers, as Wideman, Nesaule, and Mason do with their poorer relatives, Baker is not as threatened by their disadvantages and their "otherness," so he has a greater psychological ease with portraying them as rounded people.

Baker's ethical rendering of his paternal relatives is also enabled by his gender. In his particular situation, the people who most influenced his development — and therefore the people he most vividly associates with working-class life — are women. Because Baker apparently viewed Ida Rebecca as the representative figure of his paternal family, and because his memories of his father are naturally sparse since Baker was five when he died, Baker doesn't closely identify with a poor, powerless male. His generous, ethical representations of his female relatives in particular are thus enabled in part by his sense of difference from them, by his growing up with an instinctive knowledge from an early age that he wouldn't likely share their destiny. To see how threatening it can be for a young person to closely identify with a same-gender role model who is powerless, one need only look at Mason's recollection of her state of mind when she left Kentucky after college. Living in Manhattan, she saw her frivolous movie-magazine job as having saved her from a life like her mother's: "I was grateful not to be sewing labels in Tony Martin jackets or canning tomatoes in a hot kitchen with brats underfoot" (132).

The absence of Baker's father from most of the author's life gives Baker the difficult task of constructing him from the thinnest threads of memory, but it also gives him the license to create a version of his father that best enables Baker to "live in the present," in Miller's words. This strategy is at work in another early memory he recounts. When Baker was four years old, he writes, his mother bought him his first book and began teaching him to read. On one summer night, when his parents are stretched out on blankets on the floor with him, his father wants to see how his reading is progressing. "They placed me between them with the opened book," Baker recalls. "I knew a few words, but under pressure to perform forgot everything" (40). His recollection suggests a less-than-tolerant reaction from his mother: "My mother was disappointed that I could do nothing but stare stupidly at the printed page." But he remembers his father rescuing the situation with a more understanding and affectionate approach:

> My father saved my pride. "Have a little patience with him," he said. Taking the book in hand, he moved me close against him and rubbed his cheek against mine. "Now," he said, pointing to a word, "you know that word, don't you?"
> I did indeed. "The," I said [41].

In a talk Baker delivered on the subject of his memoir (the talk was fittingly titled "Life with Mother") the author insisted that everything in the book is there because he actually remembers it. However, Mandel's theory that context reveals more of a "true experience of being" than literal memories is helpful here.

Certainly the context of the memoir as a whole suggests that whether or not the scene above really happened is irrelevant; the scene conveys much about Baker's relationship with his mother and the particular qualities in a father that Baker most longed for. In the scene his father provides a much-needed buffer between Baker and his mother's steep expectations. In this symbolic mini-drama, Baker conjures up precisely the kind of father figure that he sorely needed in his real life with his mother, a father whose patience and affection might have enabled achievement, yet with less anxiety. That his ideal father takes this particular shape reveals more about what was lacking in Baker's life with his mother than it does about any sketchy memories the writer has about his father from fifty or more years ago.

Further, Baker characterizes his father here as being delighted at the prospect of his son going to college one day: "Smiling down at me, he said, 'You want to go to college?' They both laughed a little at this. Maybe he liked the extravagance of the idea as much as she did" (42). The scene of Baker reading ends with his parents happily embracing the same dream for their son: "That night they let me sleep between them." Baker's choice to "remember" this scene and to frame it as representative is part of his construction of a coherent class identity in which he gets support from both parents for his class advancement. Naturally it is impossible to know how Baker's life with his father would have gone had Benny lived longer. Many working-class fathers want to see their children attend college, but that is beside the point. More than offering literal information about Baker's father, the reading scene suggests Baker's choice to construct a father who would grant his blessing on his son's radical social and cultural departure from the father's world.

In addition, Baker is able to "remember" his father as offering an ideal blend of southern patience, country simplicity, and middle-class aspirations for his son because their relationship didn't extend beyond Baker's early boyhood. The scene in which the young Baker blissfully sleeps between his parents represents Baker's choice to put his class liminality into its most positive light, in which he derives warmth and pleasure from his father's working-class simplicity, and excellent preparation for life from his mother's middle-class pragmatism. In crafting this scene Baker demonstrates the choice he is making to "happily occup[y] both worlds."

One of Baker's real achievements is the complexity with which he renders his mother and their relationship. At the heart of Baker's identity development in the text is the "battle" he and his mother fought throughout Baker's youth, in which Lucy pushed him to achieve and Baker "bowed to superior will" (14). His narration at once acknowledges that she contributed immensely to his success, and also reveals the difficult, even unhealthy, aspects of his mother's fierce drive to push him into the middle class.

Baker begins the story of his childhood with a key episode in his identity formation. The passage is characteristic in that it is comic in tone, yet replete with enough information and meaningful dialogue to convey deep psychological truths. In particular, beneath the humor the incident dramatizes the extent to which Baker and his mother became psychologically enmeshed by her determination to make him succeed professionally and redeem her own life. When he turned eight, Baker writes, his mother "began the job of starting me on the road toward making something of myself" by arranging an interview with a man who hires Baker to sell the *Saturday Evening Post* (11). Baker playfully calls it the start of his writing career: "I began working in journalism when I was eight years old. It was my mother's idea" (9).

Though not literally the start of his career as a writer, of course, the episode nonetheless marks the beginning of Baker's psychological journey from being the son of an impoverished widow to becoming a college graduate, author, and columnist for the *New York Times*. His entrance into the world of work comes two years after his father's death, and, as we learn in the book's seventh chapter, right on the heels of his mother making a crucial decision about her own future and her son's. It is 1932, and Lucy is thirty-six, living with her children in her brother's home, and unable to make a living wage; her suitor, Oluf, has "disappeared into the Depression," and Lucy's "hopes for finding love and security vanished with him" (89). Consequently, Lucy casts Baker "as the central figure" in her campaign "to come up from the bottom without help from the sort of Providence Oluf had represented" (94). As Baker tells it, his mother consciously chose to place her hopes for a successful future on her young son's shoulders:

> She would spend her middle years turning me into the man who would redeem her failed youth. I would make something of myself, and if *I* lacked the grit to do it, well then *she* would make me make something of myself. I would become the living proof of the strength of her womanhood. From now on she would live for me, and in turn, I would become her future [94–95].

Thus, in the scene with the *Post* executive Baker is not only acquiring his first job; he is also taking on the "heavy burdens" associated with becoming his mother's redeemer (95).

The comic tension in much of the book stems from Lucy's lofty expectations of her son, and Baker's insistence on being an ordinary boy, for whom "a perfect afternoon was lying in front of the radio rereading my favorite Big Little Book, *Dick Tracy Meets Stooge Viller*" (9). In the scene of Baker's job interview the comic tension comes from the fact that Lucy has misrepresented Baker's level of ambition to the man from the *Post*, and Baker designs the dialogue to emphasize the humorous contrast between his own boyish interests and the eagerness to work that his mother falsely claims for him. Baker first recounts his true desire at that time in his life: "I loved to pick through trash piles and collect empty bottles, tin cans with pretty labels, and discarded magazines" (10). He aspired to be, he writes, a garbage man. The man from the *Post* has been told differently:

> Was it true as my mother had told him, he asked, that I longed for the opportunity to conquer the world of business?
> My mother replied that I was blessed with a rare determination to make something of myself.
> "That's right," I whispered.
> "But have you got the grit, the character, the never-say-quit spirit it takes to succeed in business?"
> My mother said I certainly did [11].

The dialogue continues in this vein, with the interviewer quizzing Baker on his character and his mother providing the right answers. Baker parrots his mother's responses, proving to be, as he later describes his younger self, "pliable" raw material (96). Yet, while the reader is meant to enjoy the irony of his mother's answers for him, the rest of the memoir makes clear that his mother's speaking for him in this scene has symbolic weight. Indeed, in the scene the young Baker resembles a ventriloquist's dummy. As Baker suggests in the passage cited above in which his mother decides to "live for me, and in turn, I would become her future," Baker's identity at the age of eight becomes to a large extent fused with his mother's.

Both the plot and the light tone of *Growing Up* assure us that Baker will eventually prevail in the struggle with his mother over the ownership of his life. As a child, and particularly as a male child, he has only to wait out the period during which she has power over him. Nevertheless, as we see in the passage about the *Saturday Evening Post* job, there is plenty of what Albert Stone calls "autobiography's coded language" in the text that suggests that Baker's mother's determination to mold him became indistinguishable at times from an appropriation of him (*Autobiographical* 14). In addition, the young Russell sensed his mother's fight to "make me make something of myself" was in part her way of erasing Benny's lingering influence on him (10). Thus, the text suggests, Baker's resistance to his mother's upward pushing was not merely boyish laziness, but rather an attempt to preserve an autonomous self, and, more poignantly, a way of remaining loyal to his father.

Throughout the memoir Baker's criticism of his mother is rendered with a great measure of understanding. In contrast to the more judgmental and unsympathetic tone in which Nesaule relates her mother's transgressions, Baker quietly reveals the emotional costs he paid for his mother's consuming focus on him. In chapter 10, for instance, he remarks on how as a boy his "love for mischief ... had been subdued in me by too much melancholy striving to satisfy my mother's notions of manhood" (141). At another point he quietly inserts the fact that his mother's over-involvement with his homework led him to feel at times incapable of achieving on his own: "I was eleven years old and consumed with timidity and a sense of my own incompetence. I attributed my success at school entirely to my mother's schoolteacher insistence on good grades and her constant help with my studies" (121).

Baker's clear attitude toward his mother in this memoir is that the benefits he gleaned from his mother's "constant help" outweighed the pressure and melancholy he felt from the expectation of achievement she imposed on him; of course, she gave him no choice. Despite the increased stress he experienced, Baker has plainly forgiven his mother for pushing him so hard and has come to appreciate and even respect her motives. Especially in light of a comparison with Nesaule's text, this human understanding forms a distinct piece of the self-identity Baker constructs here. Elizabeth Bruss writes that "identity is composed not only by acts of self-perception but by other-perception as well" (13). It is also composed of revealed attitudes and temperaments. Nesaule writes from a perspective of unhealed emotional wounds and an undisguised lack of forgiveness. Though this attitude is most blatantly directed at her former husband, Joe, it is apparent in the text that Nesaule still feels anger toward her mother as well, though her mother had been dead for several years when Nesaule wrote *A Woman in Amber*. In many ways, the young Baker and the young Nesaule share a common predicament, with their mothers both funneling their own ambition into sacrificing for their children's success.

As does Nesaule, Baker connects his mother's investment in his class advancement to her own thwarted dreams of higher education and "the better life," though he does it more implicitly than does Nesaule, merely by telling his mother's story (14). Like Nesaule's mother, Baker's mother had plans to finish college, but after the death of her father had to work instead; however, Baker records this matter-of-factly rather than with the bitterness with which Nesaule writes of her own mother's failed hopes.

Both Nesaule and Baker as young people feel simultaneously grateful to their mothers for helping them get ahead academically and are painfully aware of their mothers' expectations for them. Baker portrays his mother as a more loving and lovable woman, certainly as a woman without bitterness in spite of her hardship; Nesaule depicts her mother as a person who became hardened and acidic by her ordeals and her failure to achieve the high social status to which she felt entitled. However, the enormous difference between Nesaule and Baker in their relationships with their mothers, in their characterizations of their mothers, and ultimately, in the ethical characters of their texts, lies in the presence or absence of the authors' understanding.

Sennett and Cobb examine the "unspoken social contract demanded by sacrificial acts" by parents:

> To sacrifice for the children is to future-orient oneself, to delay gratification. The gratification will come when they, as adults, have moved up to a social position where anyone could respect them. Their future position will redeem the unsatisfying effort a parent makes now. Yet sacrifice ... means that the sacrificer is also making demands in the present on those for whom he is struggling [125–26].

The contract that Baker's mother imposes in which she will live for him and he will in turn become her future creates deep ambivalence in him toward her during his youth. As Sennett and Cobb note, "The tragedy of loving as sacrifice is that those who are pushed to feel grateful cannot. Sacrifice appears to the children as a way parents have of manipulating them, rather than really loving them" (134). The latter statement describes Nesaule's feelings when her mother reminds her again of her own lost opportunities and the sacrifices she's made for Nesaule's success: "I feel helpless whenever she recites her losses. Should I apologize for winning the scholarship? I try to harden myself.... Why does she have to ruin everything?" (Nesaule 186). Yet parent-child relationships can overcome the pressures exerted by parents' sacrifices.

According to Sennett and Cobb, the critical factor in the outcome of the relationship is not the success or failure of the young, but "whether love can survive under contract" (133). The answer in *Growing Up* is a resounding yes, while *A Woman in Amber* suggests that there may have been little real love between Nesaule and her damaged mother from the start. Of course, an autobiographer cannot be held responsible for the quality of one's life and relationships during one's childhood. But a writer can be held accountable for the ways in which one presents the tangles of a relationship, and whether one allows one's anger at someone to prevent one from writing truthfully.

Baker makes plain at least one invaluable gift from his mother: her instilling in him, through concrete actions such as helping him become a top student, the belief that, in spite of his working-class origins, he could aspire to a professional life. Throughout the text Baker sets his mother's unbending faith that he will somehow go to college in contrast with depictions of an environment in which such a future seems impossible. Baker uses the figure of his mother's "mythical Cousin Edwin" and his relatives' awed perception of him to characterize subtly the class psychology of his Uncle Allen's household, in which Baker lived with his mother and sister between the ages of five and eleven. The passage about Edwin shows how an inflated perception of professional people constitutes one of the psychological obstacles that working-class children must overcome in order to advance into the upper-middle class. The section is also an example of Baker's ability to depict his working-class relatives with realism and insight, yet without making them seem either oppressed, deprived, or passive.

Edwin, Baker's mother's first cousin, "had made something of himself in a big way" by becoming managing editor and a columnist for the *New York Times;* he is, Baker writes, a regular subject of conversation among Baker's relatives in spite of the fact that "they hadn't seen him in twenty years and didn't expect ever to see him again" (118). Baker's discussion of Edwin seems designed to show how elevated Edwin is in the minds of Allen, his wife Pat, and Baker's mother, Lucy, and how Edwin's professional success has, understandably, given him the status of a legend in Allen's household. As a child, Baker listens as the adults tell oft-repeated anecdotes about Edwin's rise.

In one such tale, Uncle Allen illustrates Edwin's "nerve" by recounting how Edwin got his first newspaper job, and the story, which sounds fictional, is significant for the way it portrays Edwin as possessing a mysterious self-assurance that magically opens doors in journalism. As Allen tells it, Edwin "went in for an interview with the editor. The editor looked at him and said, 'Young man, how do I know you're not a damn fool?' And Edwin said, 'That's a chance we'll both have to take.' They gave him the job on the spot" (118). In this story Edwin apparently triumphs in part because of his wit, but mostly because of his boldness in speaking to the editor as an equal.

Sennett and Cobb describe the somewhat rarefied and mystical view the blue-collar workers they interviewed hold of people with higher education:

> Since the power of professionals lies in their ability to give or withhold knowledge, they are in positions that by and large are not questioned by others; they are "authorities" themselves ... unto themselves. It is precisely the endowment of a professional with this inner-self-sufficing power that gives him a higher status than men with economic power [227].

In Baker's depiction of his relatives' talk about Edwin, they regard him as having some inherent, intangible quality that made his prestigious accomplishments inevitable: "'I hear Edwin's making $80,000 a year,' [an amount that would have been astronomical during the Depression] Uncle Allen said one evening. 'I always knew he'd amount to something. Edwin had sort of a way about him'" (118). Moreover, the adults interpret Edwin's lack of contact with them as a natural consequence of his attainment of an upper-middle class life: "He had achieved success on the monumental scale. 'Edwin's no more going to visit his poor relatives than I'm going to walk on water,' my mother said. 'You've got to realize, Lucy, Edwin's a big man,' said Uncle Allen, who had no envy in him" (118). In this scene, then, Baker reveals much about the perception of Edwin's world as distant and unattainable by most of the adults surrounding him in his childhood; as he puts it, "By New Street measures, Edwin was a big man indeed" (118).

Against this background, Baker's mother's words to her son about Edwin are noteworthy. Though Lucy participates in the adults' conversations about Edwin, when speaking to Baker she tries to demystify Edwin for him and to impress upon her son that Edwin's status is accessible: "When my mother talked of me making something of myself, Cousin Edwin was one of the models of success she had in mind. Her childhood memories of Edwin were not formidable. 'Edwin James wasn't any smarter than anybody else,' she assured me, 'and look where he is today. If Edwin could do it, so can you'" (121). With such details Baker emphasizes the importance of his mother's faith in the possibility of class mobility as a weapon against the psychological barrier to professional achievement. Baker recalls: "'Look where Edwin James is today. If Edwin could do it, you can do it.' I heard those words again and again while [my mother and I] toiled together over seventh-grade English homework" (123).

Baker's passages about Edwin also reveal some of the psychological advantages Baker enjoyed as a working-class child relative to the experiences of the other autobiographers in this study. Though Edwin was a distant figure, he nevertheless represented a model of professional success that the family could claim, and, more importantly for Russell's class advancement, that the family openly admired. Every week Baker was exposed to the *New York Times* and taught to hallow it.

The Edwin stories also underscore Baker's advantage as a male, and not only because the revered Edwin is a model of male achievement. Edwin's aloofness from his relatives, and Allen's casual acceptance of it, teaches Baker that a successful man detaches from his family. Baker's text, along with those of the other writers in this study, suggest that men, far more than women, are granted by society the freedom to distance themselves socially, culturally, emotionally, and geographically from one's family without being judged a bad child, especially if that distance is essential to their professional success. Baker admits to having made "infrequent visits" to his elderly mother, from whom he lived several states away (4). While he always makes it clear that he cared for her, he nonetheless shows that he sees his break from her as a normal course of adulthood: "When she was young, with life ahead of her, I had been her future and resented it. Instinctively, I wanted to break free, cease being a creature defined by her time, consign her future to the past, and create my own. Well, I had finally done that" (8). Though Wideman reveals a greater sense of obligation to his family than Baker, he demonstrates a similar ability to "break free" from Robby when he wants to return to his previous, separate life after finishing his memoir; businesslike, he describes "closing down the special relationship between my brother and myself that writing the book had precipitated" (199).

The women autobiographers, in contrast, depict themselves as feeling continuously responsible for the well-being of their parents and siblings. Nesaule and Mason both include chapters in which the authors help a family member move from one home to another. The chapters' dramatize the authors' intimate level of emotional and practical engagement with their relatives, including the authors' financial assistance to them. As this book's discussions of Nesaule and Mason argue, this deep sense of responsibility toward their family members engenders many of the ethical problems in their memoirs. Baker's relative detachment from his family—and his lack of guilt for leaving them—enable him to portray them with greater complexity and fuller dimensions.

As the sections in Baker's memoir about Edwin show, Baker benefited greatly from his mother's admiration of Edwin's writing career. Unlike Wideman and Mason, Baker grew up with family members, a mother especially, who valued not only intellectual achievement but specifically—and significantly—literary success. A significant way in which Lucy helped Baker over the class barrier was to foster in him the notion that he could be a writer someday. As he tells it, his mother first articulates the idea. At eleven he brings home from school a short paper with an A, and his mother's reaction is boldly optimistic:

> Reading it with her schoolteacher's eye, my mother agreed that it was top-drawer seventh grade prose and complimented me. Nothing more was said about it immediately, but a new idea had taken life in her mind. Halfway through supper she suddenly interrupted the conversation. "Buddy," she said, "maybe you could be a writer" [16].

The young Baker "clasped the idea to my heart" (16).

The manner in which this central aspect of the author's identity comes into being is representative of the way Baker portrays his development throughout the text. Baker's mother introduces something, or even pushes it on him, and then Baker chooses to make it his own, with the emphasis being upon his choosing of it. For example, Lucy for many years coerces him to excel in school: "For years she had been my tutor in everything academic, the eternal schoolteacher forcing me to learn to read when reading bored me, watching over my shoulder while I did my homework, encouraging me when I complained" (169). Once in high school, Baker makes academic success a central part of his identity; as he recalls, "I took to the rarefied scholarly air with gusto," and "I began to view myself with extraordinary respect" (169). This is a crucial moment that brings to light Baker's relative ease in his class ascension, compared to the other autobiographers.

Though just as academically gifted as Baker, Wideman, Nesaule, and Mason had very visible racial or cultural differences that set them apart from the norm and that made them feel inferior in school in spite of their good grades. The women especially were plagued by a sense of inadequacy even into graduate school. Nesaule writes that in college she was certain she would "finally be unmasked as an impostor not deserving my scholarships" and have to "leave school in disgrace" (189). Thus the texts in this study suggest that Baker's status as a white male from a mainstream-culture background made it easier for him to regard himself—and to be regarded—as smart and successful in his youth.

While the first discernible stage of Baker's identity in the text is a kind of contractual enmeshment with his mother, the next marked direction in his identity development is his emphatic separation from her and assertion of his own self. The joke that opens the book—"I began working in journalism when I was eight. It was my mother's idea"—masks an anxiety in Baker that is revealed over the course of the memoir: the fear that he is too much his mother's creation. One of the "oldest links" between them is his mother playing the role of teacher to him (170). In numerous places in the memoir we see them immersed together in his studies, from the time she teaches him to read until, as he writes, "we toiled together over seventh-grade English homework" (123). It is thus a pivotal moment when the adolescent Baker "yield[s] to an evil impulse" to show his mother that his education has finally surpassed hers (170). Baker realizes that he is "outdistancing her" as he progresses through a high school college preparatory program, and, desiring to "show her how little Latin she knew," he asks for his mother's help in translating a difficult passage for which he already has the answer (169–70). Having watched her "laboriously working out a couple of lines and getting them wrong," Baker trumps her feeble translation with relish: "'Don't you think it makes more sense this way?' I asked, and read the entire passage as the teacher had helped translate it earlier" (170).

Outgrowing his mother academically and intellectually marks a turning point in Baker's relationship with his mother. He writes: "One of the oldest links in the chain binding us together had snapped. She was no longer my ultimate schoolteacher" (170). The transformation of a child into a more educated, and thus more powerful, person than his parent is often both the fulfillment of the working-class parent's dream and a form of losing the child irretrievably. As Richard Sennett and Jonathan Cobb observe, "What this transformation invites the child to do is to desert his past, to leave it and the parents who have sacrificed for him all behind" (130–31). Baker recalls that his act of besting his mother at Latin signified a profound act of breaking from her: "Something else that had bound us together parted that night. It had been cruelly done, but I had issued my first declaration of independence from childhood" (172). This admission of cruelty, incidentally, raises an important difference in the ethical quality of Baker's text from that of the other writers.' Baker stands out in his willingness to judge his treatment of others. Though Wideman occasionally questions his own motives behind his desire to write about Robby, he is usually vague (and too self-exculpatory) when referring to his own lapses in character. Neither Nesaule nor Mason acknowledges their own acts of selfishness, unkindness, cruelty, or cowardice, while Baker convincingly admits to all of the above.

Baker's treatment of this transitional moment in his growing up is characteristic of the way he portrays himself, his mother and his other relatives, as well as his class advancement in *Growing Up*. He differs dramatically from Wideman, Nesaule, and Mason, in his lack of guilty feelings about going beyond his mother educationally and socially. Not that he *should* feel guilty about surpassing his mother in education; she has, after all, encouraged it. Simply, Baker differs from the other autobiographers in that he appears not to feel that transcending his mother in class is a betrayal of her. As Sennett and Cobb note, a sense of betrayal often comes with class mobility that resembles, in the adult child, survivor's guilt (183). Yet in this scene Baker links his advancing beyond his mother's level of education to declaring his independence, suggesting that it is similar to the normal parting from one's parents that comes with outgrowing childhood. Baker's absence of guilty feelings is certainly in large part due to his social and cultural background as a White Anglo-Saxon Protestant. In addition, his mother, because of her ambition, her one-year of college, and her general intelligence, was not as far removed from the upper-middle class world into which Baker moves as were the parents of Wideman and Mason.

Baker is refreshingly candid about the intellectual arrogance he developed in his ascension from working-class Baltimore. Yet, while he shows a certain degree of vulnerability in his working-class relatives because of their limited educations, and though he dramatizes some of their hardships, Baker differs significantly from the other authors in this study in his consistent portrayal of his family members as capable of holding their own in conflicts with himself, or in virtually any difficult situation. In the scene cited above in which Baker seeks to "punish" his mother with her lesser knowledge, the author wants us to sympathize with his mother but not to pity her (169). He lets her speak up for herself: "'If you knew it already, why did you bother to ask me?' she said. 'I thought maybe you could improve it,' I said. 'Improve it for yourself,' she said, and left the table" (172).

The text makes it clear that from the start, even though Lucy is the parent, Baker has the true power in the relationship with his mother because, as he notes in the opening pages of the book, he represents her future. Philip Slater observes that in a child-centered society such as America has been since the late nineteenth century, "The child emerges as the receptacle for future hopes and hence bears a higher status than her elders, whose authority is weakened by its doubtful relevance to this future" (61). In the future-oriented household of Baker's family, it is Baker, and not his sister, who represents his mother's hope for eventual success. Baker wryly notes his mother's perspective about her children: "Doris could have made something of herself if she hadn't been a girl. Because of this defect, however, the best she could hope for was a career as a nurse or schoolteacher, the only work that capable females were considered up to in those days" (10). Of course, Nesaule and Mason were also saddled with the defect of being a girl.

In chapter 7 there is a revealing passage in which Baker briefly recounts his mother's attempts to discipline him physically. Baker is around the age of eight, and the episode he recalls is meant to be an illustration of his inability to cry in the years following his father's death. It was his mother's belief, he writes, "that boys my age needed 'a good thrashing' when they misbehaved. These she administered with my belt, often for what seemed to me like trivial offenses such as coming home late for supper because I was having a good time sledding on the hill" (96). Though Baker is ostensibly trying to demonstrate his emotional numbness during this period of his life, his description of the showdown he has with his mother during his "thrashing" is clearly a sketch of a power-struggle between them, with his lack of tears coming not from an inability to feel deeply but as a strategy for protesting the unfairness of the punishment:

> My failure to cry during her "thrashings" enraged my mother, and I knew it. Tears would be evidence that I had learned my lesson. My sullen submission to her heaviest blows intensified her fury....
>
> I knew that faking the tears would gratify her and end the punishment, but I refused. The injustice and humiliation of being beaten rankled so powerfully that I deliberately accepted the worst she could deliver to show my contempt [97].

What is striking about the passage is how strong-willed Baker portrays his young self to be. Despite nearly a thirty-year age difference between them, mother and son in this scene are equally matched in their determination not to give in:

> Sometimes, to goad her with my contempt, I gritted my teeth and, when the belt had fallen four or five times, muttered, "That doesn't hurt me." In these moments we were very close to raw hatred of each other. We were two wills of iron. She was determined to break me; I was just as determined that she would not [97].

The passage captures the paradoxical process by which Baker matures in relation to his mother: he becomes a man both by submitting to her will and also, when necessary, by resisting it. Baker introduces the scene of his corporal punishment by noting, "The making of a man, even when the raw material was as pliable as I, often seemed brutally hard without the help of a father to handle the rougher passages" (96). To his mother, "a good thrashing" made a boy into a man. However, the scene describing Baker's defiant stoicism during the beatings shows Baker attaining manhood through fighting back, if only psychologically: "She was determined to break me; I was just as determined that she would not" (97).

The passage brings to mind the great moment of resistance in Frederick Douglass's *Narrative,* when he "resolved to fight" his slave overseer, Covey, in protest against repeated whippings and for having been "used like a brute" (298). Douglass's resistance earns him a psychological victory over Covey; he writes that it "revived within me a sense of my own manhood" (298). Douglass begins the story of this turning-point by telling his reader, "You have seen how a man was made a slave; you shall see how a slave was made a man" (294). In a more coded, implicit way, Baker also depicts himself becoming a man by refusing to submit to what he sees as unjust treatment.

It resonates with meaning that the standoff ends with Baker both winning the battle of wills, and then showing great tenderness and mercy toward his mother. In the end, he writes, "she was the one who always cried, and then, when she had flung the belt aside and collapsed on a chair weeping quietly, the anger and hatred instantly drained out of me, and overcome with pity and love, I rushed to embrace her" (97). Baker wins because, as noted earlier, he has the real power; as the potential man he has and will have the upper hand. Baker's mother would not be "determined to break" him if this were not so. Further, Baker's generosity and tenderness toward her after he prevails is symbolic of his generosity toward her, and others, as a writer; his benevolence and even his ethical representations are enabled by his longtime position of power in relation to his family. Unlike the other writers, he learned early on that, as the "man of the family," he enjoyed the upper hand but compensated for it with affection and tolerance toward his family (130).

Yet, Baker makes clear, none of his family members is passive or weak. One major difference between Baker's memoir and those of the other authors in this study is that Baker's relatives are all portrayed as having a reassuring strength. The family members of Wideman, Nesaule, and Mason are mostly represented as being either passive, troubled, or to a great extent defined by their hardships and/or their victimization. Baker almost invariably wants his reader to sympathize with the other person when he is in a conflict with someone, and he is inclined generally to portray his working-class relatives in a sympathetic manner. Yet he appears to make a conscious effort not to render his family members as pitiable, even when he is disclosing poignant information about their lives.

This effort is evident in the strategy he employs in chapter 6 to convey the brutal economic and psychological conditions of the Depression without emphasizing his own family's suffering. Though the setting for most of the book is the Depression, Baker devotes chapter 6 in particular to discussing the country's descent into "the modern equivalent of the Dark Ages" (80). Baker begins the chapter with his mother moving herself and her children into her brother's apartment in New Jersey. In describing his mother's discouraging quest for work and her waning hopes of independence, Baker is matter-of-fact in tone and detail, leaving the reader to imagine the anxiety and disappointment that must have accompanied his mother's "discovering [of] the Depression": "The story was the same everywhere. No jobs.... All that year she walked the streets, combed the classified ads, sat in offices waiting to talk to possible employers, and always heard the same refrain: No jobs" (75). Baker elaborates more extensively on his own experience during this period of the "routine miseries of childhood," leavening the chapter with humor (75).

When discussing his family in this chapter Baker focuses on the resourcefulness, fortitude, and even cheerfulness of his mother, his uncle

Allen, and his aunt Pat as they faced cramped quarters and poverty wages. Baker writes, "Like my mother, Uncle Allen believed that with hard work, good character, and an honest nature a man could make something of himself in spite of hard times, and he worked at the salesman's trade with total dedication" (68). He describes his aunt Pat as a "full-time combatant in the battle of life" who "flung herself into it with zest, and when she encountered an enemy or a challenger she gave him 'a piece of her mind'" (71).

Baker does here infuse his memoir with a vivid sense of the human devastation wrought by the Depression by reproducing several letters written to Lucy by her suitor, Oluf, an immigrant Dane. The last half of chapter 6 is devoted to Oluf's correspondence from May 1932 to May 1933, during which time he was traveling in search of work, and the missives document his decline from "a developing American success story"—he was initially a prosperous salesman and a landlord—to a man in financial and psychic ruin (76). In *Growing Up* it is Oluf, rather than any of Baker's family members, who is the face of Depression-era tragedy. Oluf's "cries of terror" articulate the despair and horror that symbolize the Depression in the book, and it is Oluf for whom the reader is led to feel pity.

Of course, Baker's use of the letters, which he later termed a "serendipitous discovery" (they were found in his mother's trunk after her death), gives him a way to write indirectly about his mother's pain (Baker, "Life" 46). Oluf is both an outsider and an integral part of Lucy's story. Baker makes it clear that Lucy has an emotional and potentially a practical stake in Oluf's disintegration. Baker introduces the section on Oluf's letters by remarking that to Lucy, the possibility of marriage to Oluf began to seem her "best hope of salvation," so that the reader understands that Oluf's losses are also, in a sense, Lucy's as well (76). As Baker notes, in Oluf's letters Lucy's half of the correspondence comes through somewhat in the "echoes and resonances in his replies" *(Growing Up* 78). Yet Baker shrewdly attributes the pathos to Oluf. It is Oluf who laments, in his last letter, "'I am lost and going and not interested in anything anymore'" (89). While this strategy of displacing the pathos of the Depression onto an ethnic succeeds in keeping Baker's family from appearing pitiable, it can be seen as ethically problematic in its own right. It also underscores the fact that Baker's admirable job of rendering his family— his sparing them from appearing pathetic—is greatly facilitated by his identification with a family who, unlike Oluf, always has hope (by virtue of their WASP status) of fitting into middle-class American society.

Still, Baker is laudable in not pleading for sympathy for his family members. When Baker depicts his mother in defeat, he does so in an understated way that also conveys her sturdiness and dignity. At the end of chapter 9, for example, Baker offers a rare glimpse of his mother in a melancholic mood when he describes the morning when he and his family are at last moving out of Allen's home. It is a quiet scene in which his mother surprises him by playing the used piano Allen has recently purchased (Baker hadn't known she could play). Something in his mother's demeanor as she plays causes "all the excitement" in Baker "to die": "My mother was facing me but didn't seem to see me. She seemed to be staring beyond me toward something that wasn't there.... Looking at my mother, so isolated from us all, I saw her for the first time as a person utterly alone" (136). He ends the passage by observing that his mother's "youth had passed without a single triumph. She was in her fortieth year" (136). But even in this moment, because of its immediate context, Lucy is not pathetic. The reader may share Baker's sympathy for Lucy here, but one never really sees her as "utterly alone" because of Baker's continuous portrayal of her as surrounded by, and engaging with, the love and support of family members. And unlike Oluf, Lucy, as Baker depicts her, is never truly "lost." She is in this scene, after all, at last moving her children into a home of their own.

Baker's approach to telling the story of his mother's early adulthood is characteristic of the balance he maintains throughout the text between helping his reader to understand his mother without creating a maudlin rendition of her hardships. The strategy he uses is to debunk his mother's dubious glorification of her father, whom Baker terms "poor mythic Papa" (19). This tactic allows him to explore the psychology behind her thirst for upper-middle-class life as well as to render additional nuances in his own complex relationship with her. He first describes the dreamy stories of her youth that his mother told of a seemingly idyllic childhood spent "in a great Virginia country house" with "sleek horses and fancy buggies" (19). As he does so, he humorously indicates the point at which as a child he lost interest in her reveries: when she began boasting about her seemingly-perfect father. Baker "couldn't abide his being such a splendid man," and "took revenge" by putting him out of his mind, until years later, when as an adult he "looked into the Papa matter" and discovered that "Papa had not made anything at all of himself. He had tried hard enough ... but he had failed disastrously" (20). This introduction to his mother's life establishes his approach to her as a narrator: to depict her as psychologically complex (and not as a liar but as a romantic), and to resist simply reproducing *her* version of her life, as well as her romantic myths of herself.

It is interesting to note that Nesaule, in contrast to Baker's handling of his mother's past, not only uncritically accepts but perpetuates the romanticization of her mother's childhood. In the second chapter of *A Woman in Amber* she narrates the story of how her mother Valda, as a twelve-year-old, "lost her beloved Russia," based on her mother's descriptions of her life before the Revolution (18). The world Nesaule paints is shamelessly idealized, in which a French governess "is stretched out on a narrow bed with delicately curved legs"; Valda and her friend Varvara, who is from "one of the best Russian families," partake in "ballet lessons, deportment lessons, Latin lessons, French lessons, English-style riding lessons"; and in the "cool mornings" ride their horses "as hard as they can, then stop to drink cold water out of the crystal-clear rivers, to find raspberries and fragrant wild melons" (14). For Baker, part of "growing up" is endeavoring, as an adult, to see around his parent's perspective, and to supplement her take on reality with his own information and judgment.

Indeed, of the four autobiographers discussed in this study, Baker by far applies the most critical and objective view of his family members, granting himself permission to filter their stories through an affectionate skepticism. It is, in fact, a theme in his relationships with relatives; he comes to see the value of learning *attitude* from his family members rather than information. While living in his Uncle Allen's house, Baker recalls, he was allowed to stay up and listen to the adults' nightly conversation until ten o'clock. He emphasizes that what he gained from those hours of listening was "the sense of family warmth that radiated through those long kitchen nights of talk" (116).

He suggests that this family warmth and emotional richness has seeped into him and shaped his own temperament as well as his love of storytelling: "There were many chords resonating beneath [their talk], and though I could not identify them precisely, I was absorbing a sense of them and storing them away in memory. There was longing for happy times now lost, and dreaming about what might have been. There was fantasy, too" (116). The fantasy included a story his mother's relatives often told about Papa trying to recover his ancestors' fortune, inherited from England's Bishop of London back in the time of Queen Anne. As Baker observes, "if the story was true it meant that we were all rightfully entitled to be rich"; but his sister's skepticism helps him to see the story as "baloney" and "after that," he writes, "I always smiled inwardly when they started talking about the great lost fortune, and for the first time I began to feel superior to them in a small way" (116–17). Baker immediately follows this story with an affirmation that his true inheritance from his family was in what he gathered "around that table, under the unshaded light bulb": "I was receiving an education in the world and how to think about it. What I absorbed most deeply was not information but attitudes, ways of looking at the world that were to stay with me for many years" (117). The attitudes he absorbed were mostly genial, he recalls: while their talk was sometimes "shaded with anger" about the Depression, "its dominant tones were good humor and civility. The anger was never edged with bitterness or self-pity" (117). The passage suggests that for Baker, because he is aware of how much he truly gained from his family members, he doesn't have to fear criticizing them or even recognizing ways in which his knowledge is more extensive than theirs.

The warmth, decency, and humor that characterize his relatives' interactions with each other permeate Baker's world view. Prominent in the "great river of talk that flowed through" Uncle Allen's house, Baker tells us, were good-spirited discussions of the people, past and present, in the adults' lives, and Baker has plainly imitated the pleasant tones of their storytelling in his memoir (115). "They spun humorous tales about relatives long dead," Baker recalls, which is what Baker himself does in *Growing Up* (118). And though Baker shapes his memoir to reflect his process of individuating from his mother, he has nonetheless embraced his mother's respect for "gumption" and has, indeed, made something of himself. Baker clearly admires and shares his mother's and Allen's belief in "hard work, good character, and an honest nature" (68). That these are Franklinesque values, not in opposition to the dominant culture, indicates, again, Baker's relatively smooth transition into the middle class.

That said, the progress of Baker's character in the second half of the text traces his growing ability to think independently from his mother. This process reaches a climax near the memoir's end, when Baker has fallen in love with Mimi, but struggles mightily over whether he should conform to his mother's low opinion of Mimi, knowing that it is based on snobbish criteria, or follow his own genuine affection and admiration for her. It is significant that at the beginning of the two-chapter section about Mimi, Baker describes both Mimi and himself as seen through his mother's eyes: "Mimi was not promising 'good woman' material. Besides using cosmetics, she lived alone, had no family, drank wine and whiskey ... and sometimes touched her hair with bleach. Any one of these defects would have been enough to condemn her before my mother" (234). Referring to himself, he employs the phrase that he has repeatedly linked to his mother's vision for his life, illustrating how deeply and entirely he has internalized it: "Could a man who wanted to make something of himself seriously consider marrying such a woman?" (234). His view of Mimi remained enmeshed with his mother's plan for his life: "Naturally I would marry later, when I was old and stuffy, and when I did I would naturally choose 'a good woman,' the sort my mother would approve" (253).

Baker writes that "Vanity fought with love for possession of my soul," and what swings the pendulum from vanity to love are two concurrent, intertwined developments that bring Baker's identity to maturity: a change in the way he sees Mimi, and a change in his relationship with his mother. In a great display of human wisdom, Baker depicts himself as being eventually won over by Mimi's strength of character, and by her ability to make him see her humanity beneath her excessive makeup and hardscrabble past. In a revealing scene, Baker has taken Mimi to Washington D.C. to educate her in order to indulge his vain notion of himself as her Professor Higgins; Mimi, however, ends up telling him her background, which includes years spent at an orphanage called The Sheltering Arms, and afterwards Baker "no longer wanted to batter her with education" (246). Her status as a real human being (rather than an Eliza Doolittle) with an interesting past of her own comes into focus for him. As Baker recalls, before the trip he "hadn't thought of her as someone who might have had a life before I knew her" (246).

Just as he was himself, he allows his reader to be won over by such traits as Mimi's admirable straightforwardness and self-respect, displayed several times when she simply but astutely identifies Baker's disrespectful treatment of her. Before one of their three or four breakups, for example, Mimi decides, Baker writes, that "it was time for her to start a new life.... There were bound to be men who would treat her more decently than I ever had" (258). He also portrays her as insightful and perceptive, being quick to read the chief reason behind Baker's ambivalence toward her. About her first meeting with his family at dinner, Baker recounts: "Mimi understood everything that Sunday night when I took her home on the streetcar. 'Your mother didn't like me,' she said" (250). Baker shows her to possess a mordant understanding of the dynamics of his relationship with his mother: whenever they haven't spoken for months, her first question to him is invariably, "How's your mother?" (263).

The major change in Baker's relationship with his mother during the course of his four-year "stalemate" over Mimi occurs when Baker resurrects his father and all that his father represents. Young adults famously have a talent for choosing mates who bring repressed family conflicts to the surface. Baker's text clearly suggests that his falling in love with Mimi was an indirect challenge to his mother's attempt to "erase" his father from his life. In chapter 17, Baker recounts how his subtle forcing of his mother to see his seriousness about Mimi leads to a confrontation with her about his father. Baker, who still lives at home while he attends college, has been frequently staying out all night, as if hoping his mother will finally voice her disapproval, which she does. When Baker admits that he has been staying at Mimi's, his mother's reaction reveals how she really feels about Baker's late father; his genetic presence in Baker represents a contaminating influence. "It's in the blood," she responds to Baker: "She focused again on me, and, with a look as close to hate as she'd ever given me, she cried, 'You're just like your father was. Just like your father'" (252). Baker, however, has unconsciously known most of his life of his mother's wish to "erase" his father's presence in him. Although she did, of course, marry Baker's father, Baker believes he hears "loathing" in his mother's evocation of his father, which causes him to realize how little she mentioned his father during his childhood:

> I'd spent most of a lifetime with her and she had rarely told me anything about my father, rarely even mentioned him. It was as if she wanted to erase him from my life.... There had been some taint in my father's blood. She had reared me in dread that it might reappear in mine ... Maybe she had hoped I could escape the taint of the blood by growing up far away from it among her own people [252].

Baker continues the passage by speculating that his mother's concern was that he would get Mimi pregnant, just as his father Benjamin had done with Lucy.

But this portrait of his parents makes it evident that Lucy's consternation about Mimi is not as much about premarital pregnancy, though that would undoubtedly be a concern, but about class, and her fear that her son would marry beneath him in class, just as she believes herself to have done. As Baker writes in the previous chapter, "My mother, at this time, had been considering what sort of woman might be qualified to help me make something of myself," and Mimi's biography "wasn't one to make her cry out with enthusiasm" (240). Baker, then, presents his eventual choosing of Mimi as a wife as a rejection of his mother's snobbery, and as proof of his having outgrown the narrow, success-oriented identity that she cultivated in him. His text also suggests that his choice to marry an "unsuitable woman" with a tenth-grade education demonstrates his integration of his working-class father into his new, expanded identity. The deceased father that Lucy wanted to "erase" from Baker's life comes back into Baker's life, in a sense, in the form of Mimi, and the impoverished, marginal background she represents.

Paul John Eakin proposes the autobiographical act "as both a reenactment and an extension of earlier phases of identity formation" (Eakin, *Fictions* 226). That is, the writing of autobiography is not merely "the passive, transparent record of an already completed self but rather ... an integral and often decisive phase of the drama of self-definition" (226). As a character, Baker betrays his mother by marrying Mimi, and as an autobiographer he betrays her in his deliberate differentiation from her way of seeing people. Of course, these "betrayals" are really just part of the natural process of Baker's separation from his mother, both then as a young man and now as an autobiographer. As Nancy K. Miller writes:

> To separate from the other, father or mother, requires the enactment of one's own difference; the more likeness is asserted, the more difference is displayed. In this sense, betrayal — as an act of differentiation: there are two of us — seems to come with the territory of the family memoir. This is where I come from but not where I am [*Bequest* 29].

Baker makes a point in his memoir of demonstrating his disagreement with his mother's tendency to regard people with less education as inferior. One example of this is the contrast between his own and his mother's interpretation of Uncle Harold's "lying." Both as a boy and as an adult narrator, Baker is able to grasp the creative impulse that lay behind Uncle Harold's frequent tall tales, while his mother simply sees him as a compulsive liar. Baker remembers:

> It didn't matter that my mother called him "the biggest liar God ever sent down the pike." In spite of his reputation for varnishing a fact, or maybe because of the outrageousness with which he did the varnishing, I found him irresistible. It was his intuitive refusal to spoil a good story by slavish adherence to fact that enchanted me [138].

Baker asserts that his uncle's scant education does not preclude Harold from being an artist at heart, if not necessarily a terrifically skilled one: "Though poorly educated, Uncle Harold somehow knew that the possibility of creating art lies not in reporting but in fiction" (138).

Baker conveys that his mother's dim view of Harold's fictionalizing is in part due to their socioeconomic context: "Our world in Baltimore hadn't much respect for the poetic impulse. In our world a man spinning a romance was doomed to be dismissed as nothing more than a prodigious liar" (144). Yet Baker also subtly makes it evident that his mother's dismissal of Harold as a liar is also due to her view of him as ignorant. Baker pointedly contrasts this with his own view of Harold as creatively fulfilling his need for the kind of stimulation that his work as a cemetery groundskeeper cannot provide. Without sentimentalizing Harold, Baker nonetheless grants him a dignity and even a modest nobility of purpose in his compulsive fictionalizing:

> We were two romancers whose desire for something more fanciful than the humdrum of southwest Baltimore was beyond the grasp of unimaginative people like Aunt Sister and my mother.... He wanted life to be more interesting than it was, but his only gift for making it so lay in a small talent for homespun fictions, and he could not resist trying to make the most of it [144].

Baker thus differentiates himself from his mother in the section about Harold by delineating her more limited view of poorly educated people and illustrating his own more expansive one.

Uncle Harold, Mimi, Lucy herself, and virtually all of the people Baker includes in his narrative share the common threads of psychological complexity and human dignity. In *Growing Up* Baker identifies himself not by aligning himself with any particular class or culture, but by demonstrating his ability to recognize and render people as individuals rather than as class representatives. Instead of either romanticizing or demonizing the working-class people of his past, Baker constructs a distinctly liminal identity as a writer who understands that education and social class bear no relation either to moral virtue or to the virtue of being interesting. Though he is inclined to depict working-class people sympathetically, he never ascribes to them a false purity, innocence, or simplicity; nor, for that matter, does he portray them as monolithic. Indeed, Baker constructs an identity that is based on his growing ability to see people from other social classes and ethnic groups not as Other but as complex, recognizable equals; as an author, he represents others from the perspective of what psychoanalytic theorist Jessica Benjamin terms "mutual recognition," in which "the subject accepts the premise that others are separate but nonetheless share like feelings and intentions" (53).

When Baker is at a critical juncture on the road to becoming his mature self and comfortable in his breadth of values that encompasses multiple classes, he must decide whether to adhere to the identity and the way of seeing working-class people that his mother instilled in him out of her own class insecurity. It is the voice of Mimi, the "dangerously unsuitable woman," who causes him to redefine the way in which he assesses people and, ultimately, to redefine himself in the process (234). "For God's sake, Russ, treat me like a human being," Mimi implores of him (264). His decision to heed her advice, and ultimately, to marry her, changed his life and informs his vision of others in his writing.

3

Inventing the Self and the (Br)Other in John Edgar Wideman's *Brothers and Keepers*

Published in 1984, *Brothers and Keepers* is John Edgar Wideman's account of his brother Robby's involvement in a murder, Robby's subsequent months as a fugitive, and Wideman's later visits with Robby at Pittsburgh's Western Penitentiary. Much of the book takes the form of a re-creation of those visits, during which Wideman and Robby re-establish a relationship after having grown apart over fifteen years. Robby's side of the "conversations," in fact, is written by Wideman as a simulation of Robby's speaking voice.

In his preface, Wideman describes the book as "an attempt to capture a process that began in earnest about four years ago: my brother and I talking about our lives" (xi). However, *Brothers,* of course, is far more ambitious and complicated a text than that description suggests. To begin with, the process of the brothers talking about their lives is completely enmeshed with the process of Wideman's gathering material for and writing the book. The conversations about their lives occur under the aegis of a literary collaboration. Even Wideman is unable to say whether the book exists because of their reunion, or if their reunion occurs because of his desire to write a book about his brother. "Was the whole thing between us about a book...?" he wonders when their collaboration is nearing its end, and well might he ask (200).

In interviews Wideman has said that the book was his own way of responding to Robby's crisis; but his impulse to respond was both emotional and intellectual: "Here was a situation in which my own brother was beckoning me, demanding that I pay attention, that I make some sense of the enormous gap between us" (Coleman 160). It is clear that *Brothers and Keepers* is engendered by complex motives on Wideman's part; in its very existence as a text, the book seeks to accomplish more than the rebuilding of a brotherly bond. Albert Stone contends that the "ultimate aim" of autobiography "remains identity, and not historical messages" (*Autobiographical* 17). This chapter will argue that *Brothers* is no less a vehicle for Wideman's re-invention of a personal and professional identity for its being a hybrid of autobiography and biography; that, indeed, Wideman uses his relationship/collaboration with Robby as a metaphorical construct through which to explore and to delineate a self in relation both to the black community and to the literary-intellectual community. This chapter will also analyze *Brothers and Keepers* as a text that employs the real-life "process" of the Wideman brothers' talking about their lives as an occasion for dramatizing Wideman's complicated relationship with his racial and class roots.

Laura Browder identifies what she calls "a central paradox of American identity": "This paradox has changed over the past 150 years and will continue to change, but it has two central features that remain constant: American belief in the fluidity of class identity and the fixity of racial and, to a lesser extent, ethnic identity" (7). However, Wideman's text suggests that for an African American, transcending one's lower-class origins can be experienced as a near-erasure of one's racial identity. With few identities made available to black males in America, as a young man Wideman didn't perceive that being a professional, middle-class black man was an option: to become middle-class, he had also to become "white." In a 1990 essay, "On Being Black and Middle Class," Shelby Steele writes about his own experience of the precise race/class dilemma in which Wideman found himself as a young man, and he explains the social and cultural reasons that keep most educated African Americans caught in an identity trap. Steele argues that "middle-class blacks in general are caught in a very specific double bind that keeps two equally powerful elements of our identity at odds with each other" (95). He observes that middle-class values, which an individual must embrace in order to become middle-class, "tell us to work hard for ourselves and our families, and to seek out opportunities"; on the other hand, what Steele calls "the particular pattern of racial identification that emerged in the sixties and still prevails today" urges blacks in the opposite direction (95–96). "This pattern asks us to see ourselves as an embattled minority," and it urges "an emphasis on ethnic consciousness over individualism" (96). Thus, "being both black and middle-class becomes a double bind when class and race are defined in sharply antagonistic terms, so that one must be repressed to appease the other" (96).

This chapter will demonstrate that as both the narrator and a character in the text, Wideman divides himself in terms of his racial and class identities. In addition to a narration of his struggle to reconcile these seemingly disparate identities, his profound sense of duality is also embedded in this highly metaphorical text. This duality is represented, for example, in his double roles in the collaboration of brother and writer. I will argue that Wideman delineates his black identity by dramatizing his role as a brother; he "proves" that he is authentically African American by relating to and identifying with Robby. Indeed, Robby's very presence in this auto/biographical text can be said to represent Wideman's own black identity, including all of the associations with that identity in Wideman's mind of criminality (which creates a large part of his identity crisis). Wideman's class identity, his self-image as a professional author and intellectual, expresses itself in his role as a writer of his brother's life.

Finally, this chapter contends that *Brothers and Keepers* is an ethically complex — and problematic — text. Wideman has created a book that successfully serves many ethical purposes; for example, he is clearly committed to gaining a deeper understanding of his brother's perspective, and by extrapolation, the perspectives of all other black prisoners. Further, the author is offering support to his brother by giving Robby a chance to voice his story (though always mediated by Wideman) to the public, an opportunity he would never have otherwise. Nevertheless, this chapter will argue that Wideman's book is at least as self-serving as it is benevolent. Wideman uses Robby's "blackness" and his status as a prisoner as part of Wideman's own re-invention of himself (Wideman 27).

Brothers was written during a period in Wideman's career in which he was undergoing a dramatic transformation in his professional identity as a writer of fiction. Indeed, Wideman's interest in reconnecting with his brother coincides—perhaps not accidentally — with Wideman's decision to emphasize his African American identity in his work. Doreatha Mbalia, along with other critics, has observed that the works published between 1967 and 1992 reflect Wideman's evolution "from one who is dominated by the history, culture, and language of Europe to one who accepts and appreciates African history, culture, and language" (15). Referring to this shift as Wideman's "reclaiming of his African personality" (that is, the African side of his African American identity), Mbalia argues that this "reclamation process occurred in developmental stages"; she notes that an important transition period for him was an eight-year hiatus from 1973 until 1981, during which the writer did not publish novels but instead began "to study African history and literature in order to discover his place within his own cultural and literary heritage and to speak to his own people" (29). Mbalia points out that the book that finally appeared in 1981 reflects a profound ideological shift in the author: "Beginning with *Hiding Place,* Wideman uses a voice distinctly African in perspective. The African community is no longer conceived through the eyes of a European. African traditions are no longer described as primitive or ugly or dirty as they are in *A Glance Away.* Rather, they are what give us our strength to endure" (32).

Wideman's comments in a 1983 interview support Mbalia's assessment. Agreeing with the interviewer Wilfred Samuels's assertion that his 1981 works reflect a "turning point" in his career, Wideman remarks that the "more explicit concern with Afro-American life" in his fiction is the result of a conscious decision he made. "I wanted, number one, to reach out to levels of audience that perhaps the earlier works had excluded," he recalls, and he indicates later that he is referring to a "black audience" (Samuels 17).

Wideman spent the late 1970's "catching up," as he tells Samuels, and "learning a new language to talk about [his] experience" (Samuels 19); subsequently, in the early 1980's, when he wrote *Brothers,* he was engaged in the task of analyzing and explaining what Mbalia refers to as his "first life," the years in which he was running from his "Africanness" and trying to emulate European modernist writers (Mbalia 30). In the interviews he gave during this time Wideman constructed a narrative about his exile from black culture and his re-connection with it through black literature. In this narrative, Wideman's alienation is an intellectual problem, a result of "a superficial acquaintance with black writing" (Samuels 18). He explains to Samuels that his early work was influenced by cultural paradigms imposed on him during his educational experiences at the University of Pennsylvania and Oxford University: "As you grow up, a value system seeps in, and so I was not consciously turning my back on Blackness; I was just getting acculturated, and the acculturation pushed my writing in certain directions" (18).

In this oral story, Wideman remedies the problem through intellectual work and study. The evolution of Wideman's fiction toward its "African-centered" perspective, he suggests, came about because of a lengthy self-imposed re-education program that included "an absolute immersion in Black literature" (Samuels 18). He also resolves it through art, by integrating black life and culture into his writing:

> In the later books also I began to understand how in using Afro-American folklore and language I didn't have to give up any of the goals that I was after when I was using more Europeanized ... devices and techniques.... I could talk about the most complicated and sophisticated and intense moments and understandings and characters in the Afro-American idiom [Coleman 150].

Thus, in the narrative Wideman constructed in interviews while he was writing *Brothers and Keepers,* his ideological shift occurs in the professional realm of his life, and only because of strenuous intellectual effort. It was "a real breakthrough," he tells James Coleman, "but it was a breakthrough that didn't come accidentally. It was a result of study and concentration, and research in fact" (150).

This change in his professional identity, and the story he tells of it, are relevant to a reading of *Brothers and Keepers* because in the latter text Wideman creates a parallel narrative about his running from his roots and his journey back to them. However, the narrative in *Brothers and Keepers* centers on the personal and emotional experience of his flight from his black identity, his family, and his community. It tells how in particular his "willed alienation" affected his relationship with Robby (27).

In *Brothers and Keepers,* Wideman dramatizes his confrontation with his inner "demons" in the realm of the personal (11). While he successfully dealt with his alienation on the intellectual and artistic levels, the text suggests that it is something else altogether, and a far more complicated process, to appraise and address the emotional roots and the human consequences of his earlier flight from home. Examining his own identity crisis as it was played out on an intimate level, Wideman writes that Robby's life-and-death crisis—his becoming a fugitive wanted for murder—was the catalyst for Wideman's re-assessment of his estrangement from his roots:

> Robby was a fugitive.... The police were hunting him, and his crime had given the cops license to kill. The distance I'd put between my brother's world and mine suddenly collapsed. The two thousand miles between Laramie, Wyoming, and Pittsburgh, Pennsylvania, my years of willed ignorance, of flight and hiding, had not changed a simple truth: I could never run fast enough or far enough. Robby was inside me. Wherever he was, running for his life, he carried a part of me with him [4].

Faced with his "outlaw brother" reminding him of "how much had been lost, how much compromised," Wideman at first, characteristically, tried to make sense of Robby's tragedy by turning it into fiction (11). This strategy failed, however, because "the interplay between fiction and fact in the piece was too intense ... finally too obscure to control" (18). Recognizing that this had been an attempt to evade complex and painful realities that still needed to be addressed, Wideman decided that "something of a different order remained to be extricated. The fiction writer was also a man with a real brother behind real bars" (18). He indicates his hope that this non-fiction collaboration with Robby will effect a re-connection between them by helping Wideman to see more clearly, more accurately, the causes of their estrangement: "So this book. This attempt to break out, to knock down the walls" (18). He's also knocking down the walls of the self he constructed, which he now sees as more of a prison.

In *Brothers*, Wideman uses the story of his history with Robby as an opportunity to explore deeper dimensions of his flight from black life and identity. In this narrative, the problem encompasses more than a lack of knowledge about a literary tradition or a culture; it stems from a treacherous brand of confusion concerning racial identity and class, a deep bind that Wideman suggests is ongoing, since it involves societal perceptions and forces larger than himself. Wideman traces the roots of his "willed alienation" from the black community and from his own black identity to a dilemma he began to experience as early as childhood: his perception that, if he transcended his class origins and became an educated professional, he could no longer be an authentic member of his family or his race (27). Having spent his first twelve years in the mostly-black Homewood section of Pittsburgh, a ghetto in which poverty was the norm, and as a member of a large, poor family, Wideman came to believe that being black meant being poor and uneducated. "Just two choices," he writes, "as far as I could tell: either/or. Rich or poor. White or black. Win or lose. I figured which side I wanted to be on when the Saints came marching in. Who the Saints, the rulers of the earth were, was clear" (27). Having ambition, a desire "to get ahead, to make something of myself," and determining that college was a necessary step, Wideman began "running away from Pittsburgh, from poverty, from blackness," in his mind, merely by doing well in school: "my exile, my flight from home began with good grades, with good English, with setting myself apart long before I'd earned a scholarship and a train ticket over the mountains to Philadelphia" (27).

In one section near the beginning of *Brothers and Keepers*, Wideman writes as if directly addressing Robby; in a confessional tone, using his relationship with Robby as a lens through which to recall his own state of mind in these earlier years, Wideman recounts the personal costs of the bind. He explains that he thought he had to choose between fulfilling his dreams of becoming a professional and maintaining an intimate relationship with his family, and in particular with Robby. Wideman confesses to Robby that "the problem was that in order to be the person I thought I wanted to be, I believed I had to seal myself off from you, construct a wall between us" (26). He remembers that, believing himself to have made the choice to sacrifice his bond with Robby, he was too uncomfortable, too beset with guilt, when around his brother even to have conversations with him. During visits home from college and later from his life as a professor in Wyoming, Wideman was threatened by Robby's presence because

Robby's "world," his "blackness," "incriminated" Wideman, making him afraid that the elements of home from which he was running would reveal their presence in himself: "Fear marched along beside guilt. Fear of acknowledging in myself any traces of the poverty, ignorance, and danger I'd find surrounding me when I returned to Pittsburgh" (27).

In many ways, *Brothers and Keepers,* even more than being a book about Robby, is about Wideman's *desire* to reconcile with his brother, and to reverse or at least to make amends for his transgressions against him. "I want your forgiveness," Wideman plainly states to Robby in their first prison visit (98). This desire for re-connection is manifested in *Brothers* in the narrative flourishes with which Wideman sets the stage for their fraternal reunion. He writes in mystical terms about his and Robby's seeking out and eventually finding each other, suggesting that both profound inner longings and mysterious outer forces were working in combination to bring about their fated coming together. He tells of how, when Robby was on the run, Wideman somehow "knew he was on his way to find me" (5). Two days before Robby actually showed up in Wideman's Wyoming town, Wideman writes, the author spontaneously began a letter to Robby, or actually a conversation on paper, and that while writing, "When I touched on home, the distance between us melted. I could sense Robby's presence, just over my shoulder, a sensation so real I was sure I could have reached out and touched him" (6). He goes on, giving the moments in which he "summoned up Robby, and he joined me" a mystical quality (7):

> Writing that Sunday, I had no reason to believe my brother was on his way to Laramie. No one had heard from him in months. Yet he was on his way and I knew it. Two men, hundreds of miles apart, communicating through some mysterious process neither understood but both employed for a few minutes one Sunday afternoon as efficiently, effectively as dolphins talking underwater with the beeps and echoes of their sonar.... I can't explain how or why but it happened. Robby was in the study with me. He felt close because he was close [6].

Incidentally, though this passage describes a kind of preternatural bond between Wideman and Robby, the scenes that follow, in which Robby and his companions spend a night at Wideman's, place this bond in a far more qualified and complex light.

The narrative of Robby's visit further dramatizes Wideman's identity confusion as a black man, as well as Robby's symbolic role in Wideman's confusion, since it illustrates the extreme poles of their lives. On one hand, Wideman at the time is living in Wyoming, in an insular, white-dominated upper–middle-class world, "the charmed circle of my life on the Laramie plains," and enjoying such middle-class trappings as, he notes, a Volvo:

"My life was relatively comfortable, pleasant, safe. I'd come west to escape the demons Robby personified" (11). But he also calls it a "compromised" life (11). The other extreme, which Robby "personifies," encapsulates two of the worst stereotypical identities of black men in America, that of a criminal and that of a fugitive. From fugitive slaves onward, the black male outlaw on the run has been a tenacious (and pernicious) image in American cultural consciousness, and Robby's presence in this form supports Wideman's implied thesis that America imposes a false dichotomy on African Americans: be a black criminal or become "white."

However, it must also be said that the story of Robby's visit as a fugitive also subverts, to an extent, Wideman's embrace of Robby, and his disparaging of his Wyoming life as compromised. Wideman's depiction of his life there as a professor with a young family emphasizes the safe and nurturing aspects of it. Just before Robby's visit, Wideman enjoys a peaceful Sunday of reading the paper, listening to music, and reflecting on his life. And when Robby is there, Wideman portrays his home life, with the family's focus on caring for their premature infant daughter, in sharp contrast to Robby and his friends. Wideman creates a palpable sense of danger in narrating the visit. Robby's friend Johnny-Boy is "small, dark, greasy," an "outsider who knew he didn't fit," and Wideman recognizes him as a threat:

> I didn't like the way his heavy-lidded, bubble eyes blinked open and searched the room when he thought no one was watching him. Perhaps sleeping with one eye open was a habit forced upon him by the violent circumstances of his life, but what I saw when he peered from "sleep," taking the measure of his surroundings, of my wife, my kids, me, were a stranger's eyes, a stranger's eyes with nothing in them I could trust [13].

It is revealing that Wideman juxtaposes a description of the mystical bond between him and Robby with a scene in which Robby brings elements of violence, danger, and criminality into Wideman's "pleasant" middle-class life. The juxtaposition demonstrates Wideman's profound and ongoing ambivalence toward his brother, suggesting that the author's desire for reconnection with Robby is perennially undercut by the troubling realities of his brother's life as well as the tragic forms of black life in America that Robby represents.

If the brothers' collaboration succeeds in knocking down the walls between them, it will be, he suggests, because it has taught Wideman to see his brother "on his own terms" (77). Wideman demonstrates his allegiance to Robby and Robby's point of view in most of the content of the text. The narrative and rhetorical material that Wideman elects to print is entirely sympathetic toward Robby's past and present. Proving himself to be a real "brother" in both the literal sense and in the African American colloquial sense, Wideman expounds at length on the deeply racist nature of American society, and at one point remarks that society is ultimately to blame for Robby's crime and his punishment: "If Robby fell because the only stardom he could reasonably seek was stardom in crime, then that's wrong. It's wrong not because Robby wanted more but because society closed off every chance of getting more, except through crime" (198). This statement, of course, contradicts the facts of the two brothers' lives: Wideman has clearly gotten "more" without being a criminal, and therefore he is adopting a double standard even between himself and his brother. Such disingenuous statements underscore the fact that Wideman's adoption of Robby's perspective in the text is a rhetorical construct and self-serving as well.

On one level, Wideman depicts himself as strongly identifying with Robby. He shares his brother's anger, or rather, he feels indignation and rage on Robby's behalf, as if he's seeing things anew through Robby's eyes. Indeed, a central purpose of the book is evidently for Wideman to lend his eloquence and his publishing power to raise his middle-class (and especially the white) readers' awareness of the grim realities facing two minority groups, blacks and prisoners. In one passage he fantasizes about delivering a tirade to factory workers in a chemical plant located near Robby's prison, after he assumes that the workers are oblivious to the prisoners' existence, that "the forty-foot-high stone walls did not exist for them." Clearly wanting to educate his readers as well, Wideman writes that he heard himself haranguing the workers: "Do you ever think about it? About that place over there?... Do you see it? Do you ever wonder what's happening inside?" (184).

Wideman emphasizes his racial identification with Robby by relating some of his own experiences of being racially discriminated against. For example, in a meditation on the ritual of strip searches, Wideman notes that this act, which often seems intended to humiliate, is visited far more frequently on blacks than on whites. He recounts two incidents in which he or his children were treated differently than whites at airports and were subjected to special searches. "Yes. I was angry both times. The stifled, gut-deep rage that's American as apple pie. The black rage that makes you want to strike out and smash somebody's face because you know they have you by the throat, killing you by inches" (187). Wideman then observes that the "law" that gives civilian authorities the power to single out or harass blacks is the same law that governs the keepers' treatment of prisoners; citing Supreme Court Chief Justice Roger Taney's 1857 declaration in the Dred Scott case that blacks "'have no rights which the white man was bound to respect,'" Wideman adds that in fact "the weak have no rights that the strong are bound to respect," and that this could be the motto of Western Penitentiary (187).

Wideman is using rhetoric falsely here. He is not the same as his brother; it's not 1857 and the Court's declaration in the Dred Scott case is long outdated; many prisoners *did* commit crimes and aren't comparable to the law-abiding. The passage suggests that Wideman has imagined a new character for himself and he's thinking like that fictional character.

The passages in which Wideman most closely identifies with Robby come near the end of the book; the structure of the text implies that Wideman's program of teaching himself to listen to Robby, which he struggles to do at the beginning of their collaboration, has worked. In fact, the story of their collaboration follows a meaningful, and familiar, plot line: Wideman sets himself to the task of re-educating himself by listening to the other by training his mind on the goal of assimilating the other's perspective; he then demonstrates the success of his research and study by integrating the other's idiom and point of view into his own writing, and even into his own identity.

However, although the book's overarching movement reflects Wideman's successful identification with Robby and their re-establishment of a bond, there is a subtext, what Albert Stone calls "the stubborn voice of the individual autobiographer," that speaks against the very identification that the book seems to embrace (*Autobiographical* 18). Wideman, in writing *Brothers and Keepers,* is seeking to accomplish two things: to effect a renewed intimacy between himself and Robby, and to write a text in which he delineates and asserts who he is. If on one hand the book is Wideman's attempt to tear down the walls between himself and Robby, it is also driven by his need to examine the nature of the walls that exist. "However numerous and comforting the similarities," Wideman writes about himself and his brother, "we were different. The world had seized on the difference, allowed me room to thrive, while he'd been forced into a cage. Why did it work out that way? What was the nature of the difference?" (77).

In authoring this text, Wideman splits himself into two people: one expresses his desire and commitment to aligning himself with Robby and all that Robby personifies; the other allows a more honest appraisal of the "enormous gap" between them to surface in the text. If one Wideman strives to establish commonalities between himself and Robby, the other — the autobiographical voice, rather than the brother or the biographer — explores and even affirms the differences between them.

The fault line on which Wideman divides himself in this text is where his racial and his class identities intersect. The dilemma which alienated

Wideman from Robby two decades before — Wideman's belief that to be an educated professional is to be an exile from the black community — is confronted in *Brothers and Keepers*. As Wideman acknowledges, the fluidity with which he oscillates between being a "brother" and being a writer (and a person pursuing his own professional interests) makes him impossible to nail down at any given moment. His sense of having a foot, and an interest, in two worlds, is actually no different than when he was fifteen or twenty years younger: "Problem is, I'm not talking about ancient history. I've changed. We've all changed. A lot's happened in the last twenty years. But what I was, I still am. You have to know this. My motives remain suspect" (34). One of the central ways in which Wideman textualizes a self-identity in this book is his implicit argument that he is, and can be, both authentically "black" and a middle-class professional at the same time.

Significantly, many of the "numerous and comforting" similarities between Wideman and Robby portrayed in the text have to do with their common experiences as black men (77). Both have lived under the arbitrary power of white society; both have suffered from racism. Sharing a family history and a cultural context, the brothers have cultural commonalities, too: they both enjoy "black" music, and they both love basketball. The differences between them that are explored in *Brothers and Keepers* have to do with individual attributes of the sort that determine a person's social class: characteristics that make a person both ambitious to transcend poor or working-class origins and capable of doing so. While Wideman is explicit in describing the experiences and qualities that make him and Robby alike, he is tactfully subtle in sketching out their differences. In fact, their similarities are described, while their differences are suggested and dramatized.

Of course, the narrative of the brothers' series of visits is an artful, and calculated, construct, as the author sometimes admits. In detailing his method of writing the book, Wideman writes that after a visit with Robby he would, "some time later, after I'd had an opportunity to absorb his words," "reproduce" on paper what he'd heard (xi). Significantly, however, he reveals that he relied on his skills as a novelist, "borrowing narrative techniques learned from fiction," and he acknowledges the book as a "mix of memory, imagination, feeling and fact" (xi). It is not a record, then, but a dramatization of the brothers' attempt at building an intimacy — and of the potential obstacles to that intimacy. Though the narrative of *Brothers and Keepers* is told from Wideman's point of view, he becomes a character in this story as much as Robby does, and Wideman's portrayal of the brothers as characters points to the differences that Wideman is hesitant to articulate nakedly. Indeed, the contrasts between the figures of Wideman and Robby in *Brothers and Keepers* suggests Wideman's answer to his own question, "What was the nature of the difference?"

Wideman characterizes himself as having an almost infinitely flexible identity. He is someone for whom adapting his persona and tailoring his perspective to the immediate situation comes easily. Interestingly, Wideman frames this quality in negative terms: "A potential for treachery remains deep inside [my] core," he warns Robby in the narrative. "I can blend with my surroundings" (34). While recognizing that his re-inventing and adapting himself is a survival mechanism, Wideman nonetheless seems to regard it as an unhealthy tactic, "the strategy of slaves, the oppressed, the powerless" (32). He recalls his college years when he was "an expert at going with the flow, protecting myself by taking on the emotional or intellectual coloring of whatever circumstances I found myself in"; he pronounces this as ultimately destructive: "I thought I was running but I was fashioning a cage" (32–33).

Though Wideman clearly and understandably laments the reasons for his having constructed false personas in his youth, and he recalls the pain and alienation that came with doing so, it is also clear that his ability to re-invent himself is one of the keys to his ongoing resilience. This capacity for self re-invention is the quintessence of American autobiographers (and Americans) from Franklin on. Wideman's understanding of this strength is embedded in the text. What he implicitly labels as falseness in himself is often one of the qualities that has brought him success, such as self-discipline, ambition, and focus. A representative passage in *Brothers and Keepers* is when Wideman is assessing "the steep price" he paid at Penn for becoming a better basketball player and "other cultural improvements"; he writes that he was "urged to bury [his] past" (227). But rather than duplicitousness, as he implies, the characteristic that emerges most strongly in this passage is his ability to use his imagination to reconcile himself to do what he must in order to survive and succeed. He remarks that, as a college basketball player,

> the prospect of beating Princeton or Yale was seldom incentive enough to inspire more effort. To keep hustling in practice and school, I'd imagine how lame I'd sound trying to explain to the older guys from the playground [in Pittsburgh] ... why I blew the chance they never had. I'd anticipate the golden summers at Mellon, the chance to show off my new skills and prove I hadn't forgotten the old ones, the only ones that mattered in my heart of hearts [227].

Wideman was able to justify succeeding as a Penn student and player, he implies, because he could imagine that he was doing it somehow for the people back home. Even if one suspects that this particular claim is more fiction than fact, the passage is meaningful in another respect. Wideman's depictions of his achievements conform to a pattern in which he is either betraying the people back home by succeeding, or, he is succeeding as a part of a tribute to them. His "hustling in practice and school" and his hard work is always framed in relation to his family and the black community. The truth is that his self-discipline and hard work transformed him into a Phi Beta Kappa graduate of Penn, a Rhodes Scholar, a PEN/Faulkner fiction winner, and so on. But while the fact that his success is due to his own work ethic may be obvious, it is suppressed in *Brothers and Keepers,* or at least it is always enmeshed with the characterizations of himself as duplicitous and false. Certainly one reason for this is that an explicit emphasis on his own self-discipline would undermine his thesis that "Robby's chance for a normal life was as illusory as most citizens' chances to be elected to office or run a corporation" (220).

This may be an instance of Wideman not trusting his reader enough. Wideman's point about oppression would be just as strong if he showed that only the truly extraordinary could make it out of a place like Homewood — that's how hard it is. Like Ben Franklin, who in his *Autobiography* claims to be an example of aspiring American young men but who is in fact far from ordinary, Wideman downplays his own extraordinary levels of intelligence, talent, and discipline.

Though Wideman is rightly aggrieved by the larger social circumstances that made his own assimilation into the university and middle-class cultures a kind of betrayal of his black identity, the text of *Brothers* suggests that it was Wideman's capacity to assimilate into a new culture that enabled him to transcend the poverty of Homewood. Robby is also characterized as having an agonized yearning to be someone. But unlike Wideman, Robby's "dream of making it big, becoming something special," was a dream he could only imagine fulfilling on the streets of Pittsburgh (195). He could only picture success in its street version. Robby relates:

> That's why the highest thing you can say about a cat is he made his from the curb. That's a bad cat. That's a cat took nothing and made something.... The glamour. The rep. That's what I wanted. Coming home one day with my pockets full of hundred-dollar bills and buying mommy a house and anything else she wants [132].

This vision of success captures the sharp contrast between the qualities Wideman had and Robby lacked, including perseverance, idealism, and/or the desire for academic or athletic excellence. It also shows Robby's lack of imagination; he can't imagine himself in another world.

One of the most conspicuous and the most important differences between Wideman and Robby, *Brothers and Keepers* suggests, is the way that each man relates to and uses language itself. In what amounts to a meta-narrative about the brothers' collaboration, Wideman characterizes himself and his brother in terms of the distinct ways in which they participate in the conversation. Wideman is depicted as having complex responses not only to what Robby is saying, but also to his own act of listening. During his visits with Robby, there are several occasions in which Wideman has to discipline himself to listen to his brother. "I had to listen, listen," he urges himself (87). But listening, as he depicts it, involves a fairly strenuous effort to suppress the habits of his own imagination. He suggests that his tendencies as a fiction writer threaten to obstruct a "pure" form of hearing what his brother is saying. When Robby talked, Wideman writes, "I'd slip unaware out of his story into one of my own. I'd be following him, an obedient shadow, then a cloud would blot the sun and I'd be gone, unchained, a dark form skulking behind him but no longer in tow" (77). It is telling that the figure Wideman uses to depict his properly-listening self is of "an obedient shadow"; when it comes to storytelling, Wideman chafes at being either obedient or a shadow, and he struggles with the passive role of listener. Ultimately, he is none of these.

"I had to teach myself to listen," Wideman writes (77). The chief tendency in himself that he has to re-train and restrain is the impulse to contaminate Robby's stories with his own inventions: "I had to root my fiction-writing self out of our exchanges ... tame the urge to take off with Robby's story and make it my own" (77). Not wanting to steal Robby's story, Wideman also appears to worry about whether it's morally right to write about Robby at all when he asks, "Wasn't writing about people a way of exploiting them?" (77). Such disarming forthrightness, however, begins to resemble a calculated rhetorical strategy when one considers that first, Wideman writes and publishes *Brothers and Keepers* in spite of his misgivings; and secondly, throughout Wideman's entire career he has appropriated the stories of his family and made fiction out of them. Wideman himself acknowledges as much when he refers to his urge to take off with Robby's story as a "habit" that would be hard to break.

Albert Stone contends that "Behind historic identity, ... beneath even the discourse of the artful storyteller, lurks another 'self' whose psychic structures and states reveal themselves symbolically through language." He adds that "autobiography's coded language speaks more truly than literal renditions of experience" *(Autobiographical* 14). Wideman's dramatization of his anxiety about listening to Robby recurs frequently enough to have symbolic resonance. A clue to its deeper meaning might be found in two juxtaposed passages in the text. In a section "told" by Robby, Robby is sharing his own love of performing and writing poetry with his brother. He says that his fellow prisoners like his poems and ask him to read to them: "They say I write about the things they be thinking" (87). Robby reflects that the popularity of his performances in prison reminds him of when his teachers used to ask him "to pacify the class" with his impressions of Ed Sullivan; altogether these memories move Robby to assert how similar are he and Wideman: "You said your teachers called on you to tell stories, didn't they? Yeah. It's funny how much we're alike. In spite of everything I've always believed that.... I always believed we was the most alike out of all the kids. I see stuff in your books. The kinds of things I be thinking or feeling" (87).

Immediately following that passage, Wideman recreates a moment in which he's "listening" to Robby but lapses into his own reverie (is he really listening?). As Robby talks,

> my imagination creates something like a giant seashell, enfolding, enclosing us.... A curving mirror doubling the darkness. Poems are Jean Toomer's petals of dusk, petals of dawn. I want to stop. Savor the sweet, solitary pleasure, the time stolen from time in the hole. But the image I'm creating is a trick of the glass. The mirror that would swallow Robby and then chime to me: You're the fairest of them all. The voice I hear issues from a crack in the glass. I'm two or three steps ahead of my brother, making fiction out of his words. Somebody needs to snatch me by the neck and say, Stop. Stop and listen, listen to him [88].

As the very existence of *Brothers and Keepers* suggests, Wideman has to fight the urge to re-write Robby's words because in truth Wideman believes that he can do a better job of telling Robby's story than Robby can — and, in truth, he can. The "enormous gap" between Wideman and Robby is exposed in the juxtaposition of these passages more poignantly than anywhere else in the book: Robby performs amateur poetry for prisoners while Wideman is a renowned author, a professional. When Robby asserts how alike he and Wideman are as writers, Wideman semiconsciously asserts his own superiority, though he chastens himself for doing it. When he realizes that he's "two or three steps ahead of [his] brother, making fiction out of his words," Wideman recognizes that the act of re-writing Robby's life is an egotistical one because it shows off how much more sophisticated and talented a writer he is.

The gap between Robby's words and Wideman's mental revisions of them is far greater than the understatement of "two or three steps" implies, and Wideman knows it. The recurring anxiety surrounding Wideman's listening seems due to the fact that listening to Robby exposes a harsh truth that is at the heart of *Brothers and Keepers:* Wideman finds his own version of Robby's stories more interesting than Robby's. In a brief but striking moment near the end of the book, Wideman indirectly confesses as much: "Once I'd gotten the book I'd come for, would I be able to sustain the bond that had grown between us? Would I continue to listen with the same attention to his stories?" (200). Good question, and Wideman's text makes it clear the answer is "no."

The double bind of being both black and middle class as described by Shelby Steele in "On Being Black and Middle Class" is the bind in which Wideman felt caught when he distanced himself from Robby and from his own "blackness" so that he could pursue a middle-class life; it is a bind that Wideman seems to have attempted to resolve by integrating African American culture and perspective into his professional identity through his writing. But in *Brothers and Keepers,* Wideman is confronting the bind on a profoundly personal level by setting himself up to interpret Robby's life and his own, side by side. Robby's crime forces Wideman to face head-on the philosophical crux of the race-and-class antagonism; Wideman has to choose between embracing either the middle-class belief in personal responsibility, or what Steele calls "the [prevailing] form of black identity" that makes "blackness and victimization virtually synonymous" (101).

Moreover, after listening to Robby's story, Wideman, in writing a book, has to, one way or the other, directly or indirectly, answer such questions as, "Why did Robby end up as a criminal?" "Is he responsible for having chosen a life of crime?" Given the social and cultural context in which Wideman is writing, with the special pressures on blacks explained by Steele, how Wideman answers these questions constitutes a declaration of identity, choosing with whom he's going to identify himself and based on which values.

In the text of *Brothers,* Wideman implicitly answers some of these questions through his characterizations of himself and Robby. To a large degree he romanticizes Robby, and he strongly emphasizes Robby's victimization by corrupt white authorities throughout his life, from school to prison. But the most powerful way in which Wideman addresses the question of why he and Robby ended up so differently is in his characterizations of them with regard to power through language. As its author is well aware, *Brothers and Keepers* is evidence of Wideman's tremendous power as a writer; as a character in the narrative, however, Wideman is self-conscious about his own strength and sophistication with language relative to Robby. The text suggests that one fundamental difference between Wideman and his brother that has led to their vastly different lives is that Wideman has the capacity to invent and re-invent himself, to write and re-write an identity, through his imaginative facility with language, while Robby's particular vulnerability has been his allowing other people, and other discourses, to define who he is.

At one point in the book Wideman observes that Robby's new girl friend Leslie "claims Robby lives through the words of songs and movies. Robby admits maybe it's true" (196). Wideman writes that, as a way of telling his brother what a particular experience of his was like, Robby sent him lyrics to a song, "Family Affair": "The song was popular at about the time Robby was breaking up with his first wife, Geraldine. For him the song says everything there is to say about that period in his life" (196). Relying on song lyrics to articulate one's pain is common for people to do, but Wideman suggests that for Robby a song can delineate his identity, and "the music Robby loves is simple; the lyrics often seem sentimental, banal" (196–197).

Robby "discovered visions of himself reflected in 'Family Affair,'" and some of the song's lines that Robby "remembered" and shared with Wideman suggest Robby's resignation to performing throughout his life the role of the family underachiever:

> One child grows up to be somebody
> who just loves to learn
> And the other child grows up to be
> somebody who just loves to burn [197–198].

Robby's notion that he's destined to be the bad child of the family likely came from Wideman's parents as well as from the song. As Wideman writes early in the memoir, "Always there. The bad seed, the good seed. Mommy's been saying for as long as I can remember: That Robby ... he wakes up in the morning looking for the party" (20).

In one section of the book, Wideman suggests that Robby's vulnerability to the discourse of victimization, especially in its form as a ritual of group identification, is what finally leads Robby to seek his fortune on the streets. Wideman writes that for Robby, the story of his involvement in the robbery and murder begins with the death of his friend Garth, who apparently died from misdiagnosed stomach cancer. While the loss of Garth clearly affected Robby, Wideman's narrative emphasizes the much more destructive effect on Robby of the way Garth's death was talked about by Garth's friends and family.

Steele contends that the discourse of victimization has become a deeply powerful unifying ritual among blacks, and he offers historical reasons for this. In the 1960s, he explains, racial identification underwent the same sort of transformation that national identity undergoes in times of war. "Certainly, there were more dimensions to the black experience than victimization, but no other had the same capacity to fire the indignation needed for war. So ... out of historical necessity, victimization became the overriding focus of racial identity" (101). Steele recalls his own experience of trying to be at one with his race by adopting the identity of a victim. He relates how in college, he and his African American classmates played a game called "nap matching," "in which we sat around outdoing each other with stories of racial victimization, symbolically measured by the naps of our hair" (102). The truthfulness or accuracy of the stories was beside the point, Steele emphasizes, for in fact he and his friends in reality had "had only a moderate experience of victimization" (they mostly traded borrowed or legendary tales, or so he claims); as a "ritual of group identification," however, Steele notes, these sessions provided him and the other black students with a special kind of power: "the sense of innocence that is always entailed in feeling victimized filled us with a corresponding feeling of entitlement, or even license, that helped us endure our vulnerability on a largely white campus" (103).

In *Brothers*, Wideman relays Robby's story of the aftermath of Garth's death, and how the talk after the funeral began to focus on blaming whites for Garth's misdiagnosis. In Wideman's version, such language is seductive and dangerous; while it bonds people together, it does so by generating an almost violent level of anger:

> Some people had been getting mad.... mad at doctors and hospitals and whites in general who had the whole world in their hands but didn't have the slightest idea what to do with it.... A short, dark man, bubble-eyed ... had railed about the callousness, the ignorance of white witch doctors who, by misdiagnosing Garth's illness, had sealed his doom. His harangue had drawn a crowd. He wasn't just talking, he was testifying, and a hush had fallen over half the room as he dissected the dirty tricks of white folks. If somebody ran to the hospital and snatched a white-coated doctor and threw him into the circle surrounding the little fish-eyed man, the mourners would tear the pale-faced devil apart [63].

Wideman traces a direct path from this group interpretation of Garth's death to Robby's surrendering of hope to make an honest living. Imagining Robby's thoughts at the time, Wideman re-creates Robby's reasoning:

> When you thought about it, Garth's dying made no sense. And the more you thought the more you dug that nothing else did neither. The world's a stone bitch.... The man had you coming and going. He owned everything worth owning and all you'd ever get was what he didn't want anymore, what he'd chewed and spit out and left in the gutter for niggers to fight over [64].

In novelistic fashion, Wideman crafts a scene in which Robby and his buddies drink to Garth and vow together, as a show of loyalty to their late friend, to fulfill Garth's dream of "making it from the curb." Significantly, as Wideman imagines the scene, Robby is semiconsciously thinking of himself as a character in a movie. "It's our time now," Robby intones to his friends. "We can't let Garth down. Let's drink this last one for him and promise him we'll do what he said we could. We'll be the best. We'll make it to the top for him. We'll do it for Garth" (66).

Framing Robby's decision to sell heroin as an act of devotion to a friend is, of course, to romanticize it and to mitigate the corrupt aspects of Robby's character that would lead him to make such an choice. Rather than absolving Robby, however, the story of Garth and its effect on Robby is arguably intended to illustrate how susceptible an ordinary young black man is to being defined, and confined, by his social context. Steele observes that the victim-focused black identity is a profound encumbrance because it "encourages the individual to feel that his advancement depends almost entirely on that of the group. Thus he loses sight not only of his own possibilities, but of the inextricable connection between individual effort and individual advancement" (87).

The text finally suggests that Robby's comparative powerlessness in creating an individual identity for himself is the weak point that led him astray. The arrangement of collaboration between the brothers itself points to this difference: Wideman has the power to write both of their lives, while Robby allows his to be written for him. This power of self-invention is seen, of course, in the brothers' different life choices. In the Wideman brothers' situation, conformity to one's environment — the Homewood neighborhood — doesn't generally result in class ascension; in this case, Wideman is the defiant one who breaks from the norm by living an upwardly mobile life while Robby more passively succumbs to his influences.

As noted earlier, Wideman briefly expresses his concern about exploiting Robby, but the text raises ethical issues concerning their collaboration that Wideman does not address. Janet Malcolm has written a fascinating analysis of a case in which the subject of a nonfiction book sued the journalist, and Malcolm uses this occasion to reflect on the ethical situation of writers and their subjects. She observes that nonfiction writers offer something irresistible to their subjects:

> In our society, the journalist ranks with the philanthropist as a person who has something extremely valuable to dispense (his currency is the strangely intoxicating substance called publicity), and who is consequently treated with a deference quite out of proportion to his merits as a person. There are very few people in this country who do not regard with rapture the prospect of being written about or being interviewed on a radio or television program [58].

During the interviewing process, writers make their subjects feel important and interesting. However, when the writer is a family member of the subject, there is often an additional "currency" with which he can make a trade: his emotional involvement, and in Wideman's case, his time and attention as a brother. Memoir writers who draw heavily on the exotic experiences (often, of course, troubles of one sort or another) of family members sometimes trade their interest in and involvement with the subject — a parent or sibling — for the subject's willingness to expose his or her shames, failures, and other human frailties. This is especially true of Wideman and his brother, since Robby is imprisoned for life, and his contacts with people from the outside are few. Because Robby has little to offer but his stories of crime and prison life (an insider's perspective), what occurs between Wideman and Robby is a more egregious example of the trade-off that happens more subtly in other writer-family member relationships.

A passage near the end of the text poignantly illustrates the desperation with which a prisoner sentenced to life tries to keep outsiders involved with his life. Robby tells Wideman about a woman he's met through a friend, and that he's fallen in love with her. Leslie visits and writes frequently, and is expecting to marry Robby, but the relationship — and Leslie's continuing investment — is based on a lie, as Robby informs his brother: "We got a chance. One thing, though.... I got this problem. See, Leslie thinks I'm coming out the joint in a year or so" (213). Wideman advises Robby to tell Leslie the truth about his life sentence, knowing it would end the romance; but at the same time he also acknowledges how extraordinary and precious the experience of requited love is for a man doing life:

> After all, he's caged. His sentence is life. The bars are real. The romance he's describing has found a way around all that. He's tickled because he knows he shouldn't even entertain notions of love and marriage, let alone expect such goodies to actually fall in his lap. He's getting away with something and can't help grinning. Rob's amazed because something's happening that ain't spozed to happen. Prisons are organized to prevent it. He's a man in love with a woman, being loved in return. The gates remain locked but for the moment he's holding the key in his hand [212].

Robby "knows what he should do but he just can't quite bring himself to say what has to be said to his woman" (217). As Robby tells his brother, he is tormented by the guilt of his lie, but every time he tries to write the truth to Leslie in a letter, he "Keep[s] seeing her face and thinking how good she makes me feel and I'm scared of losing her. Cause I love that lady and she loves me and I'm scared of hurting her but I'm more scared of losing her, so I don't say nothing" (215).

This story demonstrates the sad reality, and Robby's awareness of it, that few people want to invest in a relationship with a man doomed to be locked up for life. But it also suggests the lengths to which people in Robby's position will go, including the manipulation of others and the compromising of his own sense of integrity, to keep people coming back, to keep them interested. This predicament sheds light on an ethical dimension of the "collaboration" between Wideman and Robby that Wideman never explicitly addresses. Robby is literally desperate for Wideman's involvement with him, and all Robby has to offer in return is his story. Significantly, before Robby tells Wideman about Leslie, he indicates his awareness that he is about to depart from the script, that in sharing a dilemma from his love life he is veering away from the unspoken contract with Wideman to talk about his crime and his time as a fugitive: "What time is it? I know you want to hear about the road but I got to talk to somebody 'bout this other thing. It's something else, Bruh. We got time, ain't we? We got another hour and fifteen minutes" (209). Robby knows that his brother is there chiefly to get *the* story, and not necessarily to chat about their immediate personal lives. Interestingly, Robby continuously postpones delivering to Wideman an account of his months on the run, perhaps as a way to forestall the conclusion of the collaboration. After all, Robby's withholding of this part of the story occurs during the time in which Wideman has begun "the business of both rendering and closing down the special relationship between my brother and myself that writing the book had precipitated" (199).

Wideman allows for the possibility that his own interest in Robby is largely a literary interest. To keep his brother's interest, Robby has to perform as a character, which means revealing and exposing things that are dramatic, and often, illicit.

Keeping a writer interested in his story is the primary, and, as Janet Malcolm notes, the somewhat anxiety-ridden, task of the subject:

> Even as [the writer] is worriedly striving to keep the subject talking, the subject is worriedly striving to keep the writer *listening*. The subject is Scheherazade. He lives in fear of being found uninteresting, and many of the strange things that subjects say to writers—things of almost suicidal rashness—they say out of their desperate need to keep the writer's attention riveted [*Journalist* 20].

Both Wideman and Robby know that Robby's interest-value as a subject lies in his role as a criminal. Wideman only blandly and generally refers to his possible exploitation of Robby (he never outright pleads guilty to it), but a more precise and thorough examination of why and how he's exploiting Robby would undoubtedly lead this highly intelligent author to some disturbing contradictions in his own motives. For example, Wideman implies that part of his task in writing *Brothers and Keepers* is to shatter the ignorant stereotypes held by white readers about black men being essentially criminal. Yet it is hard to deny that a great deal of the literary and commercial appeal of the book is its astonishing juxtaposition of two brothers' lives that could not be more different: a murderer versus an acclaimed author. As Paul Hendrickson writes about *Brothers and Keepers* in a 1990 profile of Wideman, "Some kind of family tragedy had fused itself into literary gold" (B8). Robby has to be Other for the purposes of the text. He has to perform in the role of a criminal and prisoner in order to be sufficiently interesting as a subject, and thus as a brother to Wideman. As Wideman observes near the end of the memoir, Robby is "giving me a song, holding open a door on a world I can never enter. Robby can't carry me over to the other side, but he can crack the door and I can listen" (198). Robby's perspective is only valuable in as far as it provides an inside glimpse into a world that most of the book's readers will never enter.

Robby's instinctive grasp of his role in the book manifests itself in his adoption of the confessional mode. He characterizes himself as the bad seed of the family: "I was another Wideman, the last one, the baby, and everybody knew how I was spozed to act. But something inside me said no. Didn't want to be like the rest of youns. Me, I had to be a rebel. Had to get out from under youns' good grades and do" (85). And as he releases a stream of confessions, he offers up unsolicited details of crimes. At one point he spontaneously volunteers the truth about Wideman's TV: "Been waiting to tell you this a long time. Ain't no reason to hold it back no longer. We into this telling-the-truth thing so mize well tell it all. I'm still shamed, but here it is. You know that TV of youall's got stolen from Mommy's. Well, I did. Was me and Henry took youall's TV that time and set the house to look like a robbery" (94). Of course, Robby's perception that "*we* into this telling-the-truth thing" is not quite accurate: it is only Robby's role in the collaboration to confess and expose himself (italics added). Wideman himself is remaining silent on his own "crimes," as even he admits: "His confessions make me uncomfortable. Instead of concentrating on what he's revealing, I'm pushed in considering all the things I could be confessing, should be confessing but haven't and probably won't ever.... I have no desire to tell everything about myself so I resist his attempt to be up front with me" (97).

Wideman does not in fact resist Robby's confessions, but records them. Further, Wideman refuses to reveal himself not only to Robby but also to his readers, to whom he offers up the details of "one of the worst days of [Robby's] life" (93). Wideman writes of his own guardedness in the face of Robby's revelations, "I feel hypocritical" (97). And in truth he has a separate standard of privacy for himself than he grants to Robby. As Wideman tells Paul Hendrickson in the interview, "I'm not offering up my life as material to explain anything to anyone.... My life is a closed book" (B8).

Near the end of the book there is a passage which reveals much about the give-and-take relationship that produced *Brothers and Keepers* and also suggests what each of the brothers gets from this collaboration. In this segment Wideman demonstrates his desire to give Robby a controlling voice in the book's production, but then shows that this courtesy, as it were, is nullified by Robby's inability to articulate a vision of himself or a book. Wideman tells how Robby was given the first draft of the book, and he "liked it fine, but something was missing. Trouble was, he hadn't been able to name the missing ingredient. I couldn't either but I knew I had to try and supply it" (194). To supply the missing ingredient, Wideman "asked for more from Robby. He'd responded sporadically with poems, anecdotes, meditations on his time behind bars. What he was giving me helped me turn a corner.... I was beginning to understand what had been missing in the first version of his story. I was learning to respect my brother's touch, his vision" (196).

The final statement of this passage is yet another instance of Wideman's romanticizing of Robby and his role in the collaboration, for the book has made it abundantly clear that Wideman himself is the one with the "touch" and "vision." This exchange is emblematic of the symbiotic nature of the brothers' relationship, not only in creating a book but in creating their self-identities. Each provides something indispensable to the other that the other lacks. Robby provides raw material from his own life, and in doing so grants Wideman both access to his own past and a way of writing about it. This enables Wideman to integrate his past into his present and yet keep past and present separate. By immersing himself in Robby's story, Wideman locates a part of himself, which he integrates into his present life as an author.

But Wideman gets much more from Robby than a connection to his own past. He gets to experience, vicariously, the energy and vitality of Robby's "otherness," from the agonized yearning to "be someone" that led Robby to prison, to the gritty particulars of Robby's street and penitentiary living. As Wideman writes of his need to write about Robby, "Maybe I'm inside West Pen to warm myself by his fire, to steal it" (202). In the text as in life, Wideman is able to "encounter" and identify with Robby, and then, ultimately, to leave Robby and his dangerous vitality safely behind in West Pen. Both Wideman and his text are enlivened and energized by Robby's liminality, though neither is finally destabilized by it. Wideman's identification and encounter with the other becomes contained within the text itself. "Had I identified with him," Wideman asks, "because I discovered that was the best way to write the book? Would the identification I'd achieved become a burden, too intense, too pressurized to survive once the book was completed?" (200).

However ambiguous and even-handed the author may want the textual collaboration and the real-life relationship between himself and Robby to appear, it is Wideman who is in control of shaping the texts of both their lives, of framing the interactions between them, and of turning on or off his identification with Robby. In return for "stealing" Robby's story, Wideman lends his own eloquence and rhetorical skills to transform Robby's desultory writings and dialogue into a shapely and coherent "self" on the page — a life story that will not only reach a wide, literate audience but will also likely please it (200). What remains troubling is the fact that however sympathetic the portrait of Robby is, Wideman is its creator; and, despite Wideman's having "learn[ed] to respect [his] brother's touch, his vision," the text never accords Robby the status of an equal. Robby, as reflected in this childish appellation, is never really an author here, but is rather the subject of the paternal author, and always subject to that author's control.

In the end, then, *Brothers and Keepers* exemplifies the complicated ethics in much of American working-class autobiography. Wideman performs many ethical services with his book, including edifying his readers not only about prison life but also, more importantly, about one person who ended up there and why. By humanizing and personalizing Robby for his readers, the author accomplishes a purpose larger than himself and his brother by reminding readers that every prisoner has a story, and that society is part of that story. He deepens his reader's understanding of the role race played in Robby's life, and in the lives of many prisoners, and thereby performs an important ethical duty on behalf of other African Americans.

Wideman has created a profound book, and much of its richness is due to his revealing — and exposing — portrait of Robby. The author wonders if writing about people is a "way of exploiting them" (77). As Lynn Z. Bloom has argued, writing about one's family member is not necessarily exploiting them as long as it's done truthfully. Wideman's exposure of Robby is not in itself unethical.

What is disturbing is Wideman's posture of benevolence, and his refusal to probe as deeply into his own motives as he does into Robby's. For all of the introspectiveness he carefully displays in the text, Wideman never answers the hard questions he tosses out there. What *is* he getting from his temporary re-connection with Robby? What is the cost to Robby of Wideman's use of him? The naivete and vulnerability in Robby that Wideman successfully and movingly captures make Robby susceptible to his brother's opportunistic use of him. In some ways Wideman does his best by Robby in authoring *Brothers and Keepers*. But, significantly, Wideman's career appears to have benefited the most from Wideman's renewed closeness with his brother.

4

Autobiography as Healing: Agate Nesaule's *A Woman in Amber*

In his analysis of an ethically controversial memoir—*The Kiss* by Kathryn Harrison—Paul John Eakin relates the author's claim that "an imperative of the creative imagination," in Eakin's paraphrase, compelled her to write it, "an artistic 'necessity' overriding any other consideration" (*How* 152–53). Likewise noting the creative "necessity" often given as a motive for ethically dubious prose, Wayne Booth asks whether there are limits "to the author's freedom to expose, in the service of art or self, the most delicate secrets of those whose lives provide material"; he goes on to observe that the question is generally answered by writers with "art justifies all " (*Company* 130). Eakin and Booth are clearly troubled by the suggestion that creative urgency gives writers unlimited license when it comes to representing or exposing living people in print.

Agate Nesaule has written an ethically problematic text, but, as she leads us to infer, she justifies her action by claiming that she is compelled to write in answer to a different sort of imperative: a quest for healing, for further insight into her emotional pain, and even for the reconstituting of a self that was nearly destroyed psychologically by trauma. Her text raises an important question that has not been adequately addressed by proponents of the therapeutic benefits of writing autobiography: when one turns to life-writing for emotional healing, isn't there a difference between writing and publishing? Did Nesaule need merely to write in order to heal, or was publishing her story—and, through her revelations, affecting the lives of her former husband and her son—a necessary part of her healing?

Her narrative has a two-fold purpose: on one hand it recounts her experiences in World War Two and the years afterward in which she and her family lived in refugee camps; secondly, it tells of her struggle throughout most of her adulthood to recover from the psychic wounds inflicted by the war. Nesaule bases the overarching plot of her autobiography on the premise that telling stories brings emotional healing. In the text, the more the author narrates the traumatic events of her childhood to a sympathetic audience — her lover, John, and her therapist, Ingeborg — the more she feels the burden of her past lifting, and the more able she is to express her emotions. Her ability to forge a healthy relationship and to attain a measure of peace increases commensurately with her ability to create narratives of her life. Both the plot and the purpose of the memoir, then, are psychological; the narrative both relates a story of emotional recovery and itself furthers the process.

However, the author doesn't acknowledge the enormous ethical difference between telling one's life story to a lover or a therapist and publishing it. Similarly to *Brothers and Keepers,* Nesaule's text employs the construct of personal conversation being "reproduced" (but in truth, invented, like all dialogue) as autobiography, and as being the catalyst for it. In Nesaule's case the construct emphasizes the author's motive for the original conversation — emotional healing — and obscures the professional ambition that motivates publishing.

The act of psychological rebuilding becomes a moral act first when Nesaule publishes her story, and secondly, when her story shifts from her childhood into an account of her adulthood when she is no longer a child at the mercy of brutal soldiers, but is a grown, professional woman in an infelicitous marriage; the narrative then focuses on demonstrating the inferiority of her husband. The strategies she employs effectively when writing as a survivor of war are less effective and even ethically troubling when she writes as a survivor of a husband, whom she renders as an alien and oppressive Other, largely through a class-oriented characterization. I propose to examine *A Woman in Amber* as a text that illuminates the ethical pitfalls of writing as a survivor/victim, such as the author's inability to incorporate a reflective strain of personal responsibility into a narrative that attempts to demonstrate the psychological mutilation of dehumanizing experience. In this chapter I also explore the ethical questions that this autobiography engenders concerning the treatment of former proximate others, such as spouses, in life writing. While critics have begun to explore the ethical dimensions of autobiography in general, the ethical issues inherent in writing nonfiction about former spouses have been only scantily addressed.

In addition, I consider the problems raised by Nesaule's simplistic representation of a working-class person in her text (a text which reifies Nesaule's own establishment in a high-culture, intellectual metier), especially when the author has a vested interest in demonizing him. Other autobiographers analyzed in this study generally render working-class family members sympathetically, even at times risking romanticizing or apologizing for them. Conversely, Nesaule's text brings to light the ethical predicament of an upper-middle-class writer who holds the power — and responsibility — of representing in print a working-class person for whom his or her feelings have soured. Thus, I devote some attention in this chapter to class characterization in autobiography that amounts to an act of aggression, if not revenge.

Nesaule prefaces the story of her wartime years with a depiction of herself in a session with her therapist, Ingeborg. This narrative frame relates the author's deep resistance over five decades to facing the pain of the war, and the many layers of denial that had to be peeled away before she could begin to tell her story. As a therapy session that leads into Nesaule's narrative, the frame positions the memoir as a continuation of Nesaule's healing process, placing the reader in the room, so to speak, with the patient and with the movingly empathetic Ingeborg, whose kind words cause "more words [to] rise to [Nesaule's] lips" (33). The therapy frame also reveals the psychological point of view from which Nesaule composes the memoir that follows; as a metaphorical construct, the patient-therapist scenario signals that we are about to read the life story of a damaged woman, and that the center of the story is the wounds she's received, how and when she received them, and the shape their scars have taken.

A solipsistic vision can constitute part of the meaning of an autobiography that recounts shattering trauma. It is problematic, though, when such an autobiography implicates other living people who were not involved in the writer's original trauma. Nesaule's narrative perspective moves into the realm of the ethical when the memoir shifts from telling Nesaule's own story to telling the shared story of a marriage. The merging of therapy with autobiography is a special problem in contemporary life-writing because it puts healing before "truth value," and Nesaule's work highlights some of the weaknesses in such an approach. As I suggested, the therapy frame is a construct that implies that for Nesaule, narrative-making is an act of psychological healing. Yet as Eakin and many other critics have noted, autobiography is always an act of "building an identity," to use Nancy K. Miller's phrase (*Bequest* xi). Thus in *Amber*, Nesaule's victimized narrator combines the tasks of psychic repair, of identity construction, and of relating the story of a long marriage, in which by virtue of their shared life her spouse's story also gets told.

Nesaule's text is a memoir in which the author seeks to rebuild a self by redefining her identity in relation to others. Eakin writes that "if identity is increasingly understood in relational terms, then it follows that the lives of others are centrally implicated in the telling of any life story" (*How* 157). He observes, however, that some autobiographies are especially centered on relational lives, in which "the self's story [is] viewed through the lens of its relation with some key other person, sometimes a sibling, friend, or lover, but most often a parent — we might call such an individual the proximate other to signify the intimate tie to the relational autobiographer" (86). In a variation of this form, Nesaule defines herself in relation to two key other individuals, her mother and her former husband, and the text might be said to be a reification of Nesaule's flight from identification with her ex-husband Joe and her reification of an identity in relation to her mother.

Analyzing relational memoirs in which children write about their parents, Eakin observes that the nature or quality of the parent-child bonds recorded naturally influences the kind of memoir that is produced. "When the bond is untroubled," he writes, "we are likely to get a memoir of a traditional sort, in which filial piety produces a memorial to a beloved parent" (*How* 87). However, "when the bond is conflicted ... the motive for memoir is likely to be more intense, and a great number of relational lives could be classed under the heading of 'unfinished business.'" In such cases, the autobiographical act "affords the opportunity to speak the previously unspoken, to reveal what has been hidden or repressed" (87). Nesaule's relationship with her inexplicably remote mother is terribly conflicted, and part of the business she finishes is supplying for herself, through the act of writing and after her mother's death, a mother that she never really had. Nesaule writes a relational life, though, in which two relationships, and thus two selves, literally compete with each other, and the way that she affirms the self in relation to her mother is by writing what Eakin terms an "antirelational" narrative that renounces both Joe and the self who married him (*How* 91). Nesaule seeks to escape the bond of relational identity with the working-class Joe, just as she reifies her escape from the impoverished and depressing environment in which she lived when she met and married Joe.

The text suggests that beneath Nesaule's lifelong struggle with depression was a damaged sense of self that both her divorce from Joe and her subsequent therapy with Ingeborg have transformed into a healthy self. Before undergoing therapy her self had been "cruelly reined in," "imprisoned," "constricted," and "sealed ... into amber" (249). Her life was "constricted by shame, anger and guilt" (viii), which she attributes to the "long aftermath of war, when I waited, rather than lived, the forty years spent in a motherless universe" (279). Her text provides evidence of damage to her self-identity inflicted both by the war *and* her experience of being psychologically "motherless." As will be discussed later, the psychological damage she portrays surely made her less than an ideal spouse, but this is a point that the author never acknowledges.

Susanna Egan has written that Holocaust autobiographers "risk intense solipsism" (*Mirror* 159); as with their stories, the sometimes extreme self-focus that characterizes Nesaule's memoir is itself a poignant testament to the devastation the writer suffered. One of the meanings of the scene with Ingeborg is its suggestion of the endless self-absorption that often defines the aftermath of trauma. This is manifested, for example, in the way that Nesaule describes others primarily in relation to her own pain; people are characterized as good largely through their ability to listen to and sympathize with Nesaule, and as bad through their failure in this.

Egan has noticed that Holocaust writers often describe "a void in their selves," which results in part, Egan argues, from the Nazis' attempt to deny and destroy their humanity (*Mirror* 159). Nesaule conveys a sense of worthlessness and hollowness that is reminiscent of Egan's subjects: she launches her narrative of the war with a metaphorical image of her inner self as a starving child, a void that is almost literally fatal in its pain and emptiness. As a patient she relates to Ingeborg her unsuccessful efforts to lose weight, then, a haunting dream she has had in which she must save a seven-year-old boy who is starving to death. Nesaule's connecting of the boy to her own experience of starvation at the age of seven is presented as the turning point in Nesaule's therapy, an uncovering of a central truth about herself that unlocks her grief and enables her to progress in both her self-discovery and her story. As she describes it, however, the assault on the self that has made such a lasting wound was not the physical hunger but the controlling authorities' denial of the child's human worth. She recounts the Russian soldiers' teasing of stick-limbed children begging for food, their occasional toss of "a few chunks of raw meat into my bowl" (28). "I ... I am so ashamed," she tells Ingeborg about this period. "It made me feel completely worthless to know I wasn't even worth feeding" (27). Yet the author seems unaware of the parallels between her early traumas and her treatment of her husband in life and in her text. For example, Nesaule starves Joe emotionally, and in her book implies that he is not worth feeding.

Yet the text suggests that the void in Nesaule's self is due far more to a lack of mothering than from the months of captivity in Lobethal institution. Current theories of personality and identity formation — what Eakin terms "the origins of selfhood"—firmly situate the development of self-identity within processes of interpersonal interaction. Surveying such theories, Eakin is persuaded by the relational model of identity — the notion that our selves are socially constructed — proposed by, among others, Jessica Benjamin (*How* 66). If others play a crucial role in an individual's achievement of selfhood, then failure to receive recognition of one's autonomy can create what Eakin calls an "identity deficit" (*How* 144). Nesaule repeatedly describes a mother who fails to see her as a separate, independent human being. One of Nesaule's formative moments with her mother is both harrowing and symbolic. This is the morning at the Lobethal institution when the women and girls are lined up by Russian soldiers and made to believe they are about to be shot. Nesaule's mother begins to pull her daughters with her to the front of the line: "'If they're going to shoot us, let us be the first ones,'" she urges (77). The seven-year-old Agate is horrified — "She wants me to be shot, I think" — and successfully resists, but is punished afterwards by her mother's coldness, or so the author perceives. The life-and-death struggle between them changes their relationship; as of that morning, "the whole universe was motherless during the war and remained that way for me long afterwards" (82). Of course, one could imagine other motives for Nesaule's mother's actions, such as her wanting to spare her daughters the terror they would experience as they watched the others being shot. But Nesaule's recollection of the event, which may or may not have happened as she recalls it, and her interpretation of her mother's behavior, are emblematic of her perception of her forty-two-year relationship with her mother.

Although an increased detachment, even a strain of hostility, seems to be created between them at that moment, Nesaule acknowledges later in the book that the distance between herself and her mother existed prior to that morning and had much deeper roots: "it goes back to the sandy path where I struggled with her, further back even than that, to her own early displacements and losses, to her always looking towards the horizon, away from the house" (216). Indeed, Nesaule depicts a mother who, after the war, throughout the family's five years in the displaced persons camps, and then later when they're living in Indianapolis, demonstrates virtually no maternal love for her children, especially Agate. Consequently, as a child in the camps Nesaule is "obsessive about securing [the] attention" of women without children of their own and fantasizes about being wealthy enough as an adult to purchase a beautiful home for her mother in order to win her approval (119).

The only aspect of Nesaule that draws her mother's interest is her dutiful academic progress. She is visible to her mother only as a student, and more precisely as one whose successes will reflect well on her mother

4. Agate Nesaule's A Woman in Amber

and also fulfill her mother's own frustrated academic ambitions. One evening in their camp-home Agate watches her mother dress for a party, and tries to engage her in personal conversation, which her mother resists. Craving intimacy, the daughter "wanted to fling myself into her arms and cry and let her comfort me," but does not (126). Valda ignores her questions, and addresses her only to ask, "Have you got your poem memorized?" Impersonally, she adds: "Studying is important" (128). It must be said that the coldness Nesaule portrays in her mother is mirrored in Nesaule's own treatment of Joe, who accuses her of being "a cold bitch" (235). But the author won't admit that she learned how to behave in an intimate — or a frustratingly non-intimate — relationship from her mother.

When the family must choose a country to emigrate to, Valda passionately argues for America because there her daughters "can get scholarships and go to a university. They can have a better life. They're smart, my daughters" (137). Her ambition for her daughters brings forth an uncharacteristic burst of affection from Valda. Nesaule writes: "She put her arms around my sister and me in a gesture of solidarity. It was thrilling" (138). Once they live in Indiana, Valda's game of giving and withholding love centers on Nesaule's willingness and ability to implement Valda's plan for her to "have a wonderful, exciting life, going to lectures and concerts, listening to famous professors" (186). Nesaule enjoys her mother's warm approval when she announces that she has won a scholarship large enough to attend the university. Calling her "precious," an intimate term she used in Nesaule's early childhood, Valda "flings aside her book and holds out her arms," but the invitation merely highlights the distance between them: "I start towards her, but stop halfway. It is impossible. When have we last touched, when did she last call me precious? Too long ago" (185). In this passage, incidentally, Nesaule once again inadvertently reveals her similarity to her mother in her unwillingness to forgive and in her ability to repel.

As the author portrays it, Nesaule receives identity-nurturing recognition from her mother only when the daughter appears able to fulfill Valda's dream of class mobility. "I *knew* you would [win]," Valda tells her. "You're my daughter" (186). She instills in her an imperative to succeed not only for Agate's own sake, but also to compensate for Valda's own ruined life and lost opportunities. "[Y]ou finally have a chance. You can have a different life, a larger, freer, better life. You must escape, even if it is too late for the rest of us. You can live like people were meant to live. You must not let anything stop you" (187). It's unsurprising, then, that Nesaule's rebellion against her mother gets played out in the arena of education and class, in the form of her elopement with the coarse-behaving, working-class Joe.

The choice to court and marry Joe against her mother's wishes is a central, identity-defining moment in the narrative. Nancy K. Miller finds that "the anxiety over betrayal is palpably at work" in many memoirs that deal with a parent's death (*Bequest* 13). This is true of *A Woman in Amber,* since Nesaule implicates herself in more than one betrayal of her mother. In addition to betraying her parents by marrying Joe, Nesaule sees her own success as another betrayal. Miller notes that "leaving home and changing class is one way of feeling that one has betrayed one's parents," and Nesaule clearly feels some guilt for having had the educational and professional opportunities that her mother longed for as a young woman, even though Valda urged her to take them (13). Illustrating this bind is the scene mentioned earlier, when the college-bound Nesaule informs her mother about the scholarship, and her mother responds with characteristic ambivalence, first showing delight, then invoking her own frustrated ambitions. "I always wanted to go to the university too," she laments, proceeding to recount her misfortunes. Her reverie of "if only's" makes her daughter "long to escape. I feel helpless whenever she recites her losses. Should I apologize for winning the scholarship? I try to harden myself, push the guilt away.... I would even give up my scholarship to her" (186).

Interestingly, Nesaule remembers the "helpless" feeling she would get when her mother would retell stories of her hardships, but she can't see that Joe might feel the same way when Nesaule keeps referring to her own childhood sufferings. One of her chief complaints about him is his minimizing of her experiences in the war and in the camps. In describing this aspect of the marriage she writes, "If, for strangers, he turned into jokes the few stories I had mistakenly told him early in our marriage, I turned aside and looked away" (217). Nesaule wants the reader to be appalled by Joe's callousness, and his dialogue relating to her past is indeed crude and insensitive, including his common refrain to her, "Admit it, you really loved it over there in war-torn Europe. 'Soldier, soldier, chocolate bar'— I bet you got off on saying it" (217). However, the text shows Joe usually using this approach only when he plainly feels helpless in the face of her deep pain. In one instance, Agate and Joe are flying home from a visit with her mother, when Agate suddenly begins to cry over her mother's rejection. Joe is "surprised" and tries to cheer her up with his crass "formula": "Come on, kid, cut that out. Quit dwelling on the past, that's really one of your biggest problems" (217). Nesaule only sees Joe's words as a profound insult, rather than considering that he, like herself when she was young and faced with her mother's inconsolable pain over her past, feels powerless to fix the problem. Agate responds to her mother by trying "to harden myself," while Joe responds to his wife by minimizing her suffering (186).

4. Agate Nesaule's A Woman in Amber

In the memoir Nesaule's mother is quick to blame her daughter for perceived betrayals, irrationally and cruelly holding grudges for such incidents as their wartime struggle on "the sandy path," and Nesaule's involvement as a teenager in the arrest of a man who tried to molest her. But in the text, all these imagined or real betrayals become consolidated into and represented by Nesaule's marriage to Joe. Once Joe enters the picture, he stands for all that is wrong between Nesaule and her mother, and he is made to carry the burden of responsibility for their estrangement; with Joe on the scene, Valda's perpetuation of the strained relationship with her daughter is minimized by the author, overshadowed by Nesaule's emphasis on Joe as a force that keeps Nesaule from attaining her mother's love and from being her "true self" (212).

Indeed, despite the distance between them that precedes Nesaule's relationship with Joe, and her mother's obvious inability to show maternal affection, Nesaule's narrative asserts that her elopement is the cause of her estrangement from Valda. Nesaule's acknowledgment, cited earlier, that her mother was unloving long before Nesaule's marriage, feels pallid and cursory when it comes near the book's end, given the intensity of her narrative about having been "seized" by Joe, and her implication of a forced and even violent separation from her mother (193). After her mother's explosive outburst at the news of Nesaule's marriage, the author understands that a permanent break has occurred: "If it would do any good, I would kneel in front of my mother and beg until I was forgiven and embraced." Such a gesture would be pointless, though: "Like a bone long weakened by imperfectly healed injuries, something finally breaks violently clear through. This jagged fracture will not heal" (203). Nesaule's mother does not speak to her for two years after that day.

In a book replete with suffering, including starvation, her witnessing of rape and murder, and prolonged periods of displacement, Nesaule's narrative nonetheless registers her mother's rejection of her as the most traumatic loss of all. More than once Nesaule uses the term "motherless" to contain all of the pain and depression she has experienced in her life, as if to suggest that being unloved by one's mother is the very definition of despair.

Nesaule's interpretation of the story of her courtship and marriage performs several functions. "Writing a parent's death," Miller notes, "is a way to repair a broken connection" (*Bequest* x-xi). Valda dies to Nesaule in an important sense well before her actual death, and Nesaule clearly "writes" this death, ultimately making it the emotional center of the memoir, in order to establish a relationship that was impossible while her mother lived. She seems to know that her mother's disapproval of her was/is not rational, and so there's no formula for dispelling it. Nesaule admits, for example, that neither her achieving the status of a university professor nor her coming "to share her [mother's] opinion of Joe" brought her mother's affection or admiration: "She has never acknowledged any of my three degrees with the slightest approval, let alone congratulations" (216).

But the drive to win a mother's love is powerful, often defying rational knowledge, as evidenced by the dream with which Nesaule ends her memoir. In it her now-deceased mother, who in life was unloving to the end, confesses her blindness and asks for forgiveness. Valda explains that her blindness "is why I always looked at others, away from you, while you tried so hard to find another mother" (278). Nesaule's insistence that it "matters" that "my mother and I did touch each other, if only in a dream" demonstrates Nesaule's belief that shifting one's interpretation of the past can soothe the wounds inflicted by an unloving mother (280). Eakin's observation was that memoirs about parents give autobiographers the chance "to speak the previously unspoken," but Nesaule's narrative affords her an additional opportunity as well: she can speak again what she had already spoken to her mother, but now she can make it "matter"; that is, she can finally, after her mother's death, get the response she longed for by writing that response on behalf of her mother (*How* 87). Nesaule did express her agreement with her mother about Joe, but while she lived her mother was unmoved by Nesaule's change of loyalty; now Nesaule can solidify her identification with her mother by reifying in her narrative her renunciation of Joe.

Nesaule's giving credence to the words spoken by her mother in a dream suggests the depth of emotional pain caused by her mother's rejection of her, showing as it does Nesaule's willingness to deceive herself in order to experience some semblance of her mother's acceptance. In a more general sense, it also reveals Nesaule's capacity for self-deception in her quest for emotional relief because it demonstrates her inclination to invent versions of other people in order to meet her own psychological and rhetorical needs. In addition, is it not a distortion of her mother to believe that her mother would say and do what she clearly did not while she lived? Like Wideman, Nesaule has all the power as the writer of the relationship between herself and her subject(s). This fact in itself can't be helped, as it's an unavoidable reality of auto/biographical writing. But Nesaule's pattern of finding "truth" in her dreams—it is also a dream, as will be discussed later in this chapter, that reveals to Nesaule Joe's "true" nature—is a troubling indulgence. For the purpose of solidifying her new identity, in which she is allied with her mother and the values her mother represents, and in which she is antithetical to Joe, Nesaule dreams up a mother who is more loving than she was in life, and a Joe who is almost certainly worse than he really is. Nesaule's text implies that the author believes that dreams can yield profound truths about other people, rather than truths about the dreamer's own emotions, and this belief in itself throws the author's credibility in rendering proximate others into question.

In the scene at the university in which the twenty-year-old Nesaule first meets Joe, Nesaule asserts that she and Joe are "two outsiders" (191). But her account makes significant distinctions between them in social status, values, and moral behavior, in fact portraying Nesaule as very much an insider in terms of the text's delineation of the good and the normal, and establishing Joe as both alien and antagonistic to the norm.

Nesaule renders herself as a compliant and sensible adherent of the codes and values of the system, placing her faith in education as the route to the upper-middle class. That she submits to the rules, however daunting they may seem to a poor immigrant, is evidenced in her torturous wait in the long course registration line, around which the scene itself is constructed. Her experience in the line, like her experience of the university, is characterized by her anxious determination to meet the school's and her parents' expectations of her. Counting the people ahead of her, Nesaule worries about failure: "I will not be admitted, I will not get enough credits to satisfy the scholarship committee … I will have to leave school in disgrace" (189). We learn (through Joe's complaints) that she studies "all the time," that she dutifully reports to her scholarship committee if she gets a B, and that she does "look and try to act like an American" (191).

Joe, in contrast, truly is an outsider. He looks different from the other undergraduates: "[h]is long dark hair curls over his frayed shirt collar, he wears jeans and cowboy boots instead of neatly pressed slacks and polished loafers like the other students" (189). He is older, and already divorced; as he tells an official overseeing the line, he is a "grown-up, not a damn college kid." Naive to campus life and its middle-class trappings, he mistakes Nesaule's inexpensive wool sweater with its pearly trim for cashmere and "knockout pearls," which lead him to assume that Nesaule is in "one of the best sororities" (190). Joe is also an outsider to university values. "He does not think much of the students or professors," nor does he desire a genuine education: "He's only at the university to learn enough so that he can keep his own accounts when he sets off to Alaska or California to make his fortune" (191).

As Nesaule renders him, Joe is also an outlaw in the world of the university. He handles the long line differently than she does, by trying, in manipulative "stage-whispers," to "convince the official to let him through the turnstile ahead of everybody else" (190); later he insults the guard who helped him cut in front, audibly referring to him as a "dumb bastard" (191). Imbuing Joe with a strain of menace, Nesaule writes that as she is leaving, Joe "steps into my path" to introduce himself. He is hostile and profane, and worse, in the value-system of the text, he expresses hostility in the language of class envy. He ridicules the students who submit to "the lousy system" by calling them "dumb shits." Significantly, Nesaule refers to the students that Joe mocks as "*my* classmates" rather than "our," even though Joe clearly is registering for courses, too (my italics). "Bunch of fucking sheep," Joe says, in dialogue meant to reveal not only his nastiness but also Nesaule's shocked schoolgirl sensibilities since his comment causes her to "draw in my breath sharply, as much at the language as at the sentiments" (190).

In *Gone Primitive,* a study of Western conceptions of the primitive, Marianna Torgovnick contends that a "generalized notion of the primitive" has existed for a long time in our culture, a notion embodied in an "ensemble of ... tropes," or, "sets of images and ideas that have slipped from their original metaphoric status to control perceptions of primitives" (22, 8). These tropes portray primitives as "our untamed selves, our id forces— libidinous, irrational, violent, dangerous." Primitivist discourse positions primitives "at the 'lowest cultural levels'; we occupy the 'highest,' in the metaphors of stratification and hierarchy commonly used" (8). Such discourse, argues Torgovnick, is "fundamental to the Western sense of self and Other" (8).

The concept of the primitive as "an inexact expressive whole — often with little correspondence to any specific or documented societies" can refer both to "societies 'out there' and to subordinate groups within the West" (20). Indeed, conceptions of the primitive are often seen in representations of women as well as of people of the working class (18). In *A Woman in Amber,* Nesaule emphasizes Joe's class status and his surly behavior; in fact, these aspects are all of him we're permitted to know. More precisely, the author exploits Joe's working-class orientation to draw him as a primitive. In this text, he is not merely unlikable. He's all meanness and bullying, always insensitive and unperceptive, consistently cynical and disrespectful: a personification of "our untamed selves, our id forces"; and Nesaule repeatedly connects his truculence and boorishness with his impoverished background and lower-class sensibilities.

In the passage following the registration scene, Nesaule describes Joe's poor origins in language that evokes a dirty, ragged, chaotic life. These details are interlaced with paraphrased rants from Joe that highlight his crude opinions and amorality. We learn that Joe "grew up in slums, in one-horse towns, in abandoned oil fields. He had to work hard for every penny he ever had, driving cabs, parking cars for nightclubs, betting on horses." Then Nesaule adds, "He had a foolproof method for winning, he says, until the crooked officials in New York kicked him off the track" (191). With a broad stroke the author suggests Joe's transient, unsheltered background: "He has lived everywhere"; "[h]e has been everywhere, seen everything, he's been around, he knows what life is like." Nesaule follows this with a display of Joe's political incorrectness: "Women are always chasing him, he says, but he doesn't think much of them, they have no principles and no loyalty, just like his goddamn ex-wife"; Joe "does not think much of foreigners either," regarding them as "funny guys in pinstriped suits, whose accents he can mimic to good comic effect" (191).

This blending of Joe's material poverty with the worst clichés of lower-class immorality occurs again in a scene at Nesaule's family's home after Joe has met her parents for the first time. Joe's dialogue is crafted to reveal details about his lower-class parents at the same time that he spouts profane, disrespectful comments about Nesaule's mother. The scene occurs the morning after Joe spent the night on the family's couch; according to Joe, Valda came home from her restaurant job around four a.m., then on seeing Joe, spoke harshly to him. Joe describes their encounter: "She said, 'Get out. I won't let you have my daughter!' Just like that. And then she said it again, as if I couldn't hear her the first time" (196). Joe's reaction to Nesaule's attempts to explain her mother's outburst is typical of Joe's dialogue:

> Yeah, yeah, don't start that song and dance about all she's been through, I'm sick of hearing it. Everybody had a lousy childhood, I sure did. Jesus, all my parents did was fight. My old lady didn't give a shit about me, all she did was whine about how hard it was for her if my old man so much as had a beer. Frankly, I'd give anything to have had a childhood like yours [197].

This kind of exposition, which deftly locates Joe's family in the "lowest cultural level"—and which, incidentally, takes the focus off Nesaule's mother's rudeness—feels strategical, as if this vivid evocation of Joe's harsh upbringing is meant to solidify the author's characterization of him as a jerk.

An interesting comparison to Nesaule's portrayal of Joe is Tennessee Williams's rendering of Stanley Kowalski in *A Streetcar Named Desire*. Stanley's actions in the play are worse than Joe's—he strikes his pregnant wife and rapes his sister-in-law Blanche—but he's portrayed with a degree of sympathy that's completely absent from Nesaule's portrait of Joe. The chief difference is that, in Williams's treatment, Stanley's comparative lack of education and his working-class origins and perspective give him some vulnerability. He is intimidated and shamed by Blanche's relative sophistication, and her labeling of him as "bestial" and "ape-like" clearly strikes such a sensitive nerve in him that it sets him on a course of vicious revenge against her (Williams 82–83). Stanley is shown to be made painfully aware, at some level, through Blanche's opinion of him, of his lower status in a society that values education, money, and social mobility.

In contrast to Williams, Nesaule works assiduously to avoid engendering any degree of the reader's sympathy for Joe, his impoverished origins notwithstanding. Though Joe, like Stanley, is shown to be aware of his disadvantaged class status in relation to others, particularly his wife's family, his self-consciousness about it is always overshadowed by his victimizing of Nesaule. For example, when he visits Nesaule's family and we learn through his dialogue about his hard childhood, the context in which he divulges this information places the focus on Joe's minimizing of Nesaule's early traumas and his insults to Nesaule's mother. Nesaule never allows us to see Joe as a vulnerable person. As both a character in and author of her text, Nesaule is too absorbed in her own pain and vindictiveness to acknowledge her husband's vulnerability.

An exaggerated, demonizing portrait of a real person is a risky business, as Janet Malcolm observes: "Reporting ill of another is one of the most difficult and delicate of rhetorical operations; to be persuasive, to leave the reader with an impression of X's badness and of one's own disinterestedness and goodness, requires great skill. One cannot just blurt out ... how awful X is. All this achieves is to arouse the reader's sympathy for X" (*Silent* 48). Moreover, it lacks the ring of truth. A demonizing representation of someone, like Nesaule's of Joe, signals a fundamental dishonesty at work, a militant refusal by the author to grant the represented person a complicated, multifaceted self. This rhetorical problem takes on ethical dimensions when there is a class, and thus power, disparity between the writer and subject. Primitivist discourse by definition renders subordinate people as Other, and it does so by exploiting widespread assumptions that have become powerful enough to "control perceptions of primitives" (Torgovnick 22). The dominant middle-class culture has been conditioned more readily to accept that a man will be aggressive, profane, and threatening if he "grew up in slums" with an "old lady" that "didn't give a shit" and an "old man" who liked his beer.

An essential aspect of primitivist representations of the poor is the denial of their individuality. When the working class or other subordinated segments of a population become associated with or identified as primitives, Torgovnick notes, "these Others are processed, like primitives, through a variety of tropes which see them as a threatening horde, a faceless mass, promiscuous, breeding, inferior — at the farthest edge, exterminatable" (18). Joe's dialogue, and the information he offers about his family, rely so much on stereotypical, and primitive, conceptions of working-class people that Joe and his parents become in this text the faceless, threatening, and inferior poor. This characterization is brought into relief later in the scene mentioned above, at Nesaule's family home, when Joe threatens to "wake Mama and have it out with her." Nesaule and her sister Beate try to calm him, but Joe is a seething brute, "pacing back and forth, flicking ashes carelessly in the direction of the already overfilled ashtray" (194). Though we never see him act physically violent, Nesaule perennially suggests violence churning within him. "[T]he fucking Dragon Lady," he remarks of Nesaule's mother, "she isn't even human. I'm going to put her in her place" (195). It is early morning, but Joe is dismayed that he can't have a drink: "Jesus H. Christ, no beer? No turkey for Thanksgiving, and now no beer. And that bitch driving me to drink."

Carolyn Steedman writes about the traditional thinking among Britain's cultural elite that refuses "a complicated psychology to those living in conditions of material distress " (12) and that has "made solid and concrete [an] absence of psychological individuality — of subjectivity " in working-class lives (10). Among other works, Steedman examines Jeremy Seabrook's *Working-Class Childhood,* quoting a passage — which Steedman regards as typical — in which he argues that the poor lack the leisure to engage in complex relationships or experience "ferocious personal struggles," and she notes that "an analysis like this denies its subjects a particular story, a personal history, except when that story illustrates a general thesis; and it denies the child, and the child who continues to live in the adult it has become, both an unconscious life, and a particular and developing consciousness" (10). In *A Woman in Amber,* Joe is the only working-class figure that remains so, and he is the only main character that is one-dimensional; he has a simple, knowable past, and a simple response to it — anger. In Nesaule's text, the more education and cultural sophistication people have, the more psychologically layered they are rendered, and the more their emotional depths are probed.

This is especially apparent in the manner in which she discloses a person's history. The author grants a complicated selfhood and a complex emotional past, shaped by, in Steedman's words, "a continuing reverberation of pain and loss, absence and desire in childhood," to those like herself — educated Latvians who suffered from war and displacement (10). Compared with which her simplistic depiction of Joe's history, and his uncomplicated relationship to it, appears jarringly incongruous.

With its focus on Nesaule's childhood trauma, one of the book's implied suppositions is that people's behavior should be humanely understood in view of their painful pasts. But the memoir makes a distinction between the kind of personal history that mitigates culpability and warrants compassion, and the kind that serves to support a dismissal of someone's human complexity. For the educated, middle-class people in the text, a harrowing past makes them vulnerable in spite of appearances otherwise, and their disturbing behavior should, the author suggests, be regarded as symptomatic of inner pain. Nesaule urges the reader to peer beneath the ugly surface of some of these people and to empathize with their sorrowful pasts.

For example, the rhetorical purpose of the scene (in chapter 18) depicting a party filled with Latvian immigrants is to illustrate the psychological devastation of war and to draw connections between the Latvians' troubled adult lives and their earlier hardships. In an "author's note" preceding the memoir, Nesaule writes, "I pray for an end to war, and I fervently hope for greater understanding for all its victims. I want tenderness for them long after atrocities end" (viii). The party scene is in effect a plea for sympathy for Latvian "exiles," even those whose pain has made them abusive or violent. For instance, Nesaule strongly implicates a doctor named Laimonis in the "suspicious" and brutal death of his elderly mother, but she precedes this detail with a sad, lengthy story about Laimonis's family's war trauma (223). Even as she assumes that Laimonis beat his mother to death, Nesaule nonetheless diminishes Laimonis's personal responsibility for the crime by attributing Mrs. Klava's murder to "the endless aftermath" of war (223). For being suspected of matricide, Laimonis is treated with remarkable sympathy in Nesaule's portrayal, which asks us to imagine him as a five-year-old boy who witnessed his father's agonizing death and his mother's "constant crying," and as a man who "laughs self-deprecatingly" to "cover the pain" (222–23). (Nesaule may also, at some level, sympathize with his desire to kill his mother.)

Nesaule is initially more exasperated with Uldis, her sister Beate's Latvian-born husband who drank himself into abysmal poverty and an early death; but, along with ample evidence of Uldis's liabilities as a husband, she provides a vivid counternarrative of Uldis's struggles as an immigrant, which transforms her own anger at him into pity. In fact, Nesaule structures the chapter about Uldis to suggest a movement from present to past in search of the deeper truths of Uldis's life, ultimately locating the cause of his failures in the "too many things [that] had happened to him — exile, war, unemployment, humiliation" (268). Through half the chapter, as Nesaule helps her sister clean the apartment in which Uldis died, the author is furious with Uldis's alcoholism and irresponsibility. However,

Nesaule uses a box of Uldis's personal papers as a device with which to unfold the pathetic details of her brother-in-law's history. Going through the mass of rejection letters, Nesaule writes, "I know the ice in my heart is beginning to melt" (263). Filled with compassion, she envisions him "anxious to open each letter, knowing that if there were a job offer, he would have received a telephone call, but hoping" (263). We learn about Uldis's adolescence, the long hours of work in cotton fields in Mississippi and later in meat-packing plants in Indiana, and about his sacrificing of citizenship because his parents begged him to avoid the draft. Nesaule finds herself "crying about the waste, crying about his pain," and she concludes that Uldis was not so unlike Beate, he "only expressed his pain differently": "His self-destructiveness was the dark shadowy mirror image of the compulsively hard work, unvarying cheerfulness and high achievement of so many other Latvians" (263).

Joe has no such nuances, no poignant underside, no unexpected layers. Whenever he speaks, Nesaule gives him dialogue that is always hostile and therefore unconvincing: "Why do you stand in line?" he asks her. "Why do you study all the time? Why do you think you have to tell your scholarship committee if you get a B? Tell them you got all A's. Send them someone else's transcript, just blacken out the name." When Nesaule objects, Joe goes on: "Jesus fucking Christ.... Only a jerk goes by the rules all the time" (191).

Eakin notes that the autobiographical act is "both a re-enactment and an extension of earlier phases of identity formation" (*Fictions* 226). Nesaule makes her plot a quest for a healthy self-identity, and the way she tells her story serves to further delineate and solidify her new identity. The transformation that occurs in the memoir takes the form of the author's mastery of her past; near the very end of the book she describes the successful culmination of her journey: "Gradually the silent oppressive images inside me have become words. The past takes on meaning and shape, loses its power to paralyze, silence and shame" (277). However, just as Joe is made to represent Nesaule's broken relationship with her mother, he also embodies the psychic pain caused by Nesaule's war experiences; thus, the text posits her divorce from Joe as the final, and most essential step in her recovery.

One of the rhetorical and political benefits of primitivist discourse is its silencing of the "primitives" being portrayed, and the consequent malleability of their image and identity. For those writing about the primitive, the "needs of the present determine the value and nature of the primitive. The primitive does what we ask it to do. Voiceless, it lets us speak for it. It is our ventriloquist's dummy — or so we like to think" (Torgovnick

9). Likewise, by attributing to the working-classes a "psychological simplicity," they can be molded to fit into an author's thesis (Steedman 7). By depriving Joe of a separate, realized identity, of an autonomous selfhood, Nesaule is able to make him an abstract extension of herself, a manifestation of her own pain. As she depicts it, her marriage to Joe has no meaning in itself — indeed, it is not a story worth telling, she implies. We see only its very beginning and its very end, and nothing of the twenty-two years in between, which is only, she suggests, an extension of her war trauma. Even when they first meet, she suggests, she isn't genuinely attracted to him, only perversely and neurotically drawn to him because (as we learn near the book's end) of his resemblance to the Mongolian soldiers who terrorized her family:

> I stare at him, and he briefly catches my look before I drop my eyes. I scarcely notice that he would be considered handsome, even desirable. Something about him is so totally familiar that I can barely stop myself from greeting him in recognition. I have never seen him before in my life, and yet I am certain that I have known him or someone like him somewhere before. I cannot place where, and this familiarity is both vaguely unpleasant and compelling [189–90].

The author provides an elaborate psychological rationale for her participation in the courtship and marriage, in which she is unconsciously re-enacting her worst moments in the war through her relationship with Joe. It is not unreasonable to suppose that her post-marital therapy provided her with this explanation. "Dazzled by the intensity of Joe's attention, afraid of his anger, oblivious to his belittling, I sit as if mesmerized, when I should try to escape while there is still time" (192). While she waits for Joe to "grow tired, lose interest, go away," her dreams replay terrifying events from the war: "The drunken soldiers kick over the half-filled bowl of milk for which I have had to beg. Who do I think I am? I should have known I am not worth feeding." It is in this damaged, distorted frame of mind, she implies, that she agrees to date and marry Joe: "I wake with tears streaking my cheeks and determined not to hurt Joe any more by my remoteness and coldness. It would be terrible if Joe were as powerless as my father was, it would be all my fault. It never occurs to me that Joe's situation is in no way parallel to my father's. It is beyond me to consider that I may be the one who has been seized" (193). Ultimately, Nesaule explains her marriage by stating simply that "Deep down I know that I do not deserve any better" (192).

The effect of this representation of her relationship with Joe is to remove the element of her own agency in the marriage. Indeed, the new self-identity that Nesaule constructs and reifies in this memoir is that of a victim, and it is built through her discovery of the extent of her victimization. The epiphany towards which the narrative moves is Nesaule's realization that she has been as much a victim in her marriage as she was in the war. This epiphany, of course, is Nesaule's new awareness, which comes in the chapter she calls "The Second Escape," that Joe and the Mongolian soldiers are one and the same. It is the culmination of many spurious parallels she draws between the war and her marriage.

The locus of the primitive in *A Woman in Amber* is the Mongolian soldiers. Nesaule distinguishes the Mongolians from the rest of the Russian soldiers, making much of their poverty and ignorance and focusing on them as the fiercest source of terror. Nesaule immediately establishes the Mongolians as "peasants for whom mirrors, running water and electricity were new" (72). Interestingly, the information Nesaule offers about them comes from her mother, who "had known people like them during her childhood in Siberia," and Nesaule accepts and relays her mother's perception of Mongolian people as completely Other: "She used to talk about them loving and caressing their horses but striking their women and about their wearing heavy dark clothing during the summer, which they said kept out the heat. Another story she told was about a peasant who kept trying to bring daylight into his windowless hut in a bucket. She knew their language, but otherwise she did not have much in common with them" (72).

Nesaule paints the Mongolians with tropes commonly used for depicting the primitive. They are more animal than human, both savage and childlike; their "masculine traditions encouraged them to rape" but gave them "an unclearly defined respect for mothers" (60). In one scene in chapter 7, when the captive women are gathered in an orphanage building, a throng of soldiers burst through the door: "Mongolians. I would recognize the slanted eyes, the dark glistening skin and the high cheekbones anywhere. They survey the huddled women briefly, then stare at the orphan girls." Ready to rape and brutalize, the soldiers are "miraculously" stopped by a woman suddenly playing the piano. "Startled, the soldiers turn towards her. They have not expected this.... They stand frozen in the middle of the room, listening to the music." Like beasts, the soldiers are "mesmerized" by the melody, and they force the women to keep playing: "a soldier grasps the tired woman's elbow and jams her fingers back on the keys; he looks angry at the discordant chords" (75). Through her portrayal of the Mongolians, Nesaule proffers the fallacies that entire classes of people can be evil, and that evil can be identified with physical appearance. In this text, the physical features of the Mongolians become a metonym for the horrors of the war, and for evil itself. An illustration of this is when

Nesaule, describing the suicide of Hilda, a young woman repeatedly raped by the soldiers and made pregnant, envisions "the fetus clamped onto her frame, his cruel Mongolian eyes narrowed even further ... sucking nourishment out of her, pulling her downwards, strangling her" (92).

The author's association of savagery with the Mongolians' facial features becomes a strategy for superimposing the cruelty and violence of the soldiers onto the character of Joe, by revealing Joe's physical resemblance to them. As is mentioned above, Nesaule entitles the chapter in which she leaves Joe "The Second Escape," and she frames her marital separation as a final escape from the Mongolian soldiers of the war. Her recognition that Joe "has come to remind me of the Mongolian soldiers" comes in the form of a dream — the source of which, "a meaningful benign world," is likened to God. In the dream "a Mongolian soldier is viciously whipping a glossy pregnant mare.... His dark skin glistens, his slanted eyes above his high cheekbones are cruel, his thin lips are determined" (246). The message of the terrifying dream is that "you have to fight for yourself ... you must break free and run, you have to save yourself. No one else can do it for you" (246). On waking, the Mongolian soldier still "imprinted on [her] eyelids," Nesaule looks at the picture of Joe on her nightstand and the connection is made: Joe's face "has a willful vitality. His black eyes are alive above his high cheekbones, his dark skin is glossy, his narrow lips are decisive, self-assured, a little contemptuous" (248). Seeing these features in light of the dream, Nesaule has a "breath-catching" realization:

> Why have I never identified the familiarity I sensed when I first met him? How can I have failed to place him? Why have I not named the impassive cruelty of his slanted eyes? Why have I never used the word Slavic in describing Joe's high cheekbones? Looking out of the frame is Joe, but also the Russian soldiers of my childhood as well as the Mongolian soldier of my dream. The similarity is so undeniable that anyone else would see it immediately [248].

The epiphany, the new interpretation of her marriage as nothing more than a pathological continuation of the war, and her husband as the unmistakable enemy, is her key to freedom: "It is frightening but very exciting. I know I have been given a miraculous vision that I must use" (248). Nesaule's indecisiveness about ending a marriage despite her husband's pleas to save it vanishes with this new interpretation of him. Immediately after the dream she packs a suitcase and leaves her home for good, a move that the reader is meant to view as an unqualified victory of good over evil, a triumph of the oppressed over the oppressor. Another dream in which a complex, troubled relationship becomes suddenly and too neatly resolved.

4. Agate Nesaule's A Woman in Amber

Nesaule's resolve, however, comes at great expense to Joe as a figure in the text. His face, indeed his self, loses its individuality and its autonomous meaning. Joe's reality as a separate human being is obliterated as he is transformed into an abstract extension of her past. The marriage is reduced to a prolonged psychological exercise in Nesaule's coming to terms with her past; thus her marriage is handily summarized: "Did I need to live with him for twenty-two years in order to exorcise the soldiers?" (248). The passage relating the dream, the conflation of Joe with the soldiers, and her decision to separate, has symbolic force, and it illustrates on a small scale what the text as a whole is doing. Significantly, Joe's physical resemblance to the soldiers literally brackets his portrait. From the time Nesaule first meets him, Joe is represented in the light of Nesaule's later insight that he is a stand-in for the Mongolian soldiers: "He is tall and dark, his brown eyes intense above his high cheekbones. Only the too-narrow lips, pursed in a determined, almost spiteful way, keep his face from being handsome." Joe is never allowed a meaningful reality that is separate from Nesaule's, and in the book's scheme, discarding Joe is as morally justified as exorcizing the violent, raping soldiers. In this text, healing for Nesaule comes in part through the author's narcissistic interpretation of another person.

The memoir's problematic portrait of Joe reaches a troubling climax in the scene in which Joe attempts to rape Nesaule. On one hand, the scene appears to demonstrate the first true sign of malice in Joe: he aggressively and forcefully pursues sex with her. On the other hand, the scene exposes the depth and seriousness of the flaws in Nesaule's narrative, and the extent to which they imperil the author's credibility. By this point in the text, the reader is not only wary of Nesaule's perceptions of Joe, but is resistant to them as well. The reader comes to view the author as so invested in rendering Joe as an unmitigated villain and herself as a victim as to be somewhat unreliable as a narrator when it comes to her marriage. No reader wants to be in the position of resisting a woman's perception that a man would have raped her given the chance. But Nesaule's exaggerated and clearly agenda-driven portrait of Joe places her interpretation of his actions in some doubt.

Nesaule's account is, in fact, persuasive in describing Joe as trying to overpower her physically. She experiences at least a few moments of real fear:

> But he grabbed me harder than he ever had before. His fingers pressed into the soft flesh of my arms as he tried to force apart my hands. When that failed, he straddled me, digging his knee between my legs, trying to straighten my body, prying apart my limbs to get me to unclench and to pin me firmly under him [236].

She appears to have no doubt that what is happening to her is an attempt to rape: "For an instant I thought I could passively outwait even this. After all, what did it really matter if he raped me? So many women had been raped, it was hardly worth remarking on" (236).

And yet, the context of this incident, what is said and done before and after their physical struggle — which ends when Nesaule manages "to wriggle free of him and then to push him aside" (if his intention was rape, he might have persisted) — makes the accuracy of the term "rape" awash in gray. Nesaule describes the scene leading up to Joe's lunge at her as one that is "so dreadfully familiar. We had made our way through scenes like this a hundred times in our twenty-two-year-old marriage" (235). Apparently, the two have an established pattern, a long-rehearsed dance in which a fight ends with a physical, if not sexual, re-connection. Joe, coming home late after work, "would get into bed groaning and turn out the light," then try to make conversation with Nesaule, who feigns sleep: "Then he would lean over me and ask, 'Are you asleep? Come on, I know fucking well you're not. You're just pretending.' I would keep my eyes resolutely shut while he studied my face" (234). Often Joe gives up and goes to sleep himself, but this time he pushes, refusing to be ignored. Though Joe's dialogue here is characteristically obnoxious — "Might as well be drunk all the time, there's never any sex around here anyway. You're a cold bitch, just like your mother" — the subtext of his talk is his escalating frustration at his wife's remoteness: "Aren't you listening to me? Say something to me, for chrissakes…. Can't you talk to me for once in your life?" (235).

Joe's aggression with Nesaule on this particular evening occurs when she disrupts their ritual; Joe's coarse entreating and her aloofness usually dissolve with Nesaule making a physical gesture of reconciliation: "I would wait until I sensed that he was ready to quit. Then, filled with pity for his pain, I would reach over, comfort him, tuck him in" (235). This time, however, Nesaule is determined to break their cycle: "I should do that now," she writes. "But if I touched him, nothing would ever change" (235). This refusal to touch Joe is reminiscent, of course, of the moment in chapter 15 when, after announcing that she won the college scholarship, Nesaule refuses to enter her mother's arms. The parallel is significant because it underscores a tendency in Nesaule to withhold affection when she senses the other person is particularly needy for it. The scholarship win was, after all, a big triumph for Valda and a major milestone in her life, representing the fulfillment of her dreams and her sacrifices for her daughters. Nesaule's refusal to embrace her beckoning mother seems a deliberate refusal to acknowledge her mother's role in the achievement. It is possible, then, that Nesaule has unconsciously chosen a particular opportunity

4. Agate Nesaule's A Woman in Amber

to break the pattern of making-up with Joe, a moment when he may be more likely to react explosively. At any rate, although Joe's use of force on his wife is inexcusable, his manhandling of her can be seen as part of the push-and-pull nature of their routine marital dynamic. He, for his part, interprets their struggle as a normal expression of their passionate relationship: "'Come on, we wouldn't fight like this if we weren't in love. Admit it'" (237).

Nesaule's memoir raises heretofore overlooked questions about the ethics of writing about a failed marriage. When an autobiographer writes about a still-viable marriage, the interests of the relationship place certain boundaries on the material divulged and influence the presentation of that material. As Louis A. Renza notes, an autobiographer's "references to his past are subordinate to ... a narrative essentially representing the writer's present self-identity as seen also in the light of his future" (271). For example, when Russell Baker relates the story of his long and conflicted courtship with Mimi, the fact that Mimi has been his wife for decades is evident in his loving and respectful portrait of her. In fact, he presents himself during their romance as something of a cad, emphasizing his own fickleness and Mimi's steadfast affection.

In contrast, Nesaule takes upon herself the task of explaining and even justifying her divorce from Joe. However, rather than exploring the guilt over her divorce, which she admits feeling near the beginning of her text, and instead of venturing to examine the myriad ambiguities and shifting roles that characterize any long marriage, Nesaule forces the entire relationship into a Procrustean thesis. Early in the memoir Nesaule telegraphs the rhetorical strategy she will employ to contain her marriage and her guilt about its demise. Introducing the scene with her therapist, Nesaule writes: "I am talking to Ingeborg Casey, the therapist I have been seeing for help with my divorce, which I believe is my real problem" (23). The language suggests the direction the memoir will take: her experiences in the war are the real problem, and her marriage and divorce are relatively immaterial. Ingeborg's presence at the launch of Nesaule's narrative, and Nesaule's implication that the memoir springs from a session with Ingeborg, subtly suggest Ingeborg's imprimatur on Nesaule's interpretation of her life. Ingeborg, Nesaule implies, agrees that Nesaule's childhood, rather than her marriage, is the story that matters.

The realization of her status as a victim of war, so important for her healing, becomes the lens through which she processes her marriage to Joe. Paradoxically, this heightened awareness of one facet of her life appears to occlude her vision of another: the reification of her identity as a war victim steers her away from examining her participation in her marriage. For, however difficult a person Joe may be, does Nesaule bear no responsibility for a painful, unhealthy marriage? She doesn't seem to realize that all of her childhood trauma probably made her difficult to live with, emotionally ungenerous, and so on. Interestingly, Nesaule does accept a small measure of culpability, but only in regard to hurting herself. In chapter 19, after recounting the dream that catalyzes her divorce, she relates yet another insight gleaned from the dream: "I am not only the victim. I am also the one who has silenced myself, who has mercilessly forced myself to wait here in silent misery, in Joe's house, for much longer than I had to. I am the one who has cruelly reined myself in. I have imprisoned myself, I myself have constricted my life. I have sealed myself into amber" (249).

And yet, doesn't that very admission hold implications for Joe's experience of the marriage? By her own account, Nesaule was extremely alienated from her emotions until she was well into her forties; throughout her marriage she was plagued by "sleeplessness, anxiety, depressions and suicidal thoughts," which she attributes to her inability "to talk about my wartime experiences" (213). It was only the war stories of others "that saved me from suicide, because they gave me a harmless way to try to exorcise the past" (213). Nevertheless, Nesaule is resolute in her lack of reflection about how her emotional stuntedness and almost complete lack of self-knowledge may have affected Joe. Psychology research over the past twenty years has made the importance of emotional intelligence in relating to others a commonplace insight. Gabriele Lusser Rico makes the point succinctly: "Expressed, emotions lead to healing, to wholeness, to major shifts in our understanding of ourselves and others. Denied, they make us emotionally dull and unresponsive, as incapable of genuine affection as we are of honest anger" (204). A lack of understanding of our own emotions makes a person "incapable of genuine affection," and, as Howard Gardner notes, impairs one's ability to empathize with someone else. The "*intra*personal intelligence reflects an inward movement into the self in order to discriminate between emotional states and to apply this understanding to one's life." Building on this, "the *inter*personal intelligence moves outward from the self to embrace the perspectives of others, enabling us to be responsive to their personalities: their moods, desires, and intentions" (qtd in Rico, 201).

That Nesaule was "sealed in amber" for the duration of her marriage suggests her limitations as a wife. Though she acknowledges that she "inflicted [her] sadness" on her son Boris, the author avoids an honest exploration of her own shortcomings as a spouse. A fragment of Joe's dialogue, however, which follows his physical struggle with Nesaule, offers a clue to what his experience of the marriage might have been like: "The

4. Agate Nesaule's A Woman in Amber

least you could do," he tells her, "is to act cheerful and take care of me once in a while" (237). This comment is ignored by Nesaule, who, as a character in the scene, responds by telling Joe that she doesn't love him, a confession that floods her with "immense relief" (237). The exchange typifies the relationship between Joe as a character and Nesaule as the author, with Nesaule disregarding any meaning in Joe's dialogue and focusing only on her own feelings. Indeed, one subversive aspect of the text is the fact that Joe's observations, however harshly expressed, are often accurate concerning Nesaule's behavior. Nesaule tries to make him one-dimensional by portraying all of his dialogue as crude and excessive, but when his words are taken out of her context, they frequently tell the truth about Nesaule: she *is* passive, concerned overly with what others think of her, emotionally cold, and so on. Further, by the end of the memoir it becomes apparent that even Joe's excessiveness in his dialogue has meaning: he is often trying to get a reaction out of her, if only a negative one.

The point of my analysis is not, however, to take sides in the author's marriage, but to extract from her account a larger, unpleasant truth about autobiographies that tell on spouses: the privilege of interpreting the marriage goes to the person who, in Annie Dillard's phrase, "has access to a printing press" (70). This is an obvious point, but it unfolds a complicated reality about the nature of "truth" offered by any writer about a spouse who lacks the ability to tell his or her own version of the story. A marital relationship in itself raises special ethical issues for autobiography. In such a relationship, for example, there is the ultimate claim of intimacy by the author, and the ultimate loss of privacy for the spouse. Further, the writer has the implicit authority to pronounce on the character of a long-term spouse. The stakes are raised considerably, however, when the writer-spouse relationship is inflected by class difference. For, when an autobiographer such as Nesaule writes about her working-class husband, from the outset she has an extra advantage: the dominant culture for whom she writes shares her own, rather than her husband's, social-class perspective. As Carolyn Steedman observes, the delineation of normative "emotional and psychological selfhood has been made by and through the testimony of people in a central relationship to the dominant culture, that is to say by and through people who are not working class" (11).

Nesaule, for example, counts on her audience identifying with her upper-middle-class values and tastes, and she uses Joe's working-class sensibilities to strengthen her case against him. Nesaule's likely audience, as she well knows, is comprised largely of women, academics, and otherwise liberal and literate readers. Joe's speeches appear designed to alienate such readers, such as when he remarks to his wife that "I could get a piece of ass anytime I want to, the bar is full of women just asking for it. But you, you don't give a flying fuck. Poisoned by feminism" (235). Gratuitously we learn that Joe hates "goddamn environmentalists," "high-flying phony academics," and even "goddamn animal rights activists" (235). Nesaule overdoes it, but the effect remains: for all of his loud talk in the memoir, Joe as a human being is silenced.

One passage near the end of the memoir illustrates the way that class, marital discord, and the power of interpretation intersect in Nesaule's text. The story of Nesaule acquiring a container of Latvian soil is told within the story of how and why Nesaule leaves Joe, and as often happens in autobiography, this vignette, this detour in the narrative, offers an alternative, and, perhaps, truer, version of the larger narrative in which it is enclosed. It is a mini-drama about class, in which the author holds up for comparison her husband, whose blue-collar tastes prove socially embarrassing, and her fellow professor, an enlightened, sensitive man with whom she really connects.

It is during a dinner party with colleagues that Nesaule asks Jim Leaver for some soil from Latvia; Jim is portrayed sympathetically, even romantically, because he appreciates the meaning of, and grants, her request: "I looked down the long dinner table and really saw him for the first time. His eyes were kind, his expression attentive and calm." The other guests understand her, too: "Next to him, Rose Mary, his wife and my good friend, smiled warmly. No one else was laughing either. They seemed interested, even encouraging" (242). All of which sets up the predictable reaction from Joe, which comes later when they're alone:

> Jesus, what a ridiculous thing to ask for. You've made yourself into a real joke this time. Dirt, for chrissakes, dirt. You should have asked for something real, some Russian caviar or vodka or even some amber jewelry. There's a chance you'd actually get those. But dirt. You might as well go piss up a rope [242].

The contrast between Jim and Joe gets played out melodramatically, with Jim taking the hero's role: he "brought the soil, just as he promised," calling it "an adventure" he wouldn't have missed, and adding to Nesaule, "And I knew it was important to you" (242). As usual, Joe is the foil to Nesaule's self-validation: "Important? Oh yeah ... ask her about her childhood in war-torn Europe.... Boo hoo."

The intended message of the story is all too transparent and hamhanded: Joe's belittling keeps Nesaule from being her true self, while Jim's supportiveness enables her to realize a fuller identity in which her Latvian heritage is affirmed. On another level, the story reinforces a truth about the author that has emerged over the course of the text: her militant resistance to any feedback about herself that doesn't nurture her self-importance as a victim. Joe's mocking of her request for dirt is his indelicate way of accusing her of romanticizing her past and using it to make people see her as a martyr or heroine. But, as in the text as a whole, Nesaule trumps Joe's puncturing of her self-romanticization with class superiority. For the three-way conversation doesn't end with Joe's "Boo hoo," routine. Nesaule goes on to show Joe being put in his place, then subtly belittled himself, by Jim Leaver:

> Jim ignored him. "Now if I could never return to America, I wonder what I would want for someone to bring me?"
> "Yeah, a McDonald's hamburger and a bottle of Jim Beam, huh?"
> "No," he continued calmly. "I might ask for sand, though I doubt it. Maybe something from Arizona, some mesquite or sweet grass, perhaps, it would be hard to decide" [243].

The soil story captures the author's identity in transition; Nesaule is in the process of shedding a bond of relational identity with Joe and aligning herself with the values and tastes of the Jim Leavers of the world. The last exchange demonstrates the new self-identity that Nesaule is reifying in her text: her language shows her approval of Jim and his dismissal of Joe. The exclusion — and humiliation — of Joe is done with Jamesian delicacy, but it is justified on the grounds of class difference (which Nesaule underlines by adding "yeah" and "huh" to Joe's dialogue). Not incidentally, the value-system being endorsed here mirrors that of Nesaule's mother, in which intelligence, good breeding, and refinement are more important than a merciful tolerance of others. Nesaule's implicit but clear support of Jim Leaver echoes her support two decades earlier of her mother's snobbish rejection of Joe. When she and Joe are about to break the news of their elopement, he complains that her parents have "made up their minds not to like me, just because I'm an American." Nesaule also knows they won't like Joe, but, she implies, it's for more reasonable cause: "If Joe's being an American were the issue, I too could be energized by indignation. But I cannot hope to explain my mother's absolute contempt for Joe without hurting him further" (199). Soon after we learn the reasons for Valda's contempt, of which Nesaule is aware: "'He isn't any good,' she says about Joe, 'he's not a real American. He's the worst America has to offer. Hostile, manipulative, crude. He's not nearly intelligent enough for you. And you're from a much better family. He'll never understand our history. He's too limited to value you'" (202).

The soil story is metaphorical for the text as a whole. We're meant to like and to trust Jim Leaver because he affirms the importance of Nesaule's

Latvian past, because he is sympathetic to her perspective in general, and because he is tasteful and sensitive. But the sympathy of the reader is encouraged to be skewed, to be directed toward Nesaule, and away from Joe. Meanwhile, Joe is marginalized because he doesn't fit into Nesaule's professional world and social class. And, in this story as in the text at large, Nesaule's ethnic identity and her past are validated at the cost of diminishing and "ignoring" Joe. Indeed, the reader is meant to feel gratified when Jim Leaver subtly affirms the truth of Nesaule's mother's "prophesy" about Joe. Elizabeth Bruss contends that:

> the assumptions the autobiographer makes about the nature of his audience also come under the scrutiny of that audience. From the way an author imagines and manipulates his readers, we are allowed to draw inferences about his mode of interaction with others. Identity is composed not only by acts of self-perception but by other-perception as well [13].

Nesaule's representation of her husband may be most revealing as a portrait of the author herself.

5

"My Folks and Their Country Culture": Inventing Authenticity in Bobbie Ann Mason's *Clear Springs*

Carolyn Barros stresses the "centrality of transformation" in autobiography, and argues for reading autobiography "as narrative of transformation": "The what happened is 'I have changed.' The elements of that change, in the very simplest of terms, are the *who* of the change; the *type* or kind of change; and the *motive force* or cause to which the change is attributed" (3, 10). There are, of course, a multitude of changes that occur over a person's lifetime. In order to have a coherent theme, a writer must choose one transformation on which to center his autobiography. That choice in itself is revealing. What purchase does a writer get from his choice of "before and after" portraits? Bobbie Ann Mason's memoir is explicitly centered on one transformation, or series of changes, while other seemingly significant changes are merely embedded in the text, plainly in evidence but neither emphasized nor addressed by the author. This strategic emphasis — and avoidance — is part of the author's construction of an identity.

Bobbie Ann Mason's memoir traces a dramatic transformation of the author's self: from being a farm girl to a doctorate-holding, renowned author. It narrates her journey from a childhood in western Kentucky, into "the wide world"—college, New York City, and graduate school — and finally, eventually, back to her home state (14). Her extensive education, her long struggle "to become sophisticated" (xi), and her (belated) discovery of her family and their rural culture as her "true sources" of fiction material, eventually lead Mason to become a respected writer, one whose novel, *In Country*, would be filmed on location in her hometown, with celebrities as its stars (177).

Yet, the transformation of self around which Mason structures her autobiography is not the profound difference between her parents and herself that is created by that journey, but rather her disillusionment with the North, and her discovery that "the deepest part of my being" is comprised of "my folks and their country culture"; in short, her re-invention of herself as a "country" southerner (xi). Barros uses the term *figura* to denote "the image or metaphor for the type of change described in the autobiography. As the mode of explanation, it figures or suggests the dominant interpretative strategy of the autobiographer's change in the narrative" (13). Figura "identifies [the] transformation in a term or phrase that accommodates the many twists and turns, complexities, contraries, and contradictions of a life inscribed. While terms like *plot* or *action* only deal with events in the story line, *figura* assumes the narrating situation, the was and is configurations of the persona, and the motive for the transformation" (13).

Mason suggests one figura for her memoir: the circular journey. At the end of her first chapter, she summarizes the arc of the story that follows: "It has been a long journey from our little house into the wide world, and after that a long journey back home" (14). The "was" of her self-portrait is her younger self who, "mesmerized, churned up by popular songs and Hollywood images that filled me with longing," sought identity and meaning elsewhere, only to discover that these were to be found in "the very resources I had left behind" (x). This is a familiar discovery, of both sentimental fiction and ethnic autobiography; it's also claimed, as seen in earlier chapters, by Wideman and, less explicitly, by Nesaule.

Thus Mason stresses the change of heart that leads her to return home rather than the changes that have set her profoundly and irretrievably apart from her family. In truth, of course, Mason's reference to her "journey back home" is a vast oversimplification, and overstatement, of her renewed identification with her family; even her literal return to Kentucky is partial: "I realized that without even considering it, I had chosen not to go all the way home. The land we bought was a long way from Mayfield. I had to keep some distance, keep my options open" (183).

This chapter examines Mason's re-invention of herself as a "country" southerner as a disingenuous construct that Mason employs as a way of avoiding a more complicated, and honest, exploration of her radical change in social class and the deep differences her advanced education and professional success have created between herself and her parents. Mason's memoir illustrates a bind inherent to writing a literary memoir about one's working-class family. How does an autobiographer validate — and celebrate — her parents' life and at the same time explain how and why she chose a vastly different life? How do you write about a way of life you left without making it seem inferior? This chapter explores the various strategies Mason uses to "resolve" this dilemma, as well as the rhetorical and ethical problems that these strategies in turn create for the text.

Mason's chief strategy is to construct disparate cultural spheres, the world of her rural family and the "wide world" outside of it; the discussion will seek to show that the author uses this dichotomizing approach to delineate a liminal self-identity of one who is an insider of one world, yet possesses the detachment and authority of the dominant culture. Mason reconciles her identity as an author with her need to identify with her parents and their rural culture by positioning herself as a kind of ethnographer who records and textualizes a way of life that is both "other" and more "real" than middle-class suburban or urban American life. In Barros's approach, analyzing an autobiography's figure includes a close examination of the context in which the transformation occurs. A backdrop of loss pervades the narrative of *Clear Springs:* the death of Mason's father, the looming mortality of her mother, and the inexorable passing of farm life and the family farm itself. Mason's spiritual journey homeward, as well as her textualization of her family's culture, become strategies against those losses. Consequently, as autobiographer Mason often adopts the nostalgic pose that James Clifford finds common to early-twentieth-century ethnographic practice, which enacts what he calls the "allegory of salvage" ("Ethnographic" 112). Fieldworkers of that era saw themselves as preserving the "otherness" of vanishing cultures lost to industrialization: "The other is lost, in disintegrating time and place, but saved in the text" (112).

As part of her dichotomizing strategy, Mason portrays her bucolic origins as authentic, centering on her mother as the representative of this authenticity. It's a way of valorizing Mama's otherwise unremarkable life, and a way of validating Mason's own role as spokesperson/ethnographer of this "other" world. Mason romanticizes Mama and the rural South, sparing both the kind of clear-eyed, analytical treatment she brings to her fictional portrayals of southerners. Thus, this discussion will examine the ethical issues created when an autobiographer's self-identity relies upon sustaining his or her family's exotic "otherness."

Mason's interpretive strategy allows her to align herself with her family and their world, to write autobiography as an act of solidarity with people she has in many ways left behind, and yet at the same time to convey the costs to her family and herself— albeit through "coded imagery"— of her social mobility (Stone, *Autobiographical* 14). I will demonstrate that Mason's construct of an external, dominating force of urban sophistication, in forms ranging from the "chicken tower" facing the farm to the film crew that steals family photographs, often serves in the text as a stand-in for her own relationship with her family, and the vast disparity of power therein.

North versus South

Earlier I said that one figura for Mason's narrative is the circular journey. However, a perhaps more precise figura for *Clear Springs* is suggested by a metaphorical story in the middle of the memoir that proves to be a turning point for the narrator: a failed seduction. The poet Robert Hazel, Mason's writing professor at college in Kentucky and later her literary mentor in New York City (he coincidentally takes a new job in New York when Mason is living there), becomes a figure in the text who embodies the allure of the North for Mason, as well as her fantasies about a bohemian literary life. Her idolizing of him and her embrace of his literary vision are passionate but temporary, and her disillusionment with him coincides with the end of her infatuation with urban sophistication. To Mason when she was his student, Robert Hazel was "a seductive personality, an engaging man" with "brooding, handsome" looks; he "embodied the glamour of the writing life" (116). When Mason's relationship with him is nearing an end, however, and she's beginning to grasp his shallowness, his dazzling manner is "beginning to fade, like a worn-out couch" (132). Though she had previously admired him, she is appalled when, after she has graduated from college and is living in New York, he asks her to be his "mistress" (136). We now see his "boozy complexion," and she offers an unflattering glimpse of Hazel at dinner eating "sloppily, drunkenly" (136). That Mason makes a tawdry, would-be seducer the key figure in her soured love-affair with New York resonates with meaning. She goes from idealizing him to being repulsed by his pretensions and his condescending attitude toward her origins.

The drama of infatuation and disillusionment is the central pattern of what Mason now calls the "nightmare" of her journey north (177). Throughout her childhood, beginning with her first introduction to the Yankees in her Little Colonel books, Mason develops an intense admiration for all things northern. Though taught to have a dim view of northerners, "secretly I was attracted to them. They were mysterious and foreign. They spoke a different language, rough and superior. And they were the winners" (72). She traces the many influences by which the North, and New York City in particular, "burned its authority in my brain" (116). And the North becomes inseparable from her intellectual and literary ambitions, a notion that is reinforced by the advice of Hazel — when Mason is a college student in Kentucky — to "Get out of this backwater Podunk" (116).

In the section of the book that covers Mason's time up north, she narrates a process of "trying to get over my culture" (155). However, her account makes her return south just as plainly inevitable. It's clear in these chapters that the Mason who is narrating her past no longer renounces the South, but instead, now renounces her former reverence of Yankees as "superior" and "the winners." The northerners she encounters don't fare well in her rendition of her "nightmare journey." In these chapters, Mason ironically contrasts her naive glamorization of the North with depictions of people who, like Robert Hazel, prove unworthy of her desire for their acceptance. And in her text Mason treats virtually all the northerners as she does Hazel, deconstructing their "glamour" and painting them as the antithesis of what she now values.

All of the relationships with northerners she recalls for the reader conform to a pattern in which Mason's admiration is repaid with belittling, berating, and rejection. The exception is her future husband, Roger, who, she stresses, isn't "truly a Yankee" (155). Hazel, a professor eighteen years older than she, abuses her need for a role model and guide by crudely propositioning her, even when she is still his undergraduate student. But he also, as she depicts it, seeks to make her ashamed of her family. She implies that he urges her to make a choice between being a writer and being loyal to the people back home. "You'll have to resist sentimentalizing 'good country people' if you're really going to be a writer," he tells her. "They're too nice. You need to get tough" (137). Determined to keep Hazel a symbol of the villainous North, Mason doesn't acknowledge the wisdom of Hazel's advice here (inspired, no doubt, by Flannery O'Connor's acidic and ironically titled story), but instead interprets his words to mean that decent country people like her parents aren't interesting enough to write about.

In the two "defining episodes" of her postgraduate career, Mason portrays herself as believing "wholeheartedly in my own inferiority," and being "treated ... accordingly, like a wadded-up dishrag" (146). As with Robert Hazel, Mason interprets her first boyfriend, Larry, as imposing his seemingly-sophisticated taste and his version of authenticity on her, and as disparaging her more simple and utilitarian taste. Like Hazel, Larry "was an artist, passionate about what was tasteful and genuine." Larry, too, is a snob, and he shares Hazel's "little mean streak" (136): "When he scoffed at the curtains I'd bought at a discount place, I saw instantly, through his eyes, that they were inauthentic, like something in Lucy Ricardo's kitchen. The design was tasteless, the colors too loud" (147).

Mason's reference to Lucy Ricardo is revealing. Apparently meant to illustrate just how vulgar her curtains looked in light of Larry's opinion, Mason's comparison of herself with Lucy nonetheless positions her as the heroine — lovable, sympathetic — in the situation. This is the role for herself the author cultivates throughout her narrative of her time in the North.

On a whim, Larry drops her casserole dish from her balcony; using language that frames the shattered dish as an extension of herself, Mason writes that Larry's act makes her feel that "I deserved to have such an inferior dish broken, even though it was hard-earned and very useful" (147–48). While Mason presents Hazel and Larry, not to mention other northerners in the memoir, as being unfairly critical of her values, it must be said that her depictions of these men are designed to make the reader invariably and immediately critical of *their* values. Because they are one-sided portraits informed by her North versus South agenda, they are not entirely reliable. When Mason shows Larry a quilt made by her grandmother, a "simple creation with its five-point stars, pieced from the print dresses I had worn as a child," Larry pronounces it "'Ugly!'" (147). Larry's snobbery, as Mason frames it, bullies Mason into seeing her family and their culture in a new and harsher light, confirming her sense of inferiority: "Of course I could see, now that he mentioned it, how crude and primitive it was. Granny hadn't been to art school. I had so much to learn" (147). Mason is being ironic, but she is also unfairly blaming him for his reaction to her quilt. The widespread appreciation of quilts and other domestic arts was a cultural trend yet to happen, even in the South.

In the second such episode of this period, two fellow students, John and Carolyn, whom Mason admires "exceedingly," break off their friendship with her (148). Like Hazel and Larry, John and Carolyn are portrayed as arrogant, cruel, and domineering, with a superficial disgust for unadorned simplicity. As the couple are delivering their rebuff, Mason shows Carolyn "casting a disdainful eye around my nondescript apartment" (148). In this instance of rejection, also, the northerners' mistreatment of Mason is echoed in their disregard for her homemade things: they "marched onto my hooked rug in their snowy boots" (148). As Mason renders it, she is never rejected as an individual but as a representative of her native region and of homespun values.

In Mason's depiction of her experiences up north, she persistently portrays herself as passive, feminized, and victimized, while the northerners are "cruel," "mean," "smug," and "shallow." In all these relationships, Mason perceives that her culture is under attack. Larry, in breaking her dish, she believes, was "testing me, cruelly and deliberately," trying to provoke her into a northern-style display of anger: "I realized later that I was supposed to get angry, show some fire. I was supposed to be real, authentic. But Southern girls aren't taught to be real. I had learned modesty and submissiveness, the veneer of my rebellious streak" (148). Mason likewise frames John and Carolyn's rejection of her as a cultural misunderstanding. When they accuse her of not "being honest," she tries "to explain how Southerners expressed themselves differently" (149).

There were undoubtedly cultural differences between herself and John and Carolyn that led to their break with her, and Mason's insight into southerners' less-direct style of communication rings true. One implicit theme of *Clear Springs* is the conflict between Mason's subtle way of expressing herself and the northerners' crude (as she portrays it) habit of misreading her by seeing only the obvious. In these different cultural styles, Mason persistently reads the boorish North as victimizing the passive South, failing to consider, for example, how frustrating indirect, "devious" forms of self-expression can be for the other person (149). Like Wideman and Nesaule, Mason sometimes uses her cultural roots to excuse personal limitations.

Even before Mason's unpleasant involvements with her fellow students as a new graduate student in upstate New York, Mason is in the throes of culture shock, as well as facing steep academic challenges for which she is under-prepared: "There I was, in the North—disoriented, out of my element, but determined to plow through" (144). But "the Northern intellectual climate" is not merely different but oppressive, the Yankees hostile to her southernness and seemingly trying to intimidate her out of herself: "All around me were Yankees, the foreigners of the Little Colonel books. If they noticed me at all, they gazed at me penetratingly, pinning me on the spot as if I were a specimen of bug. My accent betrayed me" (145). Mason places the entire burden of her culture shock on the North-South difference, when surely some of her discomfort was due to her class background. She is "expected" to perform as a scholar, she writes, the practice of which she mildly derides as pursuing "elusive and false trails," and to do it "all with a Northern accent" (144).

Mason's descriptions of her life as a graduate student in New England are interspersed with information about her family's life during this time, and the two worlds could not be more different. Mason is teaching Plato; meanwhile, her mother "wrote me about the garden and the weather and broken machinery" (149). Yet Mason doesn't elaborate on the radical chasm in social class that is being created between herself and her parents during this period. Instead, she persistently focuses her narrative on the cultural gap between herself and the northerners around her. At one point in Mason's account of her decade up north, she writes, "I was in alien territory and there was a war on" (145).

Mason's description of the cultural "war" between herself and the "alien" northerners seems magnified beyond credibility. It may have *seemed* to the young Bobbie Ann that the northerners around her would "gaze at [her] penetratingly" and be so hostile to her accent, but it's hard to believe that she was persecuted for her southernness to the extent she claims. It's more likely that Mason transforms conflicts within herself during this period, which she never fully explores, into her characterizations of Robert Hazel, Larry, the professors in New York, and the North in general. All of them represent the double-bind in which Mason, Wideman, and many working-class young people feel trapped, when their ambitions seem to require a shedding of their original class, ethnic, or regional identity. At one point Mason identifies this bind when she describes the last months of her year in New York City: "I had been feeling that my job and my ambition and my background were all a jarring and jerky mix, like Mondrian's *Broadway Boogie-Woogie*" (136).

In a manner similar to Wideman's, Mason externalizes her inward conflicts and focuses on the pressure she perceives others placing on her to renounce her background, though in truth even that pressure really comes from herself. Wideman writes of being "urged ... to bury my past" by "nearly everyone important in the white university environment" (227). Similarly, just after comparing her identity confusion to a Mondrian, Mason describes her mentor's condescending, and contradictory, attitude towards working-class people like her family: "At my job [writing for a movie fan magazine] I was exploiting people who romanticized the movies, but Bob Hazel exalted the very kind of people who loved the movies and TV—farm folks, laborers, working people—while condemning what they felt. My parents were at home watching *Gunsmoke*. Bob Hazel would have sneered" (136). Indeed, the author's recognition of her own conflicted self is couched within, and overshadowed by, the passage that derides a drunken Hazel and his advice about "good country people" (137).

Mason portrays herself as a young woman who believes that in order to become successful in the mainstream culture she has to become a Northern sophisticate. Her childhood perception of the Yankees as "the winners" is reminiscent of the teenage Wideman's view of whites: "Who the Saints, the rulers of the earth were, was clear" (Wideman 27). Both Wideman and Mason determine early in life to emulate the dominant culture, which both also perceive as oppressive to their own people. This dilemma, of course, pits the individual against his or her own family and community. In *Brothers and Keepers*, as part of his plea for Robby's forgiveness for his "betrayal" of blacks, Wideman confronts his own youthful desire to leave his family and his own "blackness" behind since he believed that being black was synonymous with social powerlessness.

But Wideman and Mason diverge in their memoirs in a subtle but crucial aspect. In a passage of almost searing honesty, Wideman describes a time when he was so insecure about his status in the university culture that he felt ashamed of his family; and he feared that any intimacy with his relatives would prevent him from maintaining his foothold in the upper middle class: "The problem was that in order to be the person I thought I wanted to be, I believed I had to seal myself off from you [Robby], construct a wall between us" (26). Mason, however, is more committed to portraying herself as remaining loyal to her family throughout her identity crisis: "Although in some ways I had renounced the South, I could not lose the ties to my immediate family" (143). Two or so decades later she realized — when her father's cousin "accused me of 'going off,' as if it were a sin to leave"— that "it was true. I didn't think of them when I was away. I was free to adventure, while my loyal parents kept a place for me" (143). But she is quick to add, "I was loyal to them too" (143). The closest that Mason comes to acknowledging feelings of having betrayed her family is when she recalls allowing Larry to make her see her grandmother's quilt as "crude and primitive."

As the passage above makes clear, Mason makes a distinction between renouncing the South "in some ways" and alienating herself from her family. The section that relates her years as a graduate student in Connecticut focuses on how her sense of self was completely turned on its head: "I questioned my intelligence, my sanity, my identity" (146). This experience would seem to be true of many Ph.D. students, irrespective of region, for higher learning almost inevitably causes one to look at oneself and one's family from a new perspective. But Mason characterizes her confusion, and her renunciation of the South, as stemming from abstract cultural reasons, rather than as reactions to her family's relative powerlessness. She portrays her desire to escape as a rejection of a generalized southern culture, in particular the region's racism. She writes:

> Images of racial violence and bigotry flooded the newsmagazines— ugly scenes of beatings and murders, especially in my homeland. More than ever, I felt ashamed of being from the South. I feared that when people saw me, they imagined a walking, mute mannequin of Southern Gothic horror in high heels and a beehive — or worse, a baton twirler with a police dog. I was afraid my teachers and colleagues thought of hillbillies eating Moon Pies and swigging moonshine on the way home from a lynching. I remembered one of Daddy's cousins talking once about the significance of the date August 8. "That was the day Abe let the niggers go," he said, as if he actually remembered the emancipation. I didn't want to be Southern anymore [146].

Mason's emphasis on the cultural differences between north and south is a strategy that enables her to avoid the subject and the realities of class difference, between her family and the academic world in which she is immersed, and between her family and herself. She repeatedly stresses that she wanted to leave behind the broad social problems of her region, as when she remarks, "I believed I was meant to be in New England, in Carolyn and John's sophisticated world. I couldn't live in the South, where so much ignorance and prejudice persisted" (150).

Yet she doesn't explicitly address her unspoken but fierce rejection of her own working-class roots. Similarly, the author virtually elides the subject of racism from the world of her childhood. It may or may not be that Mason conceals racist attitudes in her immediate family, but her failure to confront her own family's attitude toward this foundational aspect of southern country life is in itself revealing. Lynn Z. Bloom finds that, with a few exceptions, all twentieth-century southern autobiographies "deal with the pervasive experience of racial segregation and its searing effects on blacks and whites alike. This does not mean that segregation is exclusively southern, but that it is inclusively southern. No child, black or white, can escape it; no autobiographer can ignore it" ("Coming" 113). Mason's suppression of any personal experience she has with racism allows her to frame her differences with the South as abstract and detached from her own life in the South. (Indeed, Mason's emphasis on her and her parents' "country" identity is a way of evading the connotations of bigotry that come with being "southern"; further, significantly, she omits any discussion or analysis of her parents' attitude toward blacks.) Thus, however noble and reasonable are the reasons that Mason gives for renouncing the South during this period, her invoking them is also a way of avoiding direct discussion of conditions closer to home that a bright and ambitious young woman might be seeking to escape.

Unexamined Class Conflicts

The intensity of Bobbie Ann's determination to remain in the North, in spite of her difficulties there, suggests that there are more dimensions to her rejection of "the South" than a principled, intellectual disgust with endemic racism. Her self-portrait of this period is notable for its emphasis on her perseverance: "But I persevered," she writes (145); elsewhere, she was "determined to plow through" (144); and again: "Still, I paddled bravely along in an uncertain current" (149). Such language echoes her description of herself earlier in the memoir, when she recalls that "my diligence in school was absurd" (76). Certainly a love of learning and a sharp intelligence help to account for her studiousness; but surely her obsession with achievement, exemplified by her refusal to join the Girl Scouts because they "didn't take scouting seriously," has more complex psychological roots (98). What makes a child from a family with no inclination for higher learning so desperately driven? Mason never adequately probes the psychology behind her intense yearning for social mobility, though her text hints that the social vulnerability of her parents, and their inability to exert control over their lives, made a profound impact on her.

Earlier in the text, when Mason is recounting her "adolescent fretting," she locates the cause of her rebellion in the family's powerlessness against the whims of nature (89). "We were at the mercy of nature, and it wasn't to be trusted. My mother watched the skies at evening for a portent of the morrow.... Our livelihood — even our lives— depended on forces outside our control" (83). She goes on: "I think this dependence on nature was at the core of my rebellion. I hated the sense of helplessness before vast forces, the continuous threat of failure. Farmers didn't take initiative, I began to see; they reacted to whatever presented itself. I especially hated women's part in the dependence" (83).

In a figurative, rather than a direct, way, Mason reveals her acute awareness of her parents' passivity in social and interpersonal interactions as well. The chief example, of course, is their complete submission to Mason's grandparents, and her parents' inability to establish autonomy in their own household and lives. Further, throughout the text are embedded images of the relative powerlessness of her parents because of their class and education levels. In one instance, Mason tells about her father reading an insult in a car salesman's innocuous (or so Mason assumes it to be) question. After her father showed interest in a car, the salesman had asked how he intended to pay for it, which struck a nerve of insecurity in her father: "Daddy bristled. He assumed the salesman didn't believe he could afford a car and would have to borrow. He was a farmer, in his jeans and feed cap" (205). Her father walked out of the dealership. Mason's assumption that the salesman's question was harmless, that her father was a victim of his own insecurity and not of snobbery, suggests how painfully conscious she is of her parents' perennial sense of inferiority.

There is ample evidence in *Clear Springs* that Mason's life, like her text, is an attempt to reverse in particular the defeated quality of her mother's life. In her preface Mason writes that this book "truly centers on my mother"; this is especially accurate in that her mother's shattering powerlessness is the psychological context for Mason's determination to persevere in her education (xi). The submissive regression of Christy Mason's life, exemplified by her following her husband back into his mother's cramped house after his father dies, is the reverse image of the ambitious Mason in the text. Dominated in her marriage, and bound day and night to chores, Mason's mother represents to the young Bobbie Ann the unthinkable alternative to education and professional work. Significantly, when Mason is living in New York City and writing for a movie magazine, she defends her job to Robert Hazel (who derides it) by describing it as the antithesis of her mother's life: "I told him I was grateful not to be sewing labels in Tony Martin jackets or canning tomatoes in a hot kitchen with brats underfoot" (132).

Mason doesn't explicitly connect the powerlessness of her mother to her own drive to escape working-class farm life, but the structure of her account of her postgraduate years suggests that her mother's oppressed life exerted a strong psychological influence on Mason. These passages about her struggles with northern culture, which also implicitly trace, though she suppresses it until the very end of the chapter, her academic achievement, are juxtaposed with sections about her mother's life growing increasingly bleak and constricted. In one place Mason draws a parallel between her own passivity with northerners and her mother's subjugation: "Mama coped. She dealt with what was handed her. Yet I didn't realize that I was behaving just like her. In my own style, I was subservient, bowing to authority. Yankee culture sat on me like the rocks Mama set on the lid of a pickle crock to hold the pickles down in the brine" (149). But the analogy is shaky, resembling Wideman's comparison of his identity conflicts amidst white culture with Robby's attempt to escape poverty through crime. Unlike her mother, Mason is acting and achieving; she has choices, and is in control of her life. Indeed, Mason ends the chapter on a note of triumph: with "a new blitz of confidence, I finished my degree.... A while later, my thesis was published" (157).

Conversely, as she relates a few pages later, her mother meanwhile has fallen into a severe state of depression:

> She was only fifty years old, but she spoke wearily, with resignation. She said, "I don't have but ten, or maybe twenty, years left." She cried, and at first I thought she was crying because she believed her life was nearly over, which hardly seemed credible, but then I realized how troubled she was. She saw her life being extinguished, her identity faded out like the pale moon in the evening. She was in the prime of her life, but it was being taken from her [161].

Mason doesn't explore the possibility that her mother's depression was in any way related to Mason's own Ph.D. achievement, but Mason was clearly painfully aware of her mother's emotional crisis during this time.

Early in the memoir, Mason mentions her mother's lack of education and the lack of opportunity that came with it: "Mama had quit school in the tenth grade, but she always regretted it, and she wanted me to get an education so I could have the chances she missed" (70). But beyond this, the author doesn't comment directly on the class situation of her parents. As for her mother's submissiveness as an adult, which Mason refers to as "sacrifices" for her husband's mother, Mason implicitly attributes it to her mother's early loss of her parents (177). In a moving conversation Mason has with her mother near the end of the memoir, her mother says, "I just never had a chance at anything." "That's because you didn't have parents to bring you up," Mason replies, "but we did" (274).

Some writers who reflect on their working-class parents, such as Carolyn Steedman and Richard Rodriguez, make a point of openly recognizing that their parents are socially and culturally disadvantaged because they lack higher education. In fact, as Chapter 1 explained, Rodriguez's autobiography, *Hunger of Memory*, is in many ways an extended argument that higher education automatically makes a person relatively powerful and privileged. Rodriguez boldly identifies a tool he has which his parents lack: a capacity for self-expression and self-knowledge. He calls their inability to express thoughts and feelings "an extraordinary oppression" (185), and also candidly notes that they would never write their autobiographies because "they lack the skill" to do so (188). He also implies that their shame, their sense of inferiority, makes them fiercely private.

But both Steedman and Rodriguez have very different kinds of relationships with their parents than Mason claims to have with hers, and this appears to allow them to be more analytical and clear-eyed than Mason about their parents' limitations. Steedman had been estranged from her mother for years when her mother died. Rodriguez plainly cares deeply for his parents, but he is somewhat alienated from them.

In contrast, Mason proclaims her bond with her mother to be an extremely close one. Late in the text, when Mason learns that her mother needs surgery, Mason is "mute" with anxiety: "The only important thing is not to lose her. She is my center. I'm only twenty-one years younger than she. She always says she was just a girl when she had me. I was so close to her that she often said she couldn't wean me. Now I can't face the ultimate weaning. I want her here.... She is the source of my being. How can I *be*, without her?" (245). This claim of complete emotional, even ontological, dependence on her mother is melodramatic, even in the context of her mother's precarious health. Mason has, of course, been away from Mayfield for virtually all of her adulthood, and has a whole life outside of her relationship with mother. But Mason's text is designed in part to reify her re-identification with her mother, and this purported near-fusion with her mother limits Mason's ability to view her mother with any objectivity.

"Country" as an Ethnic Identity

Intensely loyal to her remaining parent, and now purportedly infused with an appreciation for "all the things I wouldn't let her teach me in the past," Mason clearly does not want to insinuate in any way that her mother's life can be defined by what it has lacked (245). In one of their final conversations in the text, Mason reveals her urgent need to assure her mother of her worth: "I don't know how to speak my gratitude for her sacrifices without sounding sentimental — which would be fine with her. But I try. I need to make her believe her worth, to know how proud I am of her for her strength and resilience." Mason then tells her mother, "You've had an *extraordinary* life"; and the memoir seems designed in part to prove this (274). As an autobiographer Mason invests herself in validating not only southern life but "country people" in particular, and, of course, especially her parents. This scheme allows little room for explicit reflection on the limitations of working-class life, or life without the tools of higher learning.

In another strategy to avoid a close examination of her social mobility, Mason constructs what amounts to an ethnic identity, being "country," and sets it apart from social class: "We weren't poor, but we were country" (83). As noted earlier, "country," in Mason's rendering, is different than "southern," the former connoting innocence, vulnerability, and simplicity. A country person, in Mason's text, has a distinct temperament, certain personality traits, and a store of knowledge that is both instilled from experience and instinctual. For example, it is, Mason claims, her "country reserve" that keeps her from being able to "serve on a committee or run for office or feel easy at a cocktail party. The rural temperament still has a hold on me" (279). She argues that a rural person has a vastly different view on life than others, constructing highly debatable categories: "A country person's social isolation can be stunting, but then again he may have a chance at clearer glimpses of the ultimate — like the hummingbird that slammed into my window. A city dweller has more faith in human possibility ... but a rural person knows life's limits" (281). Mason also delineates a brand of innate knowledge which she argues to be unique to country people, that comes from generations of close association with the land: "Mama always knows where the moon is, and when to plant seed potatoes, and what potion to paint on a sick child's chest. She knows how to read the sky. My father knew when to expect birds to arrive or cows to calve; he knew how to fix almost anything without spending a cent. He could tell time in his head. He claimed he could approach any dog without fear" (282).

Country people in Mason's memoir are oppressed; she depicts them as socially marginal, and thus subject to the prejudices of urban people and to their own "ingrained sense of shame" (145). She writes that, as a child living on the edge of town (the town later expanded to encompass her farm), "I was acutely conscious of being country. I felt inferior to people in town because we grew our food and made our clothes, while they bought whatever they needed. Although we were self-sufficient and resourceful and held clear title to our land, we lived in a state of psychological poverty" (83). Throughout the text Mason repeatedly suggests that her sense of inferiority comes from cultural roots, from "being country," rather than from her social class situation. She recalls that the "overconfidence" she developed from being nurtured at home was replaced by a crippling sense of inferiority whenever she left the farm:

> I wanted desperately to live near the stores and the library, yet I was so unsure of myself when I went to town that I didn't know how to act. I wouldn't talk to anyone or look anyone in the eye. One version of me was a little queen on a throne. But another was a clodhopper. At heart was the inferiority country people felt because they worked the soil. Making my small forays out from the farm, I began to feel the centuries of shame [97].

Later in high school, she claims, she "was a nobody—an outsider, a country girl" (103).

Mason's memoir performs many of the functions that Laura Browder attributes to ethnic autobiographies. It seeks to validate an "ethnic" way of life—country life and country people—which is a common aim of the genre; as Browder observes, "In a culture in which minority citizens have often had to struggle for their rights, ethnic autobiography states a case for citizenship and for the value of the ethnic self.... Ethnic autobiographies have often been constituted as arguments for inclusion by their authors—and by extension the group to whom their authors belong—in the imagined community of the United States" (4–5). But being "country" is not widely considered an ethnic identity in America. Mason has also to make a case for a rural essence, and to do this she stresses the authenticity and the essential immutability of a country identity. You can take the girl out of the country, Mason suggests, but the rural temperament maintains its hold. In one of the many examples Mason gives to support this, she notes that "one of my primary traits," the "refusal to seek advice or ask directions," comes "from the independent spirit of generations of farm people" (115). Mason strains, and ultimately fails, to construct a convincing rural essence; she never adequately explains, for example, the apparent contradictions within the type she delineates, such as the "independent spirit" she claims for the country people whom she also portrays as passive.

Locating the "Truly" Authentic

Significantly, the chapter on Mason's tutelage under Robert Hazel in New York City features several ironic references to Hazel's idea of the authentic. In fact, Mason is most derisive of Hazel when it comes to his notions of authenticity. Ironically observing that "authenticity was essential in that period," Mason describes Hazel's shallow equation of the dark and sordid with the authentic: "He eschewed bourgeois values. His poems juxtaposed the lyrical and the cynical, and he admired the brutally physical and sordid. His novels were lurid. In one of them, rats ate a baby's face in a New York apartment" (133). She also wryly records Hazel's "rules about food. It had to be authentic, such as Spanish peasant fare, with wine" (136). Later, her Yankee boyfriend Larry scoffs at her curtains for being "inauthentic" (147). In these moments Mason may seem to be waxing critical of these men for their presumption to know what is and is not authentic, for their assumption that authenticity exists as an objectively identifiable quality. But later it becomes clear that Mason is merely disputing their ideas about what constitutes authenticity because these passages occur near the turning point in the memoir, when the narrator moves from a rejection of someone else's idea of authenticity to an assertion of her own definition of it. As James Clifford has said, "every imagined authenticity presupposes, and is produced by, a present circumstance of felt inauthenticity" ("Ethnographic" 114)

As if in compensation for having "run off" in search of something superior, Mason balances the first half of her memoir, which traces her longing for the North and her journey there, by devoting the latter half to demonstrating the organic beauty, the sincerity, and the fundamental integrity of her parents' country life. Having punctured the northerners' self-important definitions of authenticity, Mason then sets about locating it for real in her mother, and in the family farm itself. Indeed, the process of Mason's re-connection with her past begins on a note of declaration of what is real and true: "By hand, we broke sod for our garden. When I plunged my hands into the black New England soil, I felt I was touching a rich nourishment that I hadn't had since I was a small child. It had been years since I helped Mama in the garden. Yet the feel of dirt seemed so familiar. This was real. It was true. I wheeled around and faced home" (157).

A pattern emerges in Mason's illustrations of her mother's authenticity. In each case, her mother encounters people from mainstream life, often glamorous or at least relatively sophisticated people; these encounters are initiated and mediated by Mason. Every time, Christy Mason remains her rural self, and Mason makes a point of quoting the outsider's spoken approval. That Mason invariably, in these scenes, includes the more sophisticated person's appreciation of Mama suggests that on some level she still believes that her mother's life needs validating by the dominant culture. It also seems to be part of her effort to convince the reader of Mama's "extraordinary"-ness. The pattern begins with Mason's drawing of her mother into an acquaintance with the Hilltoppers. As Mason interprets it, the Hilltoppers admire her mother because she is unchanged by their presence. They "were crazy about my mother, who didn't put on any airs just because she knew some stars" (106). And Mason's depiction of Christy in relation to the singers keeps her mother fixed as a down-home type. "I think it's nice they've got that Cadillac and ain't stuck-up," is the only comment from her mother about the Hilltoppers that Mason records, even though Mason and Christy meet with them on numerous occasions, and even though spending time with bonafide celebrities would seem to be remarkable to most people. Christy relates to the young men in pragmatic, working-class terms, offering to get them free suits from the factory where she sews labels in jackets and feeding them: "Mama made a huge catfish supper, with hush puppies and slaw and blackberry pie" (110). Mason quotes the lead singer, Don, remarking of Christy, "Your mother is an amazing woman" (110).

Much later, in chapter 17 of the memoir, when Mason is in her forties and living in Pennsylvania, she meets up with her mother in New York City, when Christy is on a fall-foliage senior bus tour. A friend of Mason's in the city is "eager to meet Mama," and treats Mason and Christy to dinner. The dinner takes place at the Four Seasons restaurant, and Mason uses this highfalutin context to delineate the contrast between the self-important sophistication of the New York scene and the authentic, homespun goodness of Mama. "We strolled past the Picasso and Rothko paintings in the large foyer," she recalls, then immediately mentions the plastic Kmart bag her mother is clutching, which contains "a painting she had done in her senior-citizens art class" that her mother plans to give Amanda. ("I love it!" Amanda cries upon seeing it.) Against a backdrop of an "extravagant and dreamlike" dinner, Mason quotes her mother listing for Amanda the foods she cooks at home and her "garden crops." Later, Mason notes that they are seated next to a young woman and her family who were celebrating the woman's promotion "in a major firm. She was giddy with her success" (178). Mason then relates how Amanda described her experience of the dinner: "Amanda told me later in detail the conversation she had overheard. A businesswoman who herself moves in powerful circles, Amanda said, 'There I was wedged between two worlds, and I heard those people talking about this big-deal promotion, and I asked myself, what was all the excitement about? *What?* So what? Your mother was more real than anybody there'" (178).

In the restaurant scene, Mason offers a telling portrait of herself as a daughter, a cultural liaison, and a writer. Apparently for Amanda's benefit, she draws out and calls attention to her mother's country perspective: "'I don't see any catfish on the menu, Mama,' I teased" (178). Intriguingly, in this scene Mason shows herself beginning to use her mother as part of her own self re-invention into a southern-country writer. Mason clearly relishes bringing together her mother, whose impression of New York City is that "The rooms ain't big enough to cuss a cat in," and an urban woman like Amanda, who has never had catfish (177), and positioning her mother as the loveable innocent who infuses others with a fresh new perspective. Mason writes, with some gratification, that "Amanda too was seeing the lights and the buildings in a new way, through heartland eyes" (179).

Significantly, the restaurant scene is couched within Mason's account of finding success as a writer. Just before the scene, Mason relates the epiphany that set her on her true course: "By this time, I had become a writer.... I had discovered that I could draw on my true sources in order to write fiction. How could I have failed to recognize them? They had claimed me all along. So much of the culture that I had thought made me inferior turned out to be my wellspring. And my mother was my chief inspiration" (177). Just after telling about the dinner with Amanda, Mason returns to the subject of writing, and she underscores the "unspoiled" nature of the "voices of my family": "It was time to return to Kentucky for good. For some time, voices from home had been calling to me in clear, beckoning tones—their speech unspoiled by P.R. consultants or professional jargon or the rules of grammar.... When I began to write stories, their lives were the ones I came back to" (179). This sentimentalizing of "unspoiled" voices, incidentally, is disingenuous; Mason would never consider her own voice as having been ruined by proper grammar or more sophisticated thought. Like Wideman, Mason has a double-standard for herself and her family.

Mason is clearly invested in depicting her mother as "more real" than anyone in the restaurant and as untainted by mainstream culture. That Mama brings her painting to Amanda in a plastic K-mart bag, for example, seems too perfect a detail; the reader can't help but suspect that in the restaurant scene, both in life and on the page, Mason is transforming Christy into a literary character. In one paragraph just before the Four

Seasons scene Mason ticks off a number of places Christy visits on senior citizens tours and records her mother's impressions of her travels. Mason's characterization of Christy's perspective omits any hint of acculturation or increased sophistication in Christy from her broader experiences. It's worth quoting nearly the entire paragraph to demonstrate the brevity with which Mason describes her mother's (amazing) U.S. and European travel, and her extremely unreflective and uncurious responses:

> She went to Hawaii. She went out West, through the Badlands.... She traveled through Europe. There, she got a kick out of the various styles of commodes. In Germany she noticed the women working in the fields while the men lazed under a tree. She wasn't surprised. The scene seemed familiar. The Swiss Alps scared her and the Italian heat smothered her. She hated European bread. "That bread would yank your teeth plumb out," she said [177].

Because it's clear from the text as a whole that Mason needs her mother's identity as a rural type, the cultural "wellspring" of Mason's fiction, to remain immutable, it's hard to know if this description of her mother's account of her travels is entirely accurate. Christy Mason may indeed be as resistant to intellectual expansion as the passage paints her, but, like the K-mart bag detail, this piece of her portrait is so true to a type that it can't be trusted.

Exploitation of Southern (and Mama's) Authenticity

Mason narrates the story of the filming of *In Country* in her hometown as a cultural encounter between city people and country folk, between a dominating, sophisticated, monied film company and the starstruck, compliant, and humble townspeople. The author dramatizes this dynamic particularly in the interaction between the film company and her mother, and she shapes the narrative of this encounter as a tale that mirrors her own experiences with northerners when she was a student. As in those relationships, the film producers are in control, and the townspeople are all too solicitous in seeking their approval.

Like the young Bobbie Ann in her admiration for Hazel, Larry, and the others, the people of Mayfield are dazzled by the filmmakers and the prospect of being "authenticated" by appearing "on celluloid" (193). When the location scouts select a "modest old house" to appropriate for the shooting, "It was as though the family had won a home-delivered sweepstakes" (186). "Everyone in town wanted to be in the movie, it seemed," Mason recalls, and "the whole town, apparently, was involved in the progress of the movie" (187). But Mason's account of the film crew's three-month stay in Mayfield subtly characterizes the filmmakers as exploitative of the townspeople's eagerness and awe. One of the main themes of Mason's story of the filming is the commodification of authenticity, and specifically of rural life. The urban outsiders are covetous of the trappings of authenticity, for the movie production, but also for their own consumption. In a somewhat wry manner Mason describes the crew's appreciation of the country landscape, and their urge to purchase the symbols of rusticity: "The film crew marveled at the way the light hit the dilapidated old corncribs and tobacco barns in the landscape. They adored quilts. Bruce and Demi were spotted emerging from an antique store with armloads of quilts" (190).

However, throughout the chapter, Mason suggests that the filmmakers' enchantment with rural life is superficial, rather than based on a true respect for the natives, and she continuously reminds us that the crew is in the business of appearances. For example, she notes that much of the movie budget "was spent trying to conjure up an illusion of old-fashioned authenticity — quaint old things like those from Granny's time. Instead of filming at McDonald's, the crew chose a cozy diner with a giant rooster on the roof. For the filming, they replicated the diner" (190).

The film company's craving for images of authenticity leads them to borrow paintings and family photographs from Mason's mother. "Then," Mason writes, "the film people realized it wasn't just the pictures and antiques in the house that were authentic goods— it was Mama herself" (187). However, the details of her mother's interaction with the film people are narrated in a way that once again reinforces the exploitative nature of the relationship. They use her mother's "irreplaceable" photos, then lose some of them. Mason explicitly links the film crew's treatment of her mother's photographs with her Connecticut boyfriend Larry's breaking of her dish two decades earlier: "Mama was upset, but she wouldn't say so.... Her abashed silence reminded me of my casserole dish sailing off a balcony years before" (192). It is not only her mother's reluctance to show anger that makes the two episodes alike, but also the casual disregard in Larry and the film crew for the things the women valued, and, by extension, the women themselves. Furthermore, both the dish, "hard-earned and very useful," and the antique photos of her mother's past, are symbols of the simple, pragmatic, authentic country culture that Mason delineates in opposition to urban superficiality and arrogance. In fact, the episodes together form such a biting indictment of cruel sophisticates that one wonders if Mason included the casserole dish incident earlier so she could mention it now.

In this passage and throughout the section about the film company's stay, Mason presents the country people of Mayfield as feminized, vulnerable, and dispensable in relation to the sophisticated Other. It is not irrelevant, after all, that Mason makes a point of mentioning that the men of the film crew "said the Mayfield women who went out with them drank more than anybody they'd ever seen, as if they were desperate for excitement," a statement redolent of images of country girls being seduced and abandoned by "trendy" city guys (190).

The casserole dish incident and the disappearance of the family photos diverge in one significant aspect. Larry had pronounced Mason's grandmother's quilt as "Ugly!," and his destruction of the dish, in Mason's interpretation, was because he found it "inferior" and worthless. In contrast, the photos, it turns out, may not have been lost but stolen because of their irresistible value as authentic goods. As Mason's sister LaNelle, a set designer for the film, tells their mother, "anyone [in the crew] could have taken them" because "A lot of people are dying to have antique pictures" (193). In the twenty-five year interim since Larry's haughty disdain for Granny's quilt, the country look has become chic and sought-after, as evidenced by the movie stars buying "armloads" of similar quilts; and the irony is not lost on Mason.

This, of course, is the theme of Alice Walker's canonical 1973 short story "Everyday Use," in which an educated young black woman, Dee, returns to her mother's home to plunder the rustic, homemade things that have become valuable antiques. The old quilts made by her grandmother, which Dee had once proclaimed "old-fashioned, out of style," she now labels "priceless!" and wants to hang in her home (Walker 57). Walker portrays Dee as dismissive, condescending, and unkind toward her family, but greedy for their homely furnishings. Echoing this theme, in *Clear Springs* Mason depicts city sophisticates as coveting the images and trappings of authentic country life, yet failing to respect country people themselves. The thematic similarities between Walker's story and Mason's book run deeper, however. Like the filmmakers, Walker's character Dee is ambitious to make "artistic" use of objects that her "backward" relatives put to "everyday use" (56–57). Mason accuses the filmmakers of this kind exploitation, but, as I will discuss later, Mason is really displacing her own guilt for this same practice onto them.

Throughout the chapter on the filming, Mason's mother is the chief representative of country culture in the encounter with the urbanites. Mason depicts her as remaining true to type, and consistently in opposition to the falseness and the wasteful, pretentious extravagance of the film company. The "cast and crew were throwing around money like chicken feed," while Mason's mother, before agreeing to pick some damsons for a prop, warns that the orchard "might charge six dollars and a half this year" for a bucket (186–87). Although Christy is compliant with the film company's requests, willingly offering up herself, as Mason puts it, as "authentic goods," Mason's narrative portrays her mother as untainted by the glamor, by the culture of the Other. Christy is invited to the movie set, but arrives late due to getting her hair done; lest the reader assume that Christy herself is putting on airs with a fancy new hairdo, Mason informs us that the hairdo was free, a prize Christy won in a hula contest at the senior citizens center, a detail that further accentuates her rural quaintness.

In Mason's depiction, her mother's reactions to the noteworthy spectacle of a movie being made echo her comments about the Hilltoppers and her travel abroad in their pragmatism and simplicity. The pie baked for a scene (made with the damsons she picked) has been wasted, in her view, because it wasn't used for actual food: "I knew that pie wouldn't be eat," she laments, "I knew it would go to waste" (189). After a catered lunch (from a restaurant in Paducah) following the scene shooting, during which she mingled with the cast, she remarks primarily on the food: "'You could have all you wanted to eat,' Mama reported to me." At times her responses are nearly childlike in their innocence, such as when she reports to Mason that Bruce Willis, who is shown digging a ditch during a scene, was only pretending to dig: "'He didn't really dig that ditch,' Mama told me later. 'He just shoveled on it when the camera was on'" (189).

In telling about the filming of *In Country*, Mason delights time and again in pointing out the difference between what is real and true and what is fake, between the genuinely authentic and the expensively-crafted illusion of authenticity. A real country person like her grandmother, Mason conveys, would not approve of "the extravagance" flaunted by the cast and crew: "I remember how Granny would never turn on her single kitchen lightbulb in the evening until it was completely dark. One of the lights on the movie set was enough to illuminate a church parking lot" (190). As if to solidify her portrayal of the film producers as being somewhat ridiculously out of touch with the culture they're seeking to represent, Mason relates a humorous incident in which the filmmakers have an egret sent in from Disney World for a scene shot at a local swamp. The bird is meant to "wing its symbolic arc gracefully through the scene," but at the appropriate time, when a pistol is fired to scare it into flight, the bird stays put: "Apparently, no one had realized that in hurricanes egrets are the last birds to leave before the storm hits. The more the commotion, the steadier their nerves" (191–92). Mason reports that the next day, the camera crew discovered an enormous flock of egrets in the next cove, which "may have been there all along." The point of the story is articulated by Mason's father, who notes that the producers could have saved themselves trouble by asking Mason or her father about the egrets at the swamp: "'I've seen them over there time and again. Big flocks of them.' He laughed, enjoying his bit of superior knowledge. 'Sending all the way to Florida for a bird!'" Mason observes that "this was the kind of irony that amused Daddy," but it clearly amuses her as well (192).

On its surface, the dichotomy between the filmmakers' shallow idea of authenticity, as Mason's portrays it, and the bona fide authenticity of Mama not only reifies the author's thesis that Mama is more "real" than sophisticated people, but it also, of course, distinguishes the filmmakers, as competing artists who presume to draw from Mason's sources for their own vision of rural Kentucky, from Mason herself. Mason's hostile depiction of the filmmakers implies that unlike Mason herself, they fail to grasp fully or to respect the essence of Mama and the townspeople. This stance privileges Mason's unique position as an artist with an insider's grasp of the natives. On a different level, however, Mason's portrayal of the filmmakers hints at Mason's identification with them. Mason's text suggests that the exploitative aspects of the filmmakers are like those within herself that the author finds disturbing.

Omissions from the Author's Self-Portrait

Mason writes that "my family and I were ... conspicuously absent" throughout most of the filmmaking in Mayfield (187). But Mason herself is curiously absent from her own account of this event. Customarily a writer does not have much involvement with a movie being made from his or her book; but in this case, with the producers filming in Mason's hometown, using photographs of Mason and her family for props, and engaging the help of her mother as well as the townspeople, Mason is certainly more "present" in the project than she lets on, if in no other way than hearing about her family's involvement.

Yet aside from briefly relating her feelings as she watches a single scene being filmed, Mason does not depict any of her own participation in or reactions to the rather significant event of having her novel made into a film. Nor does she record any conversation with her family about this radical development in her life and theirs. Mason's narrative of the filming period is constructed as a cultural encounter between two disparate worlds, one of the business-minded city people and one of the relatively innocent country folk. This dichotomy can only be sustained when

Mason contrasts her parents' rural perspective with the empowered sophistication of the film people. Mason's presence as a character in this encounter would undermine her construct of a pure, exploited country culture that is untainted by mainstream culture or the expediencies of modern life. James Clifford has said that in ethnographic texts, claims to "purity" are "always subverted by the need to stage authenticity in opposition to external, often dominating alternatives" (*Predicament* 11). Since "authenticity is relational," Mason's strategy is to assert her parents' authenticity in relation to pompous northern intellectuals, pretentious New Yorkers, and flashy movie people (11).

As the author of the novel which has engendered the movie to begin with, Mason is possessed of far more power, socially and culturally, than she attributes to her parents or herself in her characterizations of them. This reality, like her presence in the filmmakers/townspeople encounter, is suppressed in this section of the text, and indeed, throughout the second half of the memoir. Notably, Mason includes very few glimpses into her autonomous adult life after her departure from the northeast in her memoir. A fuller portrayal of her present life would depict an intellectual woman leading a professionally disciplined and financially rewarded lifestyle: a radical departure from her parents' life on the farm. The sections of the book that take place in the recent past center mostly on her visits home, when she is joining her mother in farm activities, such as clearing pondweed, or later, helping her mother to move. During these times with her mother, the women converse about family history, or about nature-related curiosities that Mason knows her mother will find interesting. In one of the last chapters she tells her mother about a hummingbird, "Then I think of something else I know will interest her," a story about a cat (283). Despite their emotionally close relationship, Mason and her mother are never shown discussing Mason's work or success as an author. This may be true to life; Mason may not want to continuously bring up subjects her mother can't relate to or may find intimidating. But Mason also wants to maintain the construct of her "country" identity and her identification with her unsophisticated mother.

Mason briefly addresses the effects of her achievements on her relationship with her parents (though she refers only to her father here) in the section about going with her family to the premiere of *In Country*. The passage is replete with the *author's* discomfort, though she projects it onto her parents, claiming to be worried for them because (she assumes) they can't handle temporarily being in the spotlight. She writes, "I was acutely aware that some attention had come to me that we could not quite accommodate" (193). Interestingly, her anxiety takes the form of resisting any of the glamorous aspects of the actual premiere because, once again, she assumes her parents couldn't enjoy them. Mason declines a limousine reserved for them because "it would make my parents uncomfortable." She goes on: "Daddy would snort and mock if he saw anyone riding around the courthouse square in a limousine, so he would have been humiliated to be seen in one himself" (193). Apparently she never even asked him, or considered that people often mock luxuries they don't expect to have, only to be thrilled if they one day do get them. This is the case with Mason's mother and the type of "Big Fine House" she derides until she has and enjoys one of her own (249). Later, at the end of the chapter, Mason reveals that her father had "a few years before" written a letter to her, saying he read her stories and was proud of her (194).

But now, with her novel on film, Mason can't savor her accomplishment for fear of her father's "disappointment" and guilt over his "embarrassment": "I was afraid Daddy was disappointed, fearful that I had somehow moved into some other realm, rejecting his world. I thought he knew I wasn't likely to move to Hollywood and start throwing wild parties.... But it wasn't corruption Daddy feared so much as falseness" (193). As proof of her anxiety about being tainted by "falseness," Mason remarks, "Yet there we were at the premiere, all duded up." Aside from this passage, Mason, like her parents, is silent on the matter of how her family has handled her success, although it seems clear, incidentally, that Mason's financial position enables her mother to buy the "Big Fine House"; Mason vaguely implies that all of her siblings are contributing to the cost, but she alone helps her mother choose the house and close the deal (214).

Mason is mostly silent on her own feelings about her success, but a brief yet revealing passage about the movie premiere suggests a layer of meaning within Mason's account of the filming period and which threads throughout the text. Mason describes a painful moment in which the power disparity between her parents and the filmmakers is made glaringly evident: "After the premiere, at a reception, my parents were too tongue-tied to speak when introduced to the director. Daddy would not congratulate him on his achievement. I was sorry for his embarrassment, and I felt guilty for causing it" (193). Like Robby in relation to Wideman, Mason's parents don't have their daughter's facility with words. But her father's refusal to congratulate the director may be due to something deeper than the "embarrassment" to which Mason attributes it; Mason may be recording — without acknowledging it — a moment of her parents' resistance to her success, which may explain in part the guilt and anxiety that apparently overshadowed her evening at the premiere. Though doing so indirectly, Mason in this scene comes closer than anywhere in the memoir to expressing the complicated feelings that her achievements have created in both herself and her parents. She also subtly suggests her identification with the sophisticated — and dominating — world of filmmaking and books.

As noted earlier, Mason implicitly takes the film company to task for commodifying and exploiting rural life for their own benefit. But Mason herself, of course, has mined her parents and their country culture for her own fictional career. Several times she alludes to the fact that the characters of *In Country* are based on her own family members. In such references, Mason renders her use of her parents for her fiction in a positive light, as if she is honoring them. For instance, the most positively portrayed aspect of the months of filming is the friendship her parents form with one of the movie's stars, Peggy Rea, who "turned to Mama" for inspiration in creating her character. Mason writes, "When Peggy learned that her role in *In Country* was partly based on my mother, she came to the farm to meet Mama," and, in explaining why Peggy doesn't intimidate Mason's parents, the author notes Peggy's "oversized dimensions" and she stresses that Peggy isn't like other well-known actors: "Mama and Daddy would have been embarrassed to spend time with silk-shrouded Hollywood stars who couldn't milk a cow if their lives depended on it" (188). Mason relates a moment when her mother uses an expression that Peggy recognizes as one of her lines in the movie, and Mason characterizes this convergence of fiction and reality as a source of gratification for her mother: "'Out here, I feel I'm in the world of the characters,' [Peggy] said. Mama was pleased" (188).

As this analysis has sought to demonstrate, however, the film company's encounter with her hometown is portrayed ambivalently at best, with the loss of Christy Mason's photographs forming the emotional center. Albert Stone observes that "autobiography's coded imagery often speaks more truly than more literal renditions of experience, for it suggests patterns of deep continuity within the author's personality" (14). It is "three of the most special" photographs that turn up missing, portraits of her parents when they were young and of her grandparents; and it is not difficult to see the pictures as symbols of her mother's life: apparently borrowed for the benign purpose of crafting fiction, but in truth stolen (192). The imagery suggests the dangers of offering yourself up (as "authentic goods") for someone else's artistic use. It also points to the Promethean aspect of writing fiction based on one's family, and even of writing auto/biography: the necessary theft involved in the creation. Annie Dillard warns aspiring autobiographers of the price one pays for textualizing one's life: "If you prize your memories as they are, by all means avoid —

eschew — writing a memoir. Because it is a certain way to lose them." One can't write autobiography without "cannibalizing" one's life for parts, she asserts. Further, she adds, the written version inevitably reconfigures one's memories — and replaces them (70). Though Mason reports that her mother is financially compensated for the "use" of the photographs, the author ends the episode on a note of irreparable loss: "'Well,' [Mama] said after a moment. 'But it won't take the place of those pictures'" (193).

There are more instances of coded imagery in the memoir that suggest Mason's identification with the forces of dominant culture and their imposition on her parents. Throughout the memoir, Mason uses what she calls "the chicken tower," a feed mill across from her family's farm, as a sign of the unwelcome encroachment of modernization, which, like the subdivisions of Mayfield, is "headed our way" (7). The chicken tower is often described in futuristic terms: "If you see it at dawn, it's hard not to think about a space-shuttle launch," she writes (7); elsewhere, "the chicken tower's reflection shines in the still pond like a magnificent tableau from a science-fiction fantasy" (280). But the feed mill, the "lord of the landscape"(7), is always a symbol of dominating power: "It is still huffing away, like Godzilla" (280). In Mason's imagery, her family's houses are depicted in relation to the tower as submissive and skeptical, such as when she observes, "Our two houses face the chicken tower like cats staring at a stranger" (14); or, in the far more biting image, the two houses stand "near the chicken tower like compliant whores" (253).

Although Mason has only bitter words for the chicken tower and its ruthless assertion of ugly modernity and cold industry into the once-pure landscape, her imagery associates Mason herself with this symbol of change. In her preface Mason describes the memoir as "the story of a family trying to come to terms with profound change" (xi). Her parents' rural life on the farm is irrevocably brought into the future with both the construction of the feed mill and their lives intersecting with Hollywood — and both events happen in the same year. Mason makes the connection in a telling postscript with which she ends the chapter about the filming: "At the end of 1989, the *Mayfield Messenger* highlighted the major stories of the year. A picture of me taken at the movie premiere was juxtaposed with a picture of the new chicken-feed mill built by Seaboard Farms across from my family's house" (194).

Mason never reflects on the practice of writing someone else's life, whether as fiction or autobiography, as an act of appropriation or an assertion of power. As Nancy Miller has said, "the memoir expresses a form of power over its subjects. Like elegy, memoir always gets the last word" (*Bequest* 14). In part, the power that writers of literary memoirs have comes from their skill in creating seemingly true-to-life "people" on their pages. As with Wideman's text, the seamlessness and skill of Mason's characterizations of her family imbue her narrative with authority and credibility. Her characterization of her mother relies heavily on her use of Christy's dialogue. As Mason writes of her mother near the beginning of the book, "Her way of talking is the most familiar thing I know, except maybe for the contours and textures of this land" (10). In this remark Mason subtly asserts the validity of her version of her mother, and her authority to represent her mother through dialogue. But as Richard Rodriguez notes, to textualize personal conversations is to transform them: "Even when I quote them accurately, I profoundly distort my parents' words. (They were never intended to be read by the public). So my parents do not truly speak on my pages" (186). Incidentally, Mason's assured familiarity with her mother's "way of talking," and her striving to be faithful to it, may in fact undermine her depiction of her mother in the text, for Mason doesn't bring her usual flair with *interesting* dialogue to Christy's speech. Christy's dialogue is not nearly as memorable as that of Mason's fictional characters, including those in *In Country*.

Wideman and Mason both imply that their task as writers is in part to give voice to their family members who lack the opportunity to speak for themselves. Mason recalls her act of writing *In Country* as putting into words what was felt but not spoken by her family: "It was as though I were summoning voices from the past to undo the silences in my own family — my grandmother's fears, my father's reticence about his war, my mother's mute pain as she was caring for her mother-in-law" (180). But as Rodriguez admits, "I do not give voice to my parents by writing about their lives. I distinguish myself from them by writing about the life we once shared" (186).

That Mason is writing about their shared life is, of course, also what distinguishes Mason from her mother. Rodriguez's comments illuminate the ethical dimension of autobiographers serving up to the public conversations that occurred in private life, words that "were never intended to be read by the public." Autobiographers generally assume that it is their right to do this. Few critics have questioned this presumed privilege of the articulate family member speaking for or about the family, and critics that have done so tend to do so only when there is an egregious violation of privacy, as in Paul John Eakin's discussions of ethics in autobiography. But Mason's text raises the more subtle ethical problems inherent in a writer's use of personal relationships and conversations for a book. For example, Mason implies that she wants as much information as she can get about her mother's parents in order to better understand herself: "Now my mind is drawn to them — a mystery that I feel compelled to explore. The hole created in my mother's life yawns so wide and deep, I am washed with a grief decades old. But more than that now, I feel the hole in my own life" (252).

However, Mason's trips to the courthouse for documents, her thorough notes and her undeterred manner of interviewing her mother, suggest that all along, this writer is also preparing a book. The question is, is Mason's mother — a reticent, private woman — aware that this "reviewing" of her childhood is not only for her daughter but also for the public? Mason never indicates. To address this matter openly would require Mason to be more honest with her readers and herself about the fact that her interactions with her mother are professionally as well as personally motivated. As with Wideman, Mason's "true sources," her family, are just that: never merely family members but also the "wellspring" of her writing (177).

Mason clearly tries to get her mother's life story down accurately; with the persistence of a journalist, Mason pushes her mother to remember details, and on a few occasions, even pressures her to revisit painful memories. The most notable instance is Mason's determination to get the story of when Christy took her baby (Mason herself) to the house of her father, who had abandoned her mother and never knew Christy. Mason "urge[s]" her mother to tell about the visit, which had plainly been a distressing one, but then Mason is not satisfied: "'Go back,' I say. I have a hundred questions. 'I'm trying to see this scene'" (262). Mason continues to "pepper her with questions" and notes, "I can tell she is thinking hard." This questioning takes place soon after her mother has moved from her home of fifty years, and Mason shows her mother's physical and emotional exhaustion: "Her face is pasty. She's still tired from the move. Yesterday she said, 'I'm as tired as old Miss Tired'" (256). But Christy complies with her daughter's urging: "Each detail has been wrested from her with a question. She strains, probing the past, trying to visualize it. I know her memory must be vague, but some images loosen from the vapor and shine clear" (262). Mason persists, making Christy "exasperated with me. Why do I want to know such trifles?" Her mother at last yields up the sad summary of her visit to her father: "There was something in me that told me I had to talk to him. I had to find him. And so I did. And I saw we had nothing in common. I knew he didn't want me." Mason then observes, "When she sighs, I hope it is a sigh of release, not pain" (263). In her persistent probing of her mother, Mason is repeating her mother's urgent need to find and talk to *her* parent. Unlike Christy, though, Mason insists on finding commonality between herself and her mother.

At one point when Mason is helping her mother pack for the move, an exchange occurs between them that makes it doubtful her mother is knowingly reminiscing for a book. Mason expresses "frustration at not getting any of my own work done. 'What work is that?' Mama asks. 'I write books.' 'Oh.' She has forgotten" (246). Christy, of course, is well aware that her daughter is an author. She hasn't forgotten that Bobbie Ann writes books; it's more likely that she doesn't consider writing to be "work." But this dialogue brings to light the fundamental gap between Mason and her mother in terms of their awareness of texts and the act of transforming lives into texts. It is also, incidentally, one of the few moments in the text, and the only one depicted in a conversation with her mother, when Mason asserts her difference from her mother, as if she is attempting to reclaim a separate identity that nostalgia and a desire to validate her mother's life keep her otherwise determined to downplay. It also bears out Mason's observation, made much earlier in her account of her graduate student years, that "Southern behavior was devious, depending on indirection, a fuzzy flirtation that relied on strategic hinting" (149).

Even if her mother ultimately approves of Mason's use of herself and their shared life for *Clear Springs,* the gap in sophistication levels between Mason and her mother produces ethical problems for the autobiography. The disparity in power between Mason and her parents is embedded throughout the text. Mason's memoir illustrates the ethical pitfalls that occur in even the most loving portrayals of family members since it points to what may be the central problem of auto/biography: the purpose of the text is always, as Elizabeth Bruss notes, "an act of constructing [the author's] identity" (164). Eakin reminds us that identity is relational, and the self-identity that Mason constructs in her memoir depends upon characterizing her parents, especially her mother, as having an ethnic essence — being "country," and also of being representatives of an authentic, disappearing culture. Mason's text reveals some guilt on her part for having "betrayed my heritage as a farmer's daughter by leaving the land and going off to see the world," but it also implies that she can compensate for the betrayal by validating, preserving, and romanticizing her parents' dying culture (3).

Mason writes an ethnographic text that seeks to capture and purvey an "other" way of life for a mainstream reader. Her first chapter begins with her in the recent past working alongside her mother at the farm and recording her mother's rural expressions. For example, Christy refers to a weed as "pig presley" and Mason pursues a more precise identification. "What does it look like?" she asks her, then she tries to find its proper name: "Purslane? Parsley?" (9). In Mason's text, everything her mother says is rural-speak: "Mama gestures to the southeast and says, 'If the wind is this way, I smell horse piss, and that way I smell cow mess, and over yonder it's tobacco curing, and from the north it's chicken feed.... If that don't beat a hen a-rootin'!" (10). Mason continuously points out that her parents' way of life is fast disappearing, such as when she notes, "My mother uses idioms that are dying out with her generation, right along with the small family farms of America" (10). In another of many such comments she writes, "What my father and my ancestors knew has gone, and their idioms linger like fragile relics. Soon my memories will be loosened from any tangible connection to this land" (13). Mason's role as delineated in the text is to value, record, and save these fragile relics. This ethnographic activity frames the memoir, and also pervades it. In both the first and the second to last chapters, Mason portrays herself in the role of ethnographer, trying to get her mother's country sayings down accurately.

Mason is invested in what Patricia Meyer Spacks calls "an organizing myth" of herself: as witness to an authentic essence and as a chronicler of the "unspoiled" voices of home (54). For Mason, this identity is not only in relation to her family but also in relation to mainstream culture. By asserting her family's otherness, Mason enjoys a unique position. Spacks has found that being contrary is a favorite identity type in our era, that "twentieth-century self-presentations often focus on a personality insistently fluid, insistently at odds with what we now call 'the establishment'" (54). And Mason shows her satisfaction in drawing on her country origins to differentiate herself from others. Near the very end of the memoir, she writes,

> In sophisticated gatherings, I'm sometimes given to conversation stoppers. I might mention the time I sang in a gospel quartet, or how my family didn't have an indoor bathroom until I was eight years old, or how I had to sleep with a pan to catch the water from the leak in the ceiling.... Usually, nobody present can identify with these memories. There's an awkward pause and then someone striving for a sympathetic connection will mention summer camp in the Adirondacks, or they'll say they always liked fresh, home-baked bread [278–79].

In this passage, Mason depicts herself as "perversely" insisting on the otherness of her background, resisting anyone's attempt to "assume that my background was basically like theirs, with regular garbage pickup and ballet lessons." Her identity is based on transforming the "inferior" status of being country into an exclusive asset: "I have grown to cultivate my idiosyncratic revelations, now that I'm no longer humiliated by them; sometimes springing them is fun, though rather unfair of me. I time the mystified pause, then the quiet scramble back to familiar conversational territory" (279).

Mason's portrayal of her parents' country culture in opposition to urban life is a convention, according to James Clifford. Drawing on the work of Raymond Williams, Clifford shows how "a fundamental contrast between city and country aligns itself with other pervasive oppositions: civilized and primitive, West and 'non-West,' future and past"; he notes that Williams traces "the constant re-emergence of a conventionalized pattern of retrospection that laments the loss of a 'good' country, a place where authentic social and natural contacts were once possible" ("Ethnographic" 113). Likewise, Mason's characterization of her parents' culture as dying and in need of textual rescue, however true, is conventional as well. As Clifford notes, "The theme of the vanishing primitive, of the end of traditional society (the very act of naming it 'traditional' implies a rupture), is pervasive in ethnographic writing" (112). In this "allegory of salvage," which Clifford terms "ethnographic pastoral," historical worlds are "salvaged as textual fabrications disconnected from ongoing lived milieux and suitable for moral, allegorical appropriation by individual readers" (114). He adds that "the most problematic, and politically charged, aspect of this 'pastoral' encodation is its relentless placement of others in a present-becoming-past" (114–15).

Clifford identifies the ethical and political problems with this approach to writing another culture. While he acknowledges "specific cases of disappearing customs and languages," as well as the value of recording such phenomena, he maintains that "Ethnography's disappearing object is ... in significant degree, a rhetorical construct legitimating a representational practice: 'salvage' ethnography in its widest sense." Clifford questions "the assumption that with rapid change something essential ('culture'), a coherent and differential identity, vanishes."

He also points to "the mode of scientific and moral authority associated with salvage, or redemptive, ethnography. It is assumed that the other society is weak and 'needs' to be represented by an outsider (and that what matters in its life is its past, not present or future)." The pose of preserving an authentic culture endows the ethnographer with a special kind of power: "The recorder and interpreter of fragile custom is custodian of an essence, unimpeachable witness to an authenticity. (Moreover, since the 'true' culture has always vanished, the salvaged version cannot be easily refuted)" ("Ethnographic" 112–13).

Mason portrays her parents' country life as pure and innocent in part for the delineation of her own identity as a writer of an exotic and vanishing culture. Mason's romanticization of "country people," however, might be best understood as her attempt to valorize her mother's life. In *One Writer's Beginnings,* Eudora Welty states why she doesn't base her fictional characters on family members: "I ... know instinctively that living people to whom you are close — those known to you in ways too deep, too overflowing, ever to be plumbed outside love — do not yield to, could never fit into the demands of a story" (109). Though referring to fiction, Welty's insight points to an essential problem faced by autobiographers who have loving relationships with their family members: how at once to express love and loyalty in depicting them, yet also craft a text of rhetorical and aesthetic integrity, in which the writer brings his or her full powers of perception, analytic insight, and intellectual honesty to the characterization of others. Welty suggests the great difficulty in pulling this off.

Simply put, Mason has chosen to write a memoir that pays tribute to her mother by portraying her as virtuous, humble, and noble: the sort of characterization that one expects to find in a personal, private discourse such as an elegy, rather than in a widely published autobiographical text by a renowned and respected author. It's as if Mason ultimately suppresses her intellectual vision, and leaves behind the sharp eye and penetrating insight she has elsewhere employed as a fiction writer.

Conclusion

John Edgar Wideman told an interviewer that he wrote *Brothers and Keepers* because he was driven to "make some sense of the enormous gap" between himself and his imprisoned brother Robby (Coleman 160). Wideman's predicament, in which his own life of comfort and professional accomplishment contrasts starkly with his brother's life of poverty, drugs, crime, and now prison, is just a more extreme version of the situation that Nesaule, Mason, and to a much lesser degree, Baker, faced: they all greatly surpassed their parents and/or their siblings in terms of achievement and affluence. This life circumstance, as well as the impulse "to make some sense of the enormous gap" between oneself and one's family members, underlies much of contemporary working-class autobiography.

One significant difference between the memoir by Baker and the books by Wideman, Nesaule, and Mason is that Baker focuses more on the story of why and how he was able to attain a good education and launch into an outstanding career, while the other three authors, in trying to make sense of the gap, focus as much on the obstacles facing their family members as they do on the reasons for their own success.

The ethical problems in the texts by Wideman, Nesaule, and Mason frequently stem from the authors' attempts to compensate for the sense of inferiority they experienced as young people and which they perceive still afflicts their family members. Too often they succumb to the temptation to romanticize their families, or to strain to make a case for their specialness. This approach sometimes results in unintended patronization or condescension. Wideman's claim, for example, that he struggles with the "truth" that "maybe [Robby's] the better man" lacks credibility, to say the least (202). We also saw how Mason stakes much of her portrait of her mother on her mother's purportedly "more real" and "unspoiled" character.

Nesaule's book disturbs not so much because of her idealization of her family, but because of her investment in seeing herself and them as perennially oppressed. Nesaule's demonization of her former husband serves the author's purpose of solidifying an image of herself and her parents as victims— not only of soldiers and of ignorant, prejudiced Americans, but also of Joe. Consequently, and astonishingly, she accepts no responsibility for her own choices or for the quality of her relationships.

The fact that Wideman, Nesaule, and Mason are more conflicted about their success accounts for much of the difference in ethical quality between their books and Baker's. Perhaps because all three of them not only had to leave their family's culture but also had to enter a dominant culture that discriminated against their community of origin, they felt— and may still feel— as if they betrayed their family by finding acceptance in the mainstream world. Baker doesn't share the other authors' sense of having betrayed his family by succeeding; indeed, as his text overwhelmingly demonstrates, with his professional success he is fulfilling his mother's deepest ambition for herself and him. He is also in accord with her value system: his discipline in academics, his career as a writer, and his appreciation of hard work and social mobility were all instilled by her.

Unlike Wideman, Nesaule, and Mason, Baker didn't have to leave a markedly different culture or way of life in order to move into the middle-class dominant culture. Nor did he feel, as the other writers felt, that by entering the dominant culture he was aligning himself with a world that oppressed his family members. Further, as he portrays them, Baker's family members had good lives and positive attitudes in spite of their economic hardships. Whether that characterization reflects selective memory or keen perception on his part, Baker plainly doesn't regard his relatives as having been mistreated or defeated by life.

There is yet another important distinction to note between the memoir by Baker and the texts of Wideman, Nesaule, and Mason. This involves the degree of shame and powerlessness felt by the authors and their families during the authors' childhoods. While Baker does recall a period during the Depression when he and his mother and sister experienced the shame of accepting government "relief," he mostly suggests that he never suffered from a deep or prolonged sense of social marginalization. After all, during the Depression poverty was fairly common. In contrast to Baker, early in life Wideman recognized his family as being among the "losers" in life because they were black. He continued to feel ashamed of being black into his young adulthood, and because of Wideman's desperate desire to blend in with white culture he was threatened by Robby's "blackness." Nesaule also records the shame she and her family felt for many reasons during Nesaule's youth: their cramped living in a poor neighborhood of Indianapolis, their accents, and her mother's menial jobs. Similarly, Mason writes of her family's perennial sense of shame for being "country"—unsophisticated and socially isolated.

Thus, while this study has identified several ethical problems in the texts by Wideman, Nesaule, and Mason, it is clear that these autobiographers have had to negotiate more complicated relationships with their pasts than does Baker, whose text exemplifies a more ethical approach to portraying one's working-class relatives.

This book has raised questions about class and autobiography that warrant further study. One concern is the way in which class difference between an autobiographer and his family affects the writer's view of his family's rights to privacy or dignity. While this matter was touched on in this study, a more focused examination, analyzing autobiographers from a range of class backgrounds as well as research into extra-textual data such as interviews and lectures, would further illuminate how autobiographers' ethical standards may vary according to the class of their subjects.

Another avenue of further study concerns the relationship between class, gender, and autobiography. The life trajectories of the autobiographers studied here suggest that gender plays a significant role not only in class mobility but in its consequences for family relationships. As high school and college students the women writers were hampered by a deep sense of inferiority not shared by the men. Behaving with a learned passivity into their young adulthood, they believed themselves to be powerless in their relationships and were consequently bullied. The women writers also felt much more responsible for their families' well-being than the men writers felt.

This book has asserted that autobiography can and should be regarded not only as art but as a "form of conduct," as the ethicist Wayne Booth refers to fictional narratives, especially when writers are representing particularly vulnerable people who cannot speak for themselves (*Company* 137). Perhaps the most sensible, general ethical standard for autobiographers put forth to date is the one articulated by Lynn Z. Bloom, who argues that creative nonfiction writers owe both their families and readers only the truth; she adds that this ethical principle "dictates an aesthetic fulfillment—that the meaning will be conveyed through character and story that will provide their own clear-eyed witness to the truth, that witness untainted by vindictiveness or special pleading" ("Living" 288).

Yet the autobiographies studied in this book demonstrate that even very good writers who are undoubtedly striving to convey their version of the truth can produce autobiographies flawed by "vindictiveness" and "special pleading." One reason is that one's idea of the truth is never simply a matter of original perception but is, in part, a social and cultural collaboration.

As is well known, a person's "truth," once it is formulated in language, is comprised of far more than that person's perception of experience, though as Susanna Egan notes, even the act of perception transforms reality: "Each [literary] work, after all, conforms not to reality but to its own laws established by the tradition within which it exists. Schemata evolve to guide perception, which is accordingly largely affected by expectation" (*Patterns* 16). Further, an autobiographer delineating an identity is inevitably influenced by cultural models of identity, including racial, class, gender, and regional types. Paul John Eakin argues that even though "there is a legitimate sense in which autobiographies testify to the individual's experience of selfhood, that testimony is necessarily mediated by available cultural models of identity and the discourses in which they are expressed" (*How* 4). To some degree the ethical problems in the texts of Wideman, Nesaule, and Mason are engendered by cultural and social notions of working-class and "other" people.

As more working-class children grow up and write literary autobiographies, the models of people negotiating complex identities will become increasingly varied and sophisticated, and autobiographers' representations of people from the working-class and "other" cultures and regions will become more heterogeneous. In addition, as critics become more sensitive to the ethical aspects of autobiographers' representations of "others," future autobiographers will eventually reflect that awareness in their work. The sub-genre of working-class autobiography will continue to evolve, proving itself as adaptable and dynamic as the people who write in it.

Works Cited

Andrews, William L. "African American Autobiography Criticism: Retrospect and Prospect." *American Autobiography: Retrospect and Prospect.* Ed. Paul John Eakin. Madison: University of Wisconsin Press, 1991. 195–215.
———. "The First Century of Afro-American Autobiography: Theory and Explication." *African American Literary Criticism, 1773 to 2000.* Ed. Hazel Arnett Ervin. New York: Twayne, 1999. 223–34.
Angelou, Maya. *I Know Why the Caged Bird Sings.* 1970. New York: Bantam, 1993.
Arvin, Newton. "An American Case History." Rev. of *Dawn*, by Theodore Dreiser. *New Republic* 5 Aug. 1931: 319–20. Salzman 614–17.
Baker, Russell. *Growing Up.* 1982. New York: Plume (Penguin), 1983.
———. "Life with Mother." *Inventing the Truth: The Art and Craft of Memoir.* Ed. William Zinsser. Boston: Houghton Mifflin, 1987. 33–51.
Baldwin, James. "Dark Days." *The Price of the Ticket: Collected Non-Fiction 1948–85.* New York: St. Martin's Press, 1985.
Barbour, John D. "Judging and Not Judging Parents." Ed. Paul John Eakin. *The Ethics of Life Writing.* Ithaca: Cornell University Press, 2004. 73–98
Barros, Carolyn. *Autobiography: Narrative of Transformation.* Ann Arbor: University of Michigan Press, 1998.
Benjamin, Jessica. *The Bonds of Love.* New York: Pantheon, 1988.
Berry, J. Bill, ed. *Home Ground: Southern Autobiography.* Columbia: University of Missouri Press, 1991.
"Black Boy" (Review). *United States Quarterly Book List* June 1945: 15–16. Reilly 171.
"Black Boyhood." Rev. of *Black Boy*, by Richard Wright. *Time* 5 Mar. 1945: 94, 96, 98. Reilly 138–39.
Bloom, Lynn Z. "Coming of Age in the Segregated South: Autobiographies of Twentieth-Century Childhoods, Black and White." *Home Ground: Southern Autobiography.* Ed. J. Bill Berry. Columbia: University of Missouri Press, 1991. 110–22.
———. "Living to Tell the Tale: The Complicated Ethics of Creative Nonfiction." *College English* 65, Number 3 (January 2003): 276–289.
Booth, Wayne. *The Company We Keep: An Ethics of Fiction.* Chicago: University of Chicago Press, 1988.
———. *The Rhetoric of Fiction.* Chicago: University of Chicago Press, 1961.
Bragg, Rick. *All Over But the Shoutin'.'* New York: Vintage, 1997.
Browder, Laura. *Slippery Characters: Ethnic Impersonators and American Identities.* Chapel Hill: University of North Carolina Press, 2000.

Bruss, Elizabeth W. *Autobiographical Acts: The Changing Situation of a Literary Genre.* Baltimore: Johns Hopkins University Press, 1976.
Burns, Ben. Rev. of *Black Boy,* by Richard Wright. *Chicago Defender.* 3 Mar. 1945: 11. Reilly 127–28.
Clifford, James. *The Predicament of Culture: Twentieth-Century Ethnography, Literature, and Art.* Cambridge: Harvard University Press, 1988.
———. "On Ethnographic Allegory." *Writing Culture: The Poetics and Politics of Ethnography.* Ed. James Clifford and George Marcus. Berkeley: University of California Press, 1986. 98–121.
Coleman, James W. *Blackness and Modernism: The Literary Career of John Edgar Wideman.* Jackson: University of Mississippi Press, 1989.
Couser, G. Thomas. *Altered Egos: Authority in American Autobiography.* New York: Oxford University Press, 1989.
———. *Vulnerable Subjects: Ethics and Life Writing.* Ithaca: Cornell University Press, 2004.
Dillard, Annie. *An American Childhood.* New York: Harper and Row, 1987.
———. "To Fashion a Text." *Inventing the Truth: The Art and Craft of Memoir.* Ed. William Zinsser. Boston: Houghton Mifflin, 1987. 53–76.
Doctorow, E. L. Introduction. *Sister Carrie,* by Theodore Dreiser. 1900. New York: Bantam, 1992. v-xi.
Douglass, Frederick. *Narrative of the Life of Frederick Douglass, an American Slave, Written by Himself. 1845. The Classic Slave Narratives.* Ed. Henry Louis Gates, Jr. New York: Signet, 1987. 294–298.
Dreiser, Theodore. *Sister Carrie.* 1900. New York: Bantam, 1992.
———. *Dawn: A History of Myself.* New York: Horace Liveright, 1931.
Du Bois, W. E. B. "Richard Wright Looks Back." Rev. of *Black Boy,* by Richard Wright. *New York Herald Tribune Weekly Book Review* 4 Mar. 1945: 2. Reilly 132–33.
Duffus, R. L. "Deep-South Memoir." Rev. of *Black Boy,* by Richard Wright. *New York Times Book Review* 4 Mar. 1945: 3. Reilly 133–35.
Eakin, Paul John, ed. *American Autobiography: Retrospect and Prospect.* Madison: University of Wisconsin Press, 1991.
———, ed. *The Ethics of Life Writing.* Ithaca: Cornell University Press, 2004.
———, ed. *Fictions in Autobiography: Studies in the Art of Self-Invention.* Princeton: Princeton University Press, 1985.
———. *How Our Lives Become Stories: Making Selves.* Ithaca: Cornell University Press, 1999.
Egan, Susanna. *Mirror Talk: Genres of Crisis in Contemporary Autobiography.* Chapel Hill: University of North Carolina Press, 1999.
———. *Patterns of Experience in Autobiography.* Chapel Hill, University of North Carolina Press, 1984.
Ellingson, H. K. "Theodore Dreiser." Rev. of *Dawn,* by Theodore Dreiser. *Colorado Sunday Gazette & Telegraph* 14 June 1931. Salzman 610.
Ervin, Hazel Arnett, ed. *African American Literary Criticism, 1773 to 2000.* New York: Twayne, 1999.
Fabre, Michel. *The Unfinished Quest of Richard Wright,* New York: William Morrow, 1973.
"Growing Up Black." Rev. of *I Know Why the Caged Bird Sings,* by Maya Angelou. *Newsweek* 2 Mar. 1970: 89–90.

Hakutani, Yoshinobu, Ed. *Theodore Dreiser and American Culture: New Readings.* Newark: University of Delaware Press, 2000.
Hansen, Harry. "The First Reader." Rev. of *Dawn,* by Theodore Dreiser. New York *Evening World Telegram* 9 May 1931. Salzman 592.
Hazlitt, Henry. "Another Book About Himself." Rev. of *Dawn,* by Theodore Dreiser. *Nation* 3 June 1931: 613–14. Salzman 604–07.
Hendrickson, Paul. "The Author's Inner Fire: John Edgar Wideman and the Personal Tragedies That Fuel His New Work of Fiction," *Washington Post,* 15 Oct., 1990: B8.
Henriksen, Louise Levitas. Afterword. *Red Ribbon on a White Horse: My Story.* By Anzia Yezierska. 1950. New York: Persea Books, 1987. 221–228.
Herrick, Robert. "Dreiseriana." Rev. of *Dawn,* by Theodore Dreiser. *Saturday Review of Literature* 6 June 1931: 875. Salzman 607–10.
I.W. Rev. of *Black Boy,* by Richard Wright. St. Louis *Star-Times* 8 Mar. 1945. Reilly 139–40.
Ivy, James W. "American Hunger." Rev. of *Black Boy,* by Richard Wright. *The Crisis.* April 1945: 117–18. Reilly 159.
Kaplan, Amy. *The Social Construction of American Realism.* Chicago: University of Chicago Press, 1988.
Karr, Mary. *The Liar's Club.* New York: Viking, 1995.
Kessler-Harris, Alice. Foreword. *Bread Givers,* by Anzia Yezierska. 1925. New York: Persea Books, 1999. v–xiii.
Langbaum, Robert. "Ambiguous Pilgrimage." Rev. of *Red Ribbon on a White Horse,* by Anzia Yezierska. *Commentary* Jan.-June 1951: 104–06.
Lauritzen, Paul. "Arguing with Life Stories: The Case of Rigoberta Menchu." Ed. Paul John Eakin. *The Ethics of Life Writing.* Ithaca: Cornell University Press, 2004. 19–39.
Lehmann-Haupt, Christopher. "Books of the Times: Masculine and Feminine." Rev. of *Sugar Ray,* by Sugar Ray Robinson, and *I Know Why the Caged Bird Sings,* by Maya Angelou. *New York Times* 25 Feb. 1970: 45.
Lyden, Jacki. *Daughter of the Queen of Sheba.* Boston: Houghton Mifflin, 1997.
Malcolm, Janet. *The Journalist and the Murderer.* New York: Vintage, 1990.
———. *The Silent Woman: Sylvia Plath and Ted Hughes.* New York: Vintage, 1995.
Malloy, Robert. "The Author of *Native Son* Tells of His Childhood." Rev. of *Black Boy,* by Richard Wright. *New York Sun* 2 Mar. 1945: 22. Reilly 126–27.
Mandel, Barrett J. "Full of Life Now." *Autobiography: Essays Theoretical and Critical.* Ed. James Olney. Princeton: Princeton University Press, 1980. 49–72.
Matthiessen, F. O. *Theodore Dreiser.* New York: William Sloane, 1951.
Mason, Bobbie Ann. *Clear Springs: A Memoir.* New York: Random House, 1999.
———. "Shiloh." *Shiloh and Other Stories.* New York: Harper and Row, 1982. 1–16.
Mbalia, Doreatha Drummond. *John Edgar Wideman: Reclaiming the African Personality.* Selinsgrove: Susquehanna University Press, 1995.
Miller, Nancy K. *Bequest and Betrayal: Memoirs of a Parent's Death.* New York: Oxford University Press, 1996.
———. "The Ethics of Betrayal: Diary of a Memoirist." Ed. Paul John Eakin. *The Ethics of Life Writing.* Ithaca: Cornell University Press, 2004. 147–62.
Mills, Claudia. "Friendship, Fiction, and Memoir: Trust and Betrayal in Writing from One's Own Life." *The Ethics of Life Writing.* Ed. Paul John Eakin. Ithaca: Cornell University Press, 2004, 101–120.

Mordell, Albert. "Theodore Dreiser Dares to Give Complete Picture." Rev. of *Dawn*, by Theodore Dreiser. Philadelphia *Record* 9 May 1931. Salzman 595–96.

Moyer, Marsha S. "Dreiser, Sister Carrie, and Mrs. Doubleday: Gender and Social Change at the Turn of the Century." *Theodore Dreiser and American Culture: New Readings*. Ed. Yoshinobu Hakutani. Newark: University of Delaware Press, 2000. 39–55.

Murphy, Beatrice M. Rev. of *Black Boy*, by Richard Wright. *Pulse* Apr. 1945: 32–33. Reilly 160–62.

Nesaule, Agate. *A Woman in Amber: Healing the Trauma of War and Exile*. New York: Penguin, 1995.

O'Connor, Flannery. "Good Country People." *A Good Man is Hard to Find*. 1953. *Collected Works*. New York: Library of America, 1984. 263–84.

Olney, James, ed. *Autobiography: Essays Theoretical and Critical*. Princeton: Princeton University Press, 1980.

———. *Metaphors of Self: The Meaning of Autobiography*. Princeton: Princeton University Press, 1972.

Parker, Dorothy. "Reading and Writing: Words, Words, Words." Rev. of *Dawn*, by Theodore Dreiser. *New Yorker* 30 May 1931: 69–72. Salzman 600–602.

Prescott, Orville. "Books of the Times." Rev. of *Red Ribbon on a White Horse*, by Anzia Yezierska. *New York Times* 11 Sept. 1950: 21.

"Red Ribbon on a White Horse" (Review). *New Yorker* 23 Sept. 1950: 122.

Reilly, John M., ed. *Richard Wright: The Critical Reception*. New York: Burt Franklin & Co., 1978.

Renza, Louis A. "The Veto of the Imagination: A Theory of Autobiography." *Autobiography: Essays Theoretical and Critical*. Ed. James Olney. Princeton: Princeton University Press, 1980. 268–295.

Richter, F. K. Rev. of *Black Boy*, by Richard Wright. *Negro Story* May-June 1945: 93–94. Reilly 170–71.

Rico, Gabriele Lusser. "The Heart of the Matter." *Presence of Mind: Writing and the Domain Beyond the Cognitive*. Ed. Alice Garden Brand and Richard Graves. Portsmouth, NH: Boynton/Cook, 1994. 199–214.

Rodriguez, Richard. *Hunger of Memory: The Education of Richard Rodriguez*. 1982. New York: Bantam, 1983.

Rubin, Lillian B. *Families on the Fault Line: America's Working Class Speaks About the Family, the Economy, Race, and Ethnicity*. New York: HarperCollins, 1994.

———. *The Transcendent Child: Tales of Triumph Over the Past*. New York: HarperCollins, 1996.

———. *Worlds of Pain: Life in the Working-Class Family*. New York: HarperCollins, 1976.

Salzman, Jack, ed. *Theodore Dreiser: The Critical Reception*. New York: David Lewis, 1972.

Samuels, Wilfred. "Interview with John Edgar Wideman." *Conversations with John Edgar Wideman*. Ed, Bonnie TuSmith. Jackson: University of Mississippi Press, 1998. 14–31.

Schreiber, Le Anne. "Books of the Times." Rev. of *Hunger of Memory*, by Richard Rodriguez. *New York Times*, 1 Mar. 1982: C15.

Sennett, Richard, and Cobb, Jonathan. *The Hidden Injuries of Class*. New York: Random House, 1973.

Shorris, Earl. "In Search of the Latino Writer." *New York Times*, 15 Jul, 1990: BR1.

"Sister Carrie" (Review). Louisville *Times,* 20 Nov. 1900. Salzman 1.
Slater, Philip. *Footholds: Understanding the Shifting Sexual and Family Tensions in Our Culture.* New York: Dutton, 1977.
Smith, Lillian. "Richard Wright Adds a Chapter to Our Bitter Chronicle." Rev. of *Black Boy,* by Richard Wright. *PM* 4 Mar. 1945: m15. Reilly 135–36.
Smith, Sidonie. *Subjectivity, Identity, and the Body.* Bloomington: Indiana University Press, 1993.
———. *Where I'm Bound: Patterns of Slavery and Freedom in Black American Autobiography.* Westport, CT: Greenwood Press, 1974.
Sollors, Werner. *Beyond Ethnicity: Consent and Descent in American Culture.* New York: Oxford University Press, 1986.
Soskin, William. "Books on Our Table." Rev. of *Dawn,* by Theodore Dreiser. New York *Evening Post* 8 May 1931: 11. Salzman 590–92.
Spacks, Patricia Meyer. "Stages of Self: Notes on Autobiography and the Life Cycle." *The American Autobiography: A Collection of Critical Essays.* Ed. Albert E. Stone. Englewood Cliffs: NJ: Prentice-Hall, 1981. 44–60.
Starobinski, Jean. "The Style of Autobiography." *Autobiography: Essays Theoretical and Critical.* Ed. James Olney. Princeton: Princeton University Press, 1980.
Steedman, Carolyn Kay. *Landscape for a Good Woman: A Story of Two Lives.* 1986. New Brunswick: Rutgers University Press, 1997.
Steele, Shelby. "On Being Black and Middle Class." *The Content of Our Character.* New York: St. Martin's Press, 1990. 93–110.
Stone, Albert E., ed. *The American Autobiography: A Collection of Critical Essays.* Englewood Cliffs: N.J.: Prentice-Hall, 1981.
———. *Autobiographical Occasions and Original Acts.* Philadelphia: University of Pennsylvania Press, 1982.
Swanberg, W. A. *Dreiser.* New York: Scribners, 1965.
Torgovnick, Marianna. *Gone Primitive: Savage Intellects, Modern Lives.* Chicago: University of Chicago Press, 1990.
TuSmith, Bonnie, ed. *Conversations with John Edgar Wideman.* Jackson: University of Mississippi Press, 1998.
"20 Years of Misery." Rev. of *Black Boy,* by Richard Wright. *Omaha World-Herald* 25 Feb. 1945. Reilly 118–19.
Van Zandt, T. "Pancho and Lefty." Perf. Willie Nelson and Merle Haggard. *Willie Nelson/Half Nelson.* Columbia, 1985.
Volkan, Vamik. *Bloodlines: From Ethnic Pride to Ethnic Terrorism.* New York: Farrar, Straus and Giroux, 1997.
Walker, Alice. "Everyday Use." *In Love & Trouble.* New York: Harcourt Brace Jovanovich, 1973. 47–59.
Welty, Eudora. *One Writer's Beginnings.* 1984. New York: Time Warner, 1991.
Wideman, John Edgar. *Brothers and Keepers.* 1984. New York: Vintage, 1995.
Wildes, Harry Emerson. "Of Making Many Books..." Rev. of *Dawn,* by Theodore Dreiser. Philadelphia *Public Ledger* 7 May 1931. Salzman 587.
Williams, Raymond. *Politics and Letters.* London: NLB/Verso, 1979.
Williams, Tennessee. *A Streetcar Named Desire.* 1947. New York: New Directions, 1980.
Wright, Richard. *Black Boy: A Record of Childhood and Youth.* 1945. New York: Harper & Row, 1989.

Yezierska, Anzia. *Red Ribbon on a White Horse: My Story.* 1950. New York: Persea Books, 1987.

Zinsser, William, ed. *Inventing the Truth: The Art and Craft of Memoir.* Boston: Houghton Mifflin Company, 1987.

Zweig, Paul. "The Child of Two Cultures." Rev. of *Hunger of Memory*, by Richard Rodriguez. *New York Times*, 28 Feb. 1982: BR1.

Index

Adams, Henry (*The Education of Henry Adams*) 41
African American autobiographers and the American Dream 60, 62
African American autobiography 5, 33, 41–42, 62, 67
Alger, Horatio 18, 31, 60, 62; myth structure in autobiography 60
All Over But the Shoutin' see Bragg, Rick
All Souls: A Family Story from Southie see MacDonald, Michael Patrick
An American Childhood (Dillard, Annie) 13
An American Tragedy (Dreiser, Theodore) 35
Anderson, Dave (*Sugar Ray*) 59
Andrews, William L. 5, 62, 67
Angelou, Maya (*I Know Why the Caged Bird Sings*) 33, 58–68
Arvin, Newton 40
Ashley, Don 38
The Autobiography of Benjamin Franklin see Franklin, Benjamin

Baker, Benny 76, 78, 81, 83
Baker, Doris 27, 79, 91
Baker, Ida Rebecca 76, 78, 79
Baker, Lucy 75–78, 82–83, 86–89, 91, 94–95, 99, 101
Baker, Mimi 97–99, 101, 149
Baker, Russell 1–2, 12, 20–28, 74–101, 149, 188, 190
Baldwin, James 62, 66
Barbour, John D. 16–19
Barros, Carolyn 155–57
Benjamin, Jessica 101, 132
Black Autobiography in America (Butterfield, Stephen) 59
Black Boy see Wright, Richard
Black Elk Speaks see Neihardt, John
Bloom, Lynn Z. 4, 23, 125, 164, 190
Book List 44
Booth, Wayne 5, 127, 190
Bragg, Margaret 69–73

Bragg, Rick (*All Over But the Shoutin'*) 31–32, 69–73
Bread Givers (Yezierska, Anzia) 49–50, 53–54
Brothers and Keepers see Wideman, John Edgar
Browder, Laura 103, 169
Bruss, Elizabeth 84, 154, 184
Burns, Ben 43
Butterfield, Stephen 59, 62

Campbell, Joseph 20
Casey, Ingeborg 128–30, 149
Chekhov, Anton 41
Chicago, Illinois 34, 38
Chicago Defender 43
class disparity between autobiographers and their subjects 10–13, 17–19, 127–154
class mobility, psychological consequences of 26–27
Clear Springs see Mason, Bobbie Ann
Clifford, James 157, 170, 178, 186
Cobb, Jonathan (*The Hidden Injuries of Class*) 12, 18, 26, 85–86, 90
Coleman, James 106, 188
Congress View 46
"Country" people 168–69
Couser, G. Thomas 3–4, 7, 9–11, 13, 14, 16, 68–69
The Crisis 47

"Dark Days" (Baldwin, James) 62
Daughter of the Queen of Sheba see Lyden, Jacki
Dawn see Dreiser, Theodore
The Depression 26, 74, 82, 87, 93–94, 97, 189
Dillard, Annie 12–13, 151, 180–81
Doctorow, E.L. 37
Doubleday, Page, Company 34
Douglass, Frederick (*The Narrative*) 60, 67, 92
Dreiser, Amy 38
Dreiser, Rome 36, 39

199

Index

Dreiser, Theodore (*Dawn*) 33–42, 49–50, 56, 60–61
Du Bois, Blanche (character in *A Streetcar Named Desire* by Tennessee Williams) 139–140
Du Bois, W.E.B. 43–45
Duffus, R.L. 45, 47

Eakin, Paul John 2, 3, 9, 99, 127, 129–32, 136, 143, 182, 184, 191
Egan, Susanna 20–21, 28, 131, 191
Elk, Black *see Black Elk Speaks*
ethical representations in autobiography, description of Russell Baker's 74, 101
ethics of auto/biographical collaborations with prisoners 120–23
ethics of auto/biography 9–16
ethics of publishing an autobiography 127–29
ethnic autobiographies 103, 169
ethnic identities in autobiography 7–8; re-invention 28
ethnographic autobiography, ethical problems of 186
"Everyday Use" *see* Walker, Alice

Fabre, Michael 41
"Family Affair" (Stewart, Sylvester) 118
"The First Century of Afro-American Autobiography: Theory and Explication" (Andrews, William L.) 67
Fisk University 41
Flowers, Bertha 63–64
Franklin, Benjamin (*The Autobiography of Benjamin Franklin*) 18, 20, 23, 27–28, 41, 62, 74–75, 97, 113–14

Gardner, Howard 150
Garland, Hamlin 35
A Glance Away (Wideman, John Edgar) 105
Glass, Montague 52
Gone Primitive see Torgovnick, Marianna
Growing Up see Baker, Russell
Gunsmoke 162

Hamlet (Shakespeare, William) 64
Hansen, Harry 36
Harrison, Kathryn (*The Kiss*) 127
Haymarket Riot of Chicago, of 1890 38
Hazel, Robert 158–60, 162, 166, 170–73
Hazlitt, Henry 35, 39–40
Henderson, "Momma" 60–64
Hendrickson, Paul 123–24
Henrickson, Louise Levitas 50–51, 53–54, 56
Herrick, Robert 40
Hester Street 51, 57
The Hidden Injuries of Class see Cobb, Jonathan; Sennett, Richard

Hiding Place (Wideman, John Edgar) 105
Hilltoppers 171, 176
Hollywood, California 50–53, 180
Homewood, section of Pittsburgh 27, 114
How the Other Half Lives see Riis, Jacob
Howells, William Dean 35
Hunger of Memory see Rodriguez, Richard
Hungry Hearts (Yezierska, Anzia) 49, 51, 53, 54

I Know Why the Caged Bird Sings see Angelou, Maya
I, Rigoberta Menchu see Menchu, Rigoberta
identity and ethnicity in autobiography 23–24
identity formation 3–4, 130–132
identity in autobiography 20–29
immigrant autobiographies 49
Immigration Act of 1965 8
In Country 155, 173, 176, 178, 180, 182
Indiana University 34
Indianapolis, Indiana 27, 89
informed consent of auto/biographical subjects 10–11
Ivy, James 47

James, Edwin 86–88
James, Henry 153
Johnson, Bailey, Jr. 61–62
journey pattern in autobiography 20–22

Kaplan, Amy 37–38
Karr, Mary (*The Liar's Club*) 10, 11, 33
Kessler-Harris, Alice 53–55
The Kiss see Harrison, Kathryn
Kowalski, Stanley (character in *A Streetcar Named Desire* by Tennessee Williams) 139–40

Latvian immigrants 142
Lauritzen, Paul 4, 5
Leaver, Jim 152–54
Lehmann-Haupt, Christopher 59–61
The Liar's Club see Karr, Mary
"Life with Mother" (Baker, Russell) 81
Liveright, Horace 41
"Living to Tell the Tale: The Complicated Ethics of Creative Nonfiction" (Bloom, Lynn Z.) 4
Lobethal institution, in Germany 131–32
Louisville Times 34
Lower East Side, in Manhattan 49, 57
Lyden, Jacki (*Daughter of the Queen of Sheba*) 10, 11

MacDonald, Michael Patrick (*All Souls: A Family Story from Southie*) 33
Malcolm, Janet 120, 122, 140

Index

Malloy, Robert 45
Mandel, Barrett J. 77, 81
Mason, Bobbie Ann (*Clear Springs*) 1–2, 9–10, 12, 14, 20–28, 57–58, 68, 70, 78, 80, 88–91, 93, 155–91
Mason, Christy 10, 78, 165, 171–73, 176, 180, 182–84
Mason, La Nelle 175
Matthiessen, F.O. 33
Mayfield, Kentucky 156, 167, 173–75, 181
Mayfield Messenger 181
Mbalia, Doreatha 104–5
memories, as source of autobiography 77
Menchu, Rigoberta (*I, Rigoberta Menchu*) 4
Miller, Nancy K. 14, 15, 16, 19, 75, 80, 100, 129, 134–35, 181
Mills, Claudia 15
Mississippi, state of 41–42, 47
Moers, Ellen 33
Mondrian, Piet 162
Mongolians, soldiers in World War II 144–47
Moore, Demi 174
moral judgment, demonstrated by autobiographers 16–19
morality and social class 17–19
Mordell, Albert 39
Morrisonville, Virginia 75, 79
Moyer, Marsha S. 34–35
Murphy, Beatrice M. 43

Narrative see Douglass, Frederick
The Nation 35, 39
Native Son (Wright, Richard) 41
Negro Story 46
Neihardt, John G. (*Black Elk Speaks*) 11
Nesaule, Agate 1–2, 12, 14, 20–28, 58, 68, 79–80, 84–85, 88–91, 93, 95–96, 127–154, 156, 161, 188–191
Nesaule, Valda 96, 133–36, 139, 148
New Republic 37, 40
New York Evening Post 35
New York Evening World Telegram 36
New York Herald Tribune Weekly Book Review 43
New York Sun 45
New York Times 21, 31, 50, 59, 68, 70, 82, 86–87
New York Times Book Review 45, 47, 68–69
New Yorker 41, 57
Newsweek 61
Norris, Frank 34

O'Connor, Flannery 159
Olney, James 59
Omaha World-Herald 43
"On Being Black and Middle-Class" *see* Steele, Shelby

One Writer's Beginnings see Welty, Eudora
Oxford University 105

"Pancho and Lefty" *see* Van Zandt, T.
Parker, Dorothy 41
Philadelphia Public Ledger 37
Philadelphia Record 39
Picasso, Pablo 171
Pittsburgh, Pennsylvania 106–8, 114, 120
Plato 161
PM 46
Prescott, Orville 50
The Price of the Ticket (Baldwin, James) 66
primitivist discourse: discussion 138, 145; portrayals of working-class in 138–41, 143
privacy, of subjects in autobiographies 2–3
Propp, Vladimir 20
Pulitzer Prize 31, 70, 72
Pulse 43–44

racism, in the South 43, 46, 164; in southern autobiographies 164
The Rape of Lucrece (Shakespeare, William) 65
Rea, Peggy 180
realism, as an artistic movement 37–38, 41
Red Ribbon on a White Horse see Yezierska, Anzia
Reed, Henry 64
Renza, Louis A. 149
Ricardo, Lucy 159–60
Richter, F.K. 46
Rico, Gabriele Lusser 150
Riis, Jacob (*How the Other Half Lives*) 38
Robinson, Sugar Ray 59
Rodriguez, Richard (*Hunger of Memory*) 32, 68–69, 167, 182
Rothko, Mark 171
Rubin, Lillian 6–8, 17–18

St. Louis, Missouri 62
Samuels, Wilfred 105
San Francisco, California 59, 62, 65–66
Saturday Evening Post 52, 82–83
Saturday Review of Literature 40
Schreiber, Le Anne 68
Scott, Dred, United States Supreme Court case 110–11
Seabrook, Jeremy (*Working-Class Childhood*) 141
Sennett, Richard (*The Hidden Injuries of Class*) 12, 18, 26, 85–86, 90
Shakespeare, William 63, 67
Shorris, Earl 69
Sister Carrie (Dreiser, Theodore) 34–35, 40
Slater, Philip 91
Smith, Lillian 46
Smith, Sidonie 13, 60

Smith, Susan 72–73
Sollors, Werner 28, 49
Soskin, William 35
Spacks, Patricia Meyer 185
Stamps, Arkansas 61–63, 66
Starobinksy, Jean 1
Steedman, Carolyn 141, 151, 167
Steele, Shelby ("On Being Black and Middle-Class") 63, 103, 117–20
Stone, Albert 42, 83, 103, 111, 115, 157, 180
A Streetcar Named Desire see Williams, Tennessee
Strong, Augusta J. 46
Strong, Josiah 38
Sugar Ray see Anderson, Dave
Sullivan, Ed 116
Swanberg, W.A. 35

Taney, Supreme Court Chief Justice Roger 110
Terre Haute, Indiana 37
Time magazine 47
"To Fashion a Text" (Dillard, Annie) 12
Torgovnick, Mariana (*Gone Primitive*) 78, 138, 140, 143
Toynbee, Arnold 20
"transcendent" children, characteristics of 6–7
transformation in autobiography 155–56
truth in autobiography 4–8

University of Pennsylvania 105, 113–14

Van Zandt, T. ("Pancho and Lefty") 31–32
Vanity Fair (Thackeray, William Makepeace) 18
Volkan, Vamik 24, 26

Vulnerable Subjects (Couser, G. Thomas) 3
"vulnerable subjects" in autobiographies 3–4, 10–13

Waldorf Astoria 50
Walker, Alice ("Everyday Use") 175
The Washington Star 47
Welty, Eudora (*One Writer's Beginnings*) 186–87
Western Penitentiary 102, 111, 124
Wideman, John Edgar (*Brothers and Keepers*) 1, 2, 9, 11–12, 14, 20–28, 56–58, 67–68, 79–80, 89–91, 93, 102–26, 128, 136, 156, 161–63, 166, 172, 179, 182–83, 188–91
Wideman, Robby 14, 22–23, 28, 88, 90, 102–126, 162–63, 166, 179, 188–89, 199
Wildes, Harry Emerson Wildes 37
Williams, Raymond 32, 186
Williams, Tennessee (*A Streetcar Named Desire*) 139–40
Willis, Bruce 174, 176
A Woman in Amber see Nesaule, Agate
working class: familiar characterizations 31–32; psychology 17–18
Working-Class Childhood see Seabrook, Jeremy
working-class family members, as subjects in autobiographies 10–13
World War I 32
World War II 127
Wright, Richard (*Black Boy*) 4, 5, 33, 41–48, 50, 56, 60–61, 67

Yezierska, Anzia (*Red Ribbon on a White Horse*) 33, 48–58, 60–61, 68

Zweig, Paul 68

www.ingramcontent.com/pod-product-compliance
Lightning Source LLC
Chambersburg PA
CBHW032058300426
44116CB00007B/796